Through My Eyes

THROUGH MY EYES

A NOVEL BY **ALTON GANSKY**

ChariotVICTOR
PUBLISHING
A DIVISION OF COOK COMMUNICATIONS

Victor Books is and imprint of Chariot Victor Publishing
Cook Communications, Colorado Springs, Colorado 80918
Cook Communications, Paris, Ontario
Kingsway Communications, Eastbourne England

© 1997 by Alton Gansky.
All rights reserved.
Editor: Barbara Williams
Design: Bill Gray
Cover Photo: Image Bank, John P. Kelly, Alain Choisnet
All Scripture references are from the New American Standard Bible, ● the
Lockman Foundation 1960, 1962, 1963, 1968, 1971, 1972, 1973, 1975, 1977.

Library of Congress Cataloging-in-Publication Data

Gansky, Alton
    By my hands / by Alton Gansky.
        p. cm.
    ISBN 1-56476-534-2
    1. Hospitals—Fiction.   I. Title
PS3557.A5195B9 1996
813'.54—dc20   96-4915
                                                              CIP

1 2 3 4 5 6 7 8 9 10 Printing/Year 00 99 98 97

Dedication

This book is dedicated in loving memory of my mother,
Ruby Reid, my stepfather, James Reid, and my sister,
Jackie Mills, all gone too soon.
May their experience be as rich as Rachel's.

Acknowledgments

My deepest gratitude is extended to my family, who have shown the greatest support in the writing of this book; to Dave Horton and Greg Clouse at ChariotVictor for their support and encouragement; to Pat Henson for her sharp-eyed proofreading skills; and to the various people who patiently answered my various questions.

Part 1
The Summons

In a dream, a vision of the night,
When sound sleep falls on men,
While they slumber in their beds,
Then He opens the ears of men,
And seals their instruction,
That He may turn man aside from his conduct,
And keep man from pride;
He keeps back his soul from the pit,
And his life from passing over into Sheol.
                           — Job 33:15-18

And it will come about after this
That I will pour out My Spirit on all mankind;
And your sons and daughters will prophesy,
Your old men will dream dreams,
Your young men will see visions.
And even on the male and female servants
I will pour out My Spirit in those days.
                           — Joel 2:28,29

One

San Diego, California

She . . . was . . . beautiful.

The Reverend Adam Bridger lay in bed, propped up on one arm, and silently stared at the woman next to him. He could hardly believe his eyes, and had even more trouble believing in the reality of his marriage. The wedding had been more than five months ago, but he still had not adjusted to seeing a woman, even the woman he loved, under his covers. He let his eyes slowly trace his wife's face, taking in every detail from the smallest eyelash to the one remaining freckle that stubbornly refused to give up its spot on her right temple. He doubted that Rachel knew of the freckle, but he did. He knew everything about her face, having meticulously committed to memory each crease and every pore.

She was a changed person, altered by events beyond her or anyone's understanding. Adam wondered at the marvelous metamorphosis that had occurred. She was still a woman with strong opinions, a quick wit, and fierce loyalty, but now the sharp edges of her personality had been softened, rounded to an easy edge. She no longer viewed the world through bitter eyes, no longer felt compelled to compete with all who crossed her path. Instead of constantly stirring a stew of suspicion, she now allowed room for friendship, sharing, and love.

Gently, with no more force than a butterfly might exert on a flower, Adam brushed a wayward strand of long black hair that had fallen across the bare lips of his wife. When they had first met, she wore her hair severely short to match her sometimes quick, volatile temper. Now her black hair was shoulder length and graced with gentle waves. The morning sun sifted through the drapes casting highlights on her tousled mane. Adam felt a growing sense of warmth within himself and longed to place a gentle kiss on her smooth forehead. Instead he forced himself to be content with watching his wife sleep, captivated by her rhythmic breathing. With each exhalation he felt the urge to offer a prayer of thanks for the woman he loved with every fiber of his being.

Adam watched as one eye opened just enough to reveal its hazel color. "Ya dong gin," Rachel said in a hoarse and muffled voice.

"Ya dong gin?" Adam chortled. "What is, 'ya dong gin'?"

Slowly, Rachel dragged her arm out from under the covers and pushed the feather pillow away from her mouth. "I said, you're doing it again."

"What?"

"Staring at me," she replied sleepily. "It's the same ol' me."

"That's why I keep staring. I love the same ol' you."

Rachel reached up and gently patted Adam on the cheek. "Good old Ragsy, ever the faithful companion."

"Ragsy? Ragsy? That's the Reverend Doctor Ragsy to you."

"Forgive me," Rachel giggled. "Just plain Dr. Rachel is tired. I didn't get home from the hospital until one this morning. Had an emergency come in: an auto accident. The man wasn't wearing a seat belt. He was busted up pretty good."

"So, did you save him?" Adam asked only slightly more serious than before.

Rachel rolled on her back and rubbed her eyes. "No."

"I'm sorry," Adam offered softly. "I'm sure you did your best."

"That's what makes it so hard. I did do my best. ER had him stabilized when they called me. I was sharp, in the groove. I felt like I could do no wrong. The surgery team was great, but we lost him anyway. He just slipped away, out of our reach. I don't think I'll ever get used to that."

"Are you supposed to get used to losing a patient?"

"No, I suppose not." Rachel sat up in bed. "You hungry?"

"I'm always hungry."

"Good. I'm going to shower, which should leave you time to fix some eggs."

"Me?" Adam feigned shock. "I'm a minister, a fixer of souls."

"I'm a surgeon, a fixer of bodies."

"Hmm," Adam offered, "maybe what this relationship needs is a fixer of eggs."

Rachel chuckled. "It wouldn't be the same without your artistic touch. Of course, we could take advantage of this my day off, and you could take me out for breakfast."

"Wonderful idea; bad timing. I'm teaching at the seminary today. It wouldn't do to disappoint the students, you know."

"Ah, that's right." Rachel said as she walked toward the adjoining bathroom, "this is your day to afflict the saints."

"Afflict? I'll have you know that the students love my classes."

"That's because you're an easy 'A'." Rachel cast him a devious smile.

"You wound me!" Adam replied; then, in his best Rodney Dangerfield voice he said, "Hey, I tell ya', I get no respect."

"Take me to breakfast and I'll respect you for life."

"Nope, can't do it, but I will be home about three and I might be talked into an early movie and dinner."

Rachel held up both hands, palms up as if weighing something. "Breakfast or movie and a dinner. OK, it's a deal, but I get to pick the movie."

"And I get to pick the dinner."

"Agreed. Do I still get some eggs?"

"Only because I'm such a wonderful husband."

"You are that," she replied and returned to the bed, bent over, and kissed him. "You are that, Dr. Bridger." With that she turned, slipped her nightgown off, tossed it at her husband and walked into the bathroom. A moment later Adam heard the shower running.

"Rachel, you are a tease," he said loudly, but he knew that she couldn't hear him over the roaring cascade of water. Then, more softly he commented: "And I love it."

Two plates of scrambled eggs with diced ham later, Rachel kissed Adam good-bye as he headed out the door to begin the thirty-minute drive from their new Kearny Mesa home to the city of Escondido in north San Diego County. She felt unusually good today, and a sense of well-being permeated her thoughts. It was a feeling that she experienced more and more. There was no doubt that Adam Bridger was the best thing to happen to her. Since meeting him ten months ago and marrying him five months later her life had taken on a new meaning and a new purpose.

Things to which she had previously given no thought were now a regular part of her life. She smiled more, laughed more, and enjoyed life more. The previous bitterness that had ruled her existence had been replaced with a spiritual aspect that was becoming the driving force of her existence. The cynic in her had died and been replaced with a thoughtful person.

She was still a person of science, she was still pragmatic and disciplined, but now she felt that she was part of the fabric of existence that goes beyond that which is experienced by most.

This new sense of creation had spilled over into her work. Where she had formerly considered patients as biological machines that needed repair, she now saw them as souls whose bodies come with fully integrated emotions and thoughts, and treating those emotions was part of the healing process. Such thoughts would have received a scathing rebuke from her conscience just one year ago.

Adding to her special sense of happiness this day was the realization that she had no place to be and no schedule to keep. This was one of her rare days off. No surgery. No rounds. No reports. Instead, she had planned to read a book, nap, and go for a long walk. The only other matters she had planned was to take up Adam's offer of an evening out.

The first business at hand was to change clothes. While there was nothing that required that she hang up her robe and get dressed, she still felt that the day hadn't begun until she was properly attired. Properly attired this day meant a powder blue jogging suit and sneakers. Not professional apparel, but today she was just Rachel—Dr. Rachel Tremaine-Bridger wouldn't return until seven o'clock tomorrow morning.

The phone rang, causing Rachel to cringe. "Not today," she muttered aloud. She had a sinking feeling that the person on the other end was the hospital paging service summoning her to the bedside of one of her patients. Not answering was a thought she considered for only a moment before picking up four rings later.

"Hello," she answered, struggling to keep any curtness from her voice.

"No mushy girl movies," the caller said, causing Rachel to laugh in relief. Adam had called her from the car phone.

"Are you attempting to influence my choice?"

"Uh, no," Adam replied with a snicker. "Just letting my opinion be known."

"I was thinking of some foreign film with subtitles. How's that sound?"

"Fine with me, but remember that I move my lips when I read, and that's not a pretty sight after I've been eating popcorn."

"OK, you win. No mushy girl movies. But I still get to pick what we'll see."

"If you insist."

"I do. Did you call just to tell me what kind of movie you don't want to see?"

"No. I forgot to tell you that I love you."

"No, you didn't," Rachel replied with a smile. "You said that three times before you left. I know, I counted."

"Well then, this is a bonus. Save it for some time when I'm not around."

"You're nuts, you know that don't you? You're certifiable."

"You knew that when you married me. It was in the fine print. You did read the fine print, didn't you?"

"I didn't read anything; I was blinded by your overpowering good looks." Adam guffawed. Rachel knew that Adam did not consider himself handsome by any sense of the word. He always described himself as a middle-aged man with glasses too thick that sat upon a face that was too plain. Rachel, however, considered Adam quite appealing. True, he was not every girl's dream, but his appeal lay not in his dark hair or his limited physique, but in the gentleness of his soul and the strength of his intellect. Adam's wit, understanding, and powerful character were far more attractive to Rachel than any physical quality. "How's traffic?"

"Not bad. Pretty good, actually." There was a pause. "Be careful today, OK?"

Rachel was puzzled. "Sure. But why? What's wrong?"

"Nothing. I just felt . . . It's just a feeling . . . I don't know. Just be careful."

"I will. And you too."

"I'll see you soon."

"All right, and I'll remember, no mushy movies." Adam laughed and then hung up.

On with the day, Rachel thought and made her way to the walk-in closet in the master bedroom. Removing her robe and hanging it on a hook by the closet door, she reached for the hanger that held her jogging suit. As she touched the hanger she noticed an unusual sensation. Barely perceptible at first, a tingling began at the top of her head. It felt like her head was bathed in one of those strongly medicated dandruff shampoos, except the tingling was spreading. Soon her whole head was awash in a crawling, creeping sensation, as if thousands of ants were swarming on her scalp and face.

The sensation spread rapidly, cascading down her neck and back, encompassing her arms, coating her legs. Rachel tried to scratch her scalp but she couldn't move. She was frozen in place. I'm having a stroke, she thought. I'm thirty-eight years old and I'm having a stroke.

When the first sensation manifested itself, she reflexively slammed her eyes shut. Now she struggled to open them. Her muscles were reluctant and disobedient, yet she managed to will her eyelids apart.

Immediately she wished she hadn't.

Forcing her eyes down, she stared at the floor—except there was no floor, just an empty expanse of blackness. She could see her feet dangling over . . . nothing. The jogging suit was gone as were all the clothes. The closet was gone. The house. The street they lived on. The whole world was gone. She was floating or falling or rising in the open maw of sheer oppressive blackness. No light. No sound. No heat. No cold. No sensations. The blackness felt palpable and heavy, as if it had a life of its own. It seemed to breathe, to pulse. It pressed in on her as though it were attempting to forcibly enter her mind through her eyes and seep in through her ears.

Rachel screamed, but she heard nothing.

Class had gone well and Adam felt a sense of accomplishment.

It was a familiar feeling, one he experienced each time he taught. Since becoming adjunct professor at the San Diego Theological Seminary in Escondido, Adam had relished the opportunity to teach at a level above that which he could in his church. Here he could discuss the weighty doctrines that only scholars found interesting.

As an adjunct professor he taught only twice a week. This term he was lecturing on ecclesiology, the study of the church. Since the seminary was a nondenominational organization, Adam's class was filled with students from various backgrounds. Mixing Baptists with Pentecostals with Presbyterians made for interesting and exciting class discussion.

Today's class was no exception. A spirited discussion erupted over the proper form of church government. "Should churches be congregationally led," Adam had asked, "or led by a board of elders?" For those outside the seminary environment such a discussion might be the catalyst for a wicked case of ennui, but not for a room of soon-to-be pastors. There had been no shortage of opinions.

Following the class, Adam graded papers in the library for the remainder of the morning, took lunch with Dr. Hinders from the Old Testament department, then returned to campus to prepare for his afternoon class.

Now he was driving south along Interstate 15 intent on arriving home as soon as possible. He considered stopping by the church office to see if he was needed but decided against it, knowing that his secretary, Fannie, would call him if anything important had arisen. No, today he would head straight home. Maybe he and Rachel would start their night out with a walk along the beach, one of Rachel's favorite things to do. This bright, cloudless spring afternoon would be perfect for a stroll along La Jolla Cove. Adam could already smell the salt air.

The blackness was different now, but Rachel didn't know how. She could see nothing, no stars, no reflections, just simple expansive darkness. Yet, it was different. It didn't seem as oppressive and not nearly so invasive.

So this is what it is to die, she thought, no heaven, no hell. Boy, won't Adam be surprised. But it was Rachel who was surprised by her own calmness. At first she struggled, screamed, thrashed about, but now she was indifferent. She attempted to activate her logical,

reasoning mind, but logic and reason seemed out of place here—
wherever here was.

There was no sense of falling, no spinning, just quiet suspension.
For some reason she thought of a paperweight she had seen as a child.
She had been on a cross-country trip with her parents when they
stopped at a tourist stand outside Phoenix. Displayed on a rough
and weather-beaten table was a small cube of plastic with a reddish-
brown scorpion suspended in the middle. The sight of the ugly arach-
nid frightened the young Rachel, but as her family traveled on she
began to wonder what the scorpion thought about being locked in
a cube of plastic.

Suspended as she was in her own opaque cube of black, she felt
a kinship with the scorpion.

I'm going to miss Adam terribly, she thought.

"Rachel, I'm home."

Silence.

"Rachel?"

Nothing.

Stillness.

"Come out, come out, wherever you are."

Still nothing.

Adam walked into the kitchen. The breakfast dishes were in the
sink unwashed. Strange, Adam thought. Rachel was not a metic-
ulous house cleaner, but she seldom left dirty dishes lying about. Adam
noticed something else: the light on the drip coffeemaker was
still lit. He supposed that Rachel might have left the house without turning off the coffeemaker, but it still gave him pause.

"Rachel?" Adam was beginning to feel uncomfortable. Maybe the
bathroom. Adam entered the master bedroom and peeked in the
master bath. Nothing. She must have gone out, Adam thought.
Walking past the walk-in closet, Adam made his way outside and
to the garage. The door was still closed, but all that meant was that
Adam would have to go to his car and activate the automatic garage
door opener. A moment later the roll-up door was rattling and squeaking as it rose on its tracks. Adam saw that Rachel's '56 T-Bird was
still there. He closed the door and went back into the house.

Glancing around the living room, Adam looked for any clues to
his wife's whereabouts. There was no note, nor did anything seem

16

disturbed. Adam's uneasiness grew.

Something wasn't right. Rachel may have taken a little walk or stepped over to Bob and Julie's next door. Rachel and Julie were becoming close so it was reasonable to expect that his wife might be enjoying some female company and had just let the time slip by. But somehow, Adam knew that wasn't the case. Still he should call.

It took only a few moments for Adam to dial his neighbors' phone number. He let it ring ten times before conceding that they were not home. Adam had been feeling unsettled since leaving this morning and he didn't know why. Now he was becoming really concerned.

"This is ridiculous," he said aloud. "Rachel is a grown woman and a surgeon at that; she can take care of herself." Adam attempted to squelch his rising tide of anxiety by reminding himself that there was no real reason to expect Rachel to sit home on her day off. But the car was still there. Where could she have gone?

Absentmindedly, Adam pulled the knot of his necktie away from his neck. Might as well change clothes, he thought and headed for the closet. He hadn't noticed when he walked through the bedroom before, but now he could see that the closet light was on. He heard his dad saying, "If you're not using the light, then turn it off. Save a penny here, save a penny there, it all adds up."

Stripping the tie from around his neck, Adam stepped into the little room. He gasped and dropped the tie. In front of him lay his wife, dressed only in her underclothes, her arms and legs akimbo. To her left a small blue plastic basket used to hold their dirty clothes had been knocked over, to her right, sneakers, pumps, and dress shoes were scattered about. Rachel's head rested on the carpeted floor.

Frozen, Adam stared at her for a moment. She was looking at the ceiling with a fixed gaze, her eyes wide, her pupils dilated. Adam's first thought was that she was dead, that he was looking down at the corpse of the only woman he loved. But then she blinked, rapidly. She convulsed with arms and legs trembling for a few seconds, then stopped. Her breath was ragged and hoarse.

"Rachel! Rachel, what is it? What's wrong?" Adam knelt by her and cradled her head. "Talk to me, baby. What's wrong?" Rachel didn't answer. She trembled again, took in a lungful of air in a raspy wheeze and then exhaled it. She did not move her eyes. It was as though she were looking off into the distance, studying something that only she could see. "Oh, God, oh, God," Adam prayed. The prayer wasn't elaborate or formal; instead it was the prayer of a frightened and desperate man. "Oh, God, no. Oh, God, no." Adam had prayed publicly and privately thousands of times, tens of thousands of times, but now his words were limited to a single, heartfelt, panic-stricken plea: "Oh, God, no. Oh, God, let her be all right."

Gently Adam set Rachel's head down then raced from the closet with such haste that he viciously smashed his elbow into the doorjamb, breaking the skin and sending a searing bolt of pain up his arm. Adam didn't even pause long enough to touch it. Instead, he dashed to the phone and dialed 911.

What is that? Rachel thought. In the distance she could see that the absolute blackness had been punctured by a tiny light. It started as just a barely perceptible pinprick, but now it was growing. The light, or whatever it was, shone with a pure and brilliant green, like an emerald backlit by a high-intensity light. The sight of it captivated her. But then again, it was the only thing to see.

The paramedics arrived within fifteen minutes of Adam's call—fifteen interminably, agonizingly long minutes. When they arrived, Adam, doing his best to maintain his composure, showed them to the closet. What the paramedics saw was a woman covered in a sheet who stared at the ceiling, blinking only intermittently. Adam had placed the sheet over Rachel partly out of modesty, knowing that she would want that done, and simply to have something helpful to do.

The pair of paramedics, a large woman with blond shoulder-length hair and a thin black man with kind eyes, began their work immediately, quickly checking Rachel's pulse, skin color, and temperature, flashing a light from a pocket flashlight to check pupil reaction—there was none. They attempted to talk to Rachel, but she didn't responded. They also asked questions, with the male paramedic taking the lead. He was clearly the senior of the two.

"What can you tell us?" he asked.

"Nothing," Adam replied. "I found her this way when I got home twenty minutes ago. She was fine this morning."

"Is she on medication?"

"No, none."

"Has she ever had episodes like this before?" The paramedic's voice was calm and even. He never looked up from Rachel.

"No. At least not that I know of."

"Does your wife drink?" he asked not unkindly.

"Alcohol? No, not recently anyway."

"Was she ever a heavy drinker?"

"No, not at all." Adam felt embarrassed by the question. "And she hasn't had anything like that to drink since we've been married, and for a good time before that."

"How long have you been married?"

"Five months." Adam stood in the closet doorway wishing there were something he could do. "What do you think is wrong?"

"Can't tell," the man said. "Her color is good, and she's breathing well, uneven as it appears. We've looked for injury to head and neck that might cause this, but haven't found anything."

The blond woman spoke for the first time: "What about suicide?"

The black paramedic snapped his head around and cast her a withering glare. "Look around you," he said sternly. "How many suicides do you know that choose the closet as their place to die? No, this is no suicide. My guess is that something is happening in the brain. A stroke maybe."

Adam felt the pit of his stomach plummet. "A . . . a stroke?"

"Can't be sure," the man replied. "Her pupils are equal, so that tends to rule stroke out, but she is showing some of the other indications. So, I can't say for sure. That's for the doctors to decide. One thing is for sure: we can't leave her here. We can take her to . . ."

"Kingston Memorial," Adam interjected. "She's on staff there."

"Staff?"

"She's a surgeon."

"Kingston Memorial it is." The male paramedic picked up the handset of the transceiver that would connect him to the hospital and relayed the results of his field examination. The emergency room nurse who took the call advised immediate transport, an IV of Ringer's lactate with a heparin push, as well as other things Adam didn't understand.

Adam did know that heparin was a blood thinner. That meant that the emergency room nurse was thinking of a stroke too.

"We can't get her on the gurney here in the closet; it's just too tight," the paramedic said, and then turning to his partner he gave orders: "I want the backboard. We'll strap her to that. That should give us the mobility we need to get out of here. Bring a cervical collar, too."

It took twenty-five minutes for the emergency crew to get Rachel into the back of the ambulance, which was now speeding down the road toward the hospital. In the back of the ambulance, Adam sat holding Rachel's hand, watching as she moved back and forth in time with the rocking of the ambulance. "Hang in there, baby, we'll get you taken care of. Everything will be all right." Adam wondered if he was lying.

It's spectacular, Rachel thought. The green dot in the darkness had grown. Now she could see that it was an orb, like a bright green planet. What she couldn't tell was if she was falling toward it or if it was flying toward her. In either case they were coming closer together. And that was all right with her. For some reason she found the green orb attractive; not just attractive to look at, it was certainly that, but she wanted to do more than gaze at the orb—she wanted to be on it.

The doors to the ER swung open as the two paramedics pushed the gurney down the long pale green hall. Doctors and nurses, having been alerted that it was Dr. Rachel Tremaine being brought in, had lined the corridor ready to help work on one of their own.

The woman paramedic chanted the litany of medical status: "Woman, thirty-eight years old, found unconscious in her closet at home. Pulse is seventy and strong; respiration twenty per minute but erratic; B/P is 125 over 70; no visible injury; no drug paraphernalia found; her pupils are dilated, equal, and fixed . . ." At that the ER doctor who was the recipient of all this information swore. Adam felt his heart sink. "No previous history. As instructed we started an IV of Ringer's with a heparin push."

"In here," the doctor said firmly, "Room 3."

The paramedics turned the gurney sharply and pushed it into the room. Adam followed. He watched as the paramedics helped move Rachel from the gurney to the emergency room bed. The doctor began barking out orders to the half dozen nurses in the room. Adam wondered if Rachel was receiving special treatment because she was a doctor on staff at the hospital. He hoped so.

"Sir," a nurse said to Adam, "you'll need to wait outside."

"I prefer to wait here."

"I know you do, and I know this is difficult, but you must let us do our job. Please wait in the lobby." Adam hesitated. The nurse took him by the arm and walked him out. Adam turned in time to see the doors to the emergency room swing shut, closing Rachel in and shutting Adam out.

Adam's eyes began to sting. A moment later tears began to trickle down his cheeks. "Please God, oh, please, please, God. Make her all right."

Such a pretty green, Rachel thought. So very, very, pretty.

Two

The Rural Connecticut Coast

An adult bluejay fluttered from a nearby tree and lightly landed on the late model Jaguar's hood. The jay moved its head around in jerky motions, ever alert for predators or a tasty morsel of bug. Then, as if it were a second thought, the bird turned and faced the lone man sitting in the driver's seat. The bird tipped its bright blue head first to the left and then to the right, analyzing the large creature in the metal machine. The man did not move, but only returned the gaze.

"You must be the bluebird of happiness," the driver said, knowing the bird couldn't hear him. "And you've come to cheer Pruit Bain up. Is that it?" The bird twisted its head around again. A breeze stroked the leaves of the trees, causing a symphony of rustling. Startled by the sudden sounds, the bird flew away. "Just what I thought," Bain said, "I'm too big a job for you. Well, no matter. I'm too big a job for me, too."

Pruit Bain refocused his attention on the small dirt road in front of him and visualized what the next few minutes would hold. He had done his homework, driving up and down the coastal

22

road looking for the ideal place. It wasn't easy finding just the right spot with a cliff that was high enough to do the kind of damage he needed done. It wasn't easy finding a place that would allow him a way to drive his car off the cliff so that he and the auto would take up their final resting place on the shoreline of the Long Island Sound. But Pruit Bain was an expert in research and planning.

He was creative too. There were many ways to kill oneself, but most of them were messy and lacked artistry. He could have chosen a gun or pills or a razor blade, but he wanted to end his life, like he had lived it—with élan. That's the way an advertising man should go into the great beyond. So Pruit searched for the right method, the right place, and the right time.

It was this attention to detail that had made him famous in the advertising world. As founder and CEO of Bain, Lockeridge, and Mullins he had attracted the attention of the largest companies in the world. He produced award-winning commercials and print ads that were seen by a full third of the world's population. Advertising was his universe and he was its master. It was a world that made him rich beyond his dreams.

But none of that mattered now. Soon it would be dark enough for him to proceed. The plan was easy: wait until dark when there was no chance of his car being seen as it plummeted over the cliff; dark enough so that he could see the headlights of any approaching vehicles. It wouldn't do to collide with a car coming down the crossroad; he might accidentally kill someone or, worse, be prevented from killing himself. No, he would wait patiently for his time, and when that time came he would start the powerful engine in his Jaguar XK8, drop the transmission into drive, and when he was sure no one was coming who might attempt a rescue, floor the accelerator, driving the $80,000 car across the main road and over the edge of the cliff.

The cliff itself was only 150 feet high, but that should be high enough. He had cut through his seat belt and shoulder harness so that he could unsnap the buckle and not be forced to listen to the annoying reminder chime. Knowing that the devil was in the details, as his father used to say, Pruit had even paid a street thug near his New York office to steal his driver's side air bag.

It would be another thirty minutes until it was dark enough to execute his plan. He wondered if the bluejay would still be around to watch Pruit's first and only attempt at flying.

They would be looking for him by now. The itinerary that he left with his secretary said that he would be back in New York by two that afternoon; it was now nearly six. His wife wouldn't be concerned, not yet. She and their only son were in Europe. Michael was on spring break from school and it seemed a good time to go. Pruit should have gone with them, but there was work to do. There was always work to do. In many ways, Meredith, his wife, was already a widow and his son already fatherless. His success had allowed Pruit to give them everything except a husband and a father.

Tears welled up in his eyes. How had he sunk so low? How could he have made so many mistakes? It was his fault and he knew it. He blamed no one but himself. If only he had been a little more aware, a little more on his toes, perhaps he could have seen it coming and prevented the whole thing. But that didn't happen. He didn't see it coming. He hadn't been alert. He had been too busy to take care of the simplest and most basic needs. And now he had to pay for it.

Pay for it. That was a good phrase. There was always a price to be paid for inattention, always a cost to be doled out by those who overlook the details.

He wiped away the tears. I wonder if Dad cried too? he asked himself. Pruit's father had been a successful lawyer with many famous clients. He had created the family riches that allowed Pruit to go to the finest schools, just like Michael was doing now, and take positions in the finest firms. Pruit had been proud of his father, even when he purposely overdosed on barbiturates. Now Pruit was about to travel the same path.

Contrary to Pruit's expectation, the time passed quickly. One would think that seconds would tick past like hours when one is waiting to die, but such was not the case. Already the sun had set in the west and darkness had edged ever closer to the cliff. It was so dark now that Pruit could no longer see the edge of the road. He rolled his window down and the scent of the woods, heavy with oak, seeped in. Along with it came the rhythmic antiphonal crashing of the sea against the rocks at the base of the cliff.

Pressing the buttons that would automatically roll all the windows down, Pruit felt the cool spring air. He heard the sounds of insects, and the occasional cry of birds. And the sea, always the sea, rolling and rumbling and calling him. Details, Pruit reminded himself. Make sure all the details are covered. With the windows down the ocean could plunge in just as the night air was doing now.

Pruit wiped at his face again, smearing the tears nose to ear. It was time. Flicking on the overhead, he was once again bathed in light. Glare from the overhead would reflect off the inside of the windshield, making it a little harder for him to see the edge of the cliff coming. Pruit didn't want to back out at the last second.

Step by step. He reached for the ignition key and turned it. The car roared immediately to life. The radio was on, but Pruit quickly silenced it. "The last thing I want to hear is a news report," Pruit said aloud. Slowly he reached for the gear shift lever on the console between the seats. Placing his foot on the brake, Pruit dropped the car into drive. Then he released the parking brake. Bringing his hand to the steering wheel, he braced himself for what would be his last act on earth.

The steering wheel felt funny. Wet. Maybe his hands were wet from his tears, but that didn't seem likely. Slowly Pruit brought his right hand close to his face, allowing the light from the overhead to illuminate it. His palm was wet, and not with tears but with something dark and sticky. Pruit squinted in an attempt to see better. It looked like . . . it was—blood! But how? He hadn't stuck or cut himself.

Bringing his left hand into view he could see that it too was covered in blood. Straining his eyes in the dim light, Pruit could see the source of the blood—two holes, one in each palm, were oozing the fluid. Pruit was puzzled. How could he have injured both hands and not known it? The blood was beginning to drip down his arms.

There was no pain, no burning, no tenderness. Pruit had tested the last of these by pressing a finger into the hole of one of his hands. Nothing but blood. No sensation, just blood. If he cupped his hands, the blood would form a puddle in his palm.

Turning his hand over, oblivious to the blood dripping from his hand and splattering on his trousers, he could see something else happening. Another hole was forming right before his eyes. A new hole on the back of each hand. It was as if an invisible spike was being pressed through his flesh. He watched as the skin first bulged, then perforated, oozing out a drop of blood, then a trickle, then a rivulet of red, sticky fluid.

This didn't make sense. But what did it matter? He had come here to kill himself. What difference did it make if he was bleeding before he died? He certainly would be bleeding afterward.

Placing his hands back on the now slippery steering wheel, Pruit tightened his grip, took his foot from the brake, and waited for the car to roll forward. It didn't move. He put his foot on the accelerator and depressed it slightly. Still nothing. The engine roared, but the car remained immobile, held in place by some invisible force. "What is going on here?" he said aloud. "Can't a man kill himself?"

Someone answered. Not someone in the woods or even the back seat, but someone in his head. Someone with a strong voice, a gentle voice, a firm voice. The voice uttered only one line: "Not today, Pruit."

Three

San Diego, California

The candystriper behind the visitor's counter hastily called out, "May I help you, sir?"

"Nope," came the blunt reply.

"Sir, you'll need to sign in, before . . . sir? Sir!?"

Dick Slay brushed past the counter, turning left down the first hall. It was clear that he knew where he was going and nothing was going to stop him. At the end of the hall was a pair of metal doors that opened automatically as he approached. A moment later he stood in the ER lobby. The lobby was only half full, which made locating Adam easier.

"Pastor?" Dick said. "You OK?"

Adam was sitting next to a window that looked out over the front parking lot. He had been staring out the window, watching cars pull in and out. Hearing Dick's voice, he looked up. "Dick! How did you get here?"

"I own a trucking company, remember? I have access to all kinds of vehicles."

"I mean, how did you find out?"

Dick Slay was a squat, balding, barrel-chested man who could be brusque and intimidating. He could also be sensitive and caring. A rough-and-tumble upbringing on a farm in central California, a stint in the Navy, and two decades of dealing with truckers had drop-forged him into an alloy of rugged teamster and caring friend. "Easy. Your neighbor Judy, Jammie, or . . ."

"Julie?"

"Yeah, that's it," Slay replied as he lowered himself into a chair opposite his pastor. "She pulled into her driveway as the ambulance was pulling out. She called the church to see what was going on. Fannie didn't know, so she called me."

"If Fannie knows, then I guess everyone knows," Adam said with a forced smile.

"True enough," Dick said. "But that's not a bad thing. The whole church will be praying for you." Adam nodded slowly. "Since you're sitting here in the lobby, I guess the problem's with Rachel."

"Yes. I came home from teaching my class and found her unconscious on the closet floor. Her eyes are open, but she's not conscious."

"Have the doctors said anything?" Dick inquired softly.

"No, not yet. The ER doctor looked her over and called for some tests. They're doing some kind of neurological workup right now. There's been some talk of a stroke."

Dick sat back in his chair. "A stroke? She's not even forty yet. How can she have a stroke?"

"I don't know. I guess age doesn't have anything to do with it." Adam leaned forward and rubbed his eyes. "I don't think it's a stroke. I don't know why I think that, but I do. It's something else."

"Well, if it is, they'll figure it out."

"I hope so," Adam uttered quietly. "I don't know what I would do without her. She's become my life."

"I know," Dick said, echoing Adam's soft tones. "But let's not go writing her off yet. She's tough. You're tough. Neither one of you is going to have to go through this alone. The whole church is behind you."

Adam smiled weakly. "It seems odd being on the receiving end of that line. I've uttered it to others so many times in the past."

"Was it true then?"

"Yes, of course."

"Well, it's true now too."

"Thanks, Dick. You're a great chairman of the deacons and even a better friend."

Dick allowed himself to smile. "I have a good role model."

The two men fell into silence, each wanting to say something, neither with any idea of just what to say. Dick rubbed his hands together, and Adam returned to staring out the window.

"I had better call Fannie or she'll skin me alive. I don't want to get on the wrong side of her." Dick stood. "You want me to bring you some coffee or something?"

"No thanks," Adam replied.

"I don't know why we do that," Dick continued. "Offer coffee or water or something, like they're some magic elixir."

Adam thought of the many times he had been in Dick's position and made the same offer. "It gives us something to do and a way to break the silence. It's a good thing."

Nodding, Dick said, "I'll be back in a minute." With that he turned and walked to the pay phones on the far side of the lobby. Adam was thankful to have a friend like Dick.

Green. Everywhere green. Pure, without variation or flicker. Green. Like emerald. Infinitely green in all directions. No more darkness, no more black. The green was warm and soft. The green was tangible, touchable, tactile. It was comfortable here like a womb, like a blanket of wispy down, like sunshine.

Floating and falling into the orb of green, Rachel felt no fear, no anxiety. She was flying through an unknown universe. She was alone but felt no loneliness; empty but felt full.

Rapture. Pleasure. Joy. Peace. Unity. Acceptance. Knowledge. Hope. Value. Green.

Rachel smiled.

The two men had sat in near silence for hours. The sun was beginning to fall toward the horizon. Shadows became longer, the blue sky darkened and so did Adam's spirit. He wanted to pray, but words didn't come. It wasn't that he had lost his faith, but that he had lost the capacity to concentrate on anything other than Rachel, who was somewhere in the hospital lying helpless, and there wasn't anything Adam could do.

Emotions churned within him: impotency, fear, anxiety, concern, anger. Adam Bridger, man of faith, man of action, was forced to wait . . . and wait . . . and wait.

Several times he had had to fight back tears of fear and frustration. Dick pretended not to notice. Adam was a man like most other men, uncomfortable with personal displays of emotion, ill-equipped to handle tears, uncertain how to express fears. So the emotions continued to churn and move like magma under a volcano, seeking a way out, looking for the weakest part of the earth's crust to push aside. Adam's volcano was near eruption.

"Mr. Tremaine?" a voice asked above him.

Adam looked up at a tall man with a boy's face who stood nearby. "Bridger," Adam corrected. "But I'm Rachel Tremaine's husband." He started to explain that Rachel had adopted his name when they married, but still used Tremaine at the hospital, then decided that none of that mattered. This young man, who didn't look old enough to have been through medical school, was going to tell him something about Rachel. "Please sit down." Adam motioned to the chair opposite him and next to Dick.

"I'm Dr. Metzger, a resident here in the ER." Metzger looked tired as he ran his fingers through his brown hair. "I've admitted Dr. Tremaine for observation and further tests."

"What have you discovered?" Adam asked intently.

"We haven't found anything yet," he replied, "but the good news is that we've been able to rule out a few things. We've done a CAT scan of her brain and the results are negative for any signs of cerebral hemorrhage or stroke. All her other neurological signs seem normal and her vitals are strong. That's the good news. The bad news is that we don't know why she is so unresponsive. I've sent the CAT images to several specialists in hopes that they can help solve this problem."

"You're confident that it's not a stroke?" Dick asked.

"As confident as I can be at this point. If she's had a stroke we should be able to see some deposit of blood somewhere in the brain and we don't. While she does show some signs of a stroke such as unresponsiveness and immobility, other signs make us think otherwise. Her pupils, which in the case of stroke should be unequal— that is, one pupil larger than the other—are dilated but still equal in size. My first thought was that she had some trauma."

"Trauma?" Adam asked.

"Yes, such as a blow to the head, a fall, drug overdose, something like that. But her blood workup rules out drugs and alcohol, and we can find no external signs of physical trauma."

"So what's your best guess?" Adam inquired pointedly.

"We don't like to guess," Metzger replied.

"Humor me," Adam said forcibly.

Metzger eyed Adam warily and then offered, "All right. But mind you, this is just a guess. I think she may be having a seizure of some sort. I don't know what precipitated it, but something is going on in her brain."

"What do you mean?" Adam asked.

"In addition to the CAT scan we also did an EEG. That's a test to analyze brain wave activity. She has the brain waves of someone who is wide awake."

"Awake?"

"Yes, awake." The doctor continued. "That's not unheard of, of course, but it is puzzling."

"What now?" Dick asked.

"As I said, she's been admitted and will be placed in ICU so we can keep an eye on her throughout the night. We'll continue to search for answers and get consults from neurology and others. Waiting is hard, I know, but that's all you can do now."

"What is the best-case scenario?" Adam asked bluntly.

Metzger shrugged, "She wakes up and says, 'Howdy.'"

"And worse case?" Adam was equally blunt.

The doctor paused. "There's a chance that she could slip into a deeper coma."

Adam averted his eyes. "Thank you, doctor. When can I see her?"

"Give it half an hour. She should be in ICU by then. Visitors will be limited to you and other family."

"I understand," Adam said.

"ICU is on the fifth floor," Metzger offered, then he placed a hand on Adam's shoulder. "She's getting the best-possible care. We have many excellent people on staff here, and every one of them will do everything he can to make Dr. Tremaine well again. You have my word on that."

Adam stood with the doctor and shook his hand. "I believe you, doctor. I just hope it's enough."

Dr. Metzger nodded and then turned to leave. Dick stepped to Adam's side and put an arm around his pastor and friend. "Come on," he said. "Let's go to the cafeteria for a change of scenery, then we'll go see Rachel."

"OK, I better call Fannie and let her know what's going on."

"I'll take care of that. She's already telling people not to bother you until they hear from her first. That'll keep a few hundred people off your doorstep."

"Thanks, Dick. Thanks for being here. You're a big help."

"That's what truck-driving deacons are for, my friend." Adam gave a feeble chuckle, then walked slowly from the ER lobby. Those in the waiting room saw a man walking like one who had just lost his soul.

There was now a "below." Which meant there was also an "above." The green was parting underneath her as she slowly descended through its midst. There was no sense of uncontrolled plummeting. She knew she should be terrified. She knew she should be dropping head first toward the ground below the clouds, but she wasn't, and the incongruity of that fact bothered her not at all.

Ground. There was ground below her. Clouds first, then ground. She was descending slowly like a tiny feather on a perfectly still day. Slowly. Slowly. Ever so slowly. A rose petal in the breeze; a fall leaf from an oak tree. Slowly descending. Slowly falling. Slowly. Slowly. Green above, blue below. Slowly.

Death wasn't so bad.

Four

Fort Worth, Texas

The Texas wind carried a familiar sound with it as it maneuvered its way through the tall concrete-and-steel buildings of downtown Fort Worth. The rising and falling undulations pierced the air and the window between it and the ears of Nick Stern.

At first, Nick pretended to take no notice of it. He dismissed it as something he had heard a thousand times before. It was a sound that came his way every day. That was not unusual when you lived so close to the fire station. Day in and day out, the trucks and pumpers would leave surrounded in red light and emitting their shrill call. And every time Nick heard it, he would rise, go to the window of his downtown apartment, and watch Engine Company 32 go off to work—without him.

Today would be different though. Nick was determined that nothing was going to get him out of his warm La-Z-Boy recliner. He had his coffee, his magazine, and his radio playing "the best of the sixties, seventies, and eighties." No, this time Nick was going to stay put.

The air horn on the American LaFrance pumper sounded. Its brash, guttural call was familiar to Nick. He had sounded that horn many times himself as he sat in the cab of the fire truck, first as a firefighter, then engineer, and finally as captain. He had many times ridden the red diesel into the cold Fort Worth winter nights, as well as into the hot summer days. And now he heard the horn again.

With each blast of the air horn and each undulation of the siren, Nick felt called to rise. He resisted. It was too painful to leave the chair and not just physically. Seeing the engine company race down the street only reminded him that he would never sit in the captain's seat again. He would never don the yellow Nomex jacket, never pull on the protective pants and boots, and never would he again wear that most symbolic of all firefighting garb—the helmet.

He still had the helmet from his days with the department. It was red like the truck he rode in. Red signifying his rank as captain. Another year and he would have been promoted to battalion chief and he would have worn a white helmet. But now that would never happen.

Another siren joined the first. The truck company had also been dispatched, which meant that there was a good chance that they were headed for a structure fire. Firefighters are called to many needs: auto accidents, downed power lines, toxic spills, but nothing caused the heart to beat faster than the sight of a thick column of smoke lit beneath by fingers of flame grasping for anything that would burn.

It was no use, Nick conceded. He had to look. He was compelled to rise from his chair and lumber over to the grimy window. Lowering the footrest, Nick rose from his chair, grimacing as he did. The first few steps were always the worst, as the thick stiff skin resisted any movement before becoming only slightly more pliable. He grunted with each step.

"What a pitiful man you've become, Nick ol' boy," he said to himself. He was looking at his reflection as he approached the window. The dark night and the dimly lit room had converted the window into a meager mirror. What Nick saw was a formerly six-foot-two man who was now slightly hunched; a formerly robust man of a hundred ninety pounds, now shrunken and shriveled to nearly two-thirds of that; a previously gregarious gentleman who had allowed his personality to degrade into that of a bitter curmudgeon. He cursed his reflection as he watched it mime each waddling step he took.

At the window, Nick saw the tall buildings, including the cheap flophouse he was in now, bathed in brilliant red. Sure enough, both Engine Company 32 and Truck Company 28 were responding to the unknown call. And once again, Nick was left behind.

In the distance Nick could see a faint red glow. "Structure fire all right," he said to no one. "Looks like a boomer too." He considered turning his radio scanner on, but decided against it. He could hear the radio traffic in his imagination: "This is Engine Company 32 on scene, we have smoke and flame," . . . just like last time . . . "four-story building, top two floors" . . . just like last time . . . "Truck Company 28 lay two, two-and-a-halves, position on northeast corner," . . . just like last time . . . "Better sound a second alarm on this" . . . just like last time.

He could see the captain turning to his three-man crew, "Tie two, two-and-a-halves into the hydrant, and pull the monitor; we're going to need lots of water on this one." The captain would order the truck company to set up a stream of water to protect surrounding build-ings. When the other pumper arrived, its crew would do the same. Once that was done, his men could start a direct assault on the fire itself.

Nick closed his eyes tightly and five years were stripped away. He was wearing the red helmet and speaking into his radio: "I'm start-ing a search." It was all in slow motion now as he donned his breathing apparatus, positioning its face mask and cranking the valve that would provide his air while in the hell of the burning building.

Normally a lower-ranking firefighter would be the first in, but his crew was short-handed and it took two men to set up the monitor, a large and heavy nozzle capable of delivering a waterfall's worth of water every minute.

Inside the building he raced to the third floor and found much of it involved in flame. Nick hunched over, getting as close to the floor as possible. Thick smoke obliterated any line of sight above four feet. He bellowed loudly to be heard through the plastic mask that was sealed to his face. "Anyone here? This is the fire depart-ment, anyone in here?" He scanned the hallways, opening what doors he could, looking for unconscious or trapped citizens. A large crowd had been waiting out front when the trucks arrived. Maybe everyone got out OK.

Nick raised his radio to his faceplate and spoke loudly: "Third floor is heavily charged with smoke. No one comes up without a b.a." In the old days when Nick's father was on the department, firemen never wore breathing equipment. They simply charged into the building, inhaling poisonous fumes that shortened their lives. But that was part of the job then, and more importantly, part of the image. They earned the name "smoke eaters." Without a breathing apparatus with its tank of pure air a firefighter could quickly become a victim in need of rescue.

"I'm headed to the fourth floor," Nick said. "We need a couple of lines up here as soon as possible." On the fourth floor, Nick began the same kind of systematic search, looking for unconscious people, children hiding in closets, but he found nothing. He was about to turn around and exit when he heard a muffled sound. He turned slowly, trying to get a fix on the elusive cry. It sounded like a child weeping.

Suddenly there was a teeth-rattling crash. Nick spun around with his hands up in front of his face. It was a sound down the hall, a sound of broken glass. The heat was shattering the windows. Redirecting his attention to the child's cry, he moved cautiously until he came to an apartment door. The sound was coming from in the apartment.

Nick removed the glove from his right hand and placed the back of his hand against the door; it was warm, but not hot. No backdraft situation here, but Nick was too cautious a man to take chances. He knew that if there were a smoldering fire in the room and he opened the door, the fresh influx of oxygen could ignite the flames in an explosive eruption known as a backdraft.

Crouching down close to the floor he replaced his glove, grabbed the doorknob, and prayed that it was unlocked. It was. Slowly he opened the door and listened for the sucking sound of air being drawn in by the oxygen-starved room. He heard nothing but the crying of a child. My lucky day, Nick thought. With that he threw the door open and stood up.

The room was abysmally hot. Smoke, with its invasive, permeating quality, was oozing through the cracks in the floor and around the baseboards, giving the room an eerie, haunting quality. The smoke percolating through the floor could only mean that the fire was directly below them and very hot. Across the living room, hunkered down next to the floor, was a child no more than four years old. Nick swore, and his heart pounded.

Turning to his right, Nick saw a window. Outside the window were long vicious waves of flame lapping and slapping the sides of the building. We're going to lose this structure, Nick thought. The fire is moving too fast—much too fast. I'll bet this month's salary that an arsonist did this. A moment later the window exploded as the temperature difference between the air in the room and the fire on the pane proved too much. Razor-sharp shards of glass flew everywhere.

The child screamed and grabbed his ear.

Seeing the terrified youngster holding the side of his head and watching as blood began to trickle down his arm caused Nick to forget his years of training and experience. He made a rookie mistake. Without first testing the floor between himself and the child, Nick walked in. Halfway across the room, a portion of the floor weakened by the hellish hunger of the fire below gave way.

Nick fell.

The hole in the floor caused by Nick's weight was only large enough for him to drop down to his shoulders. He was stuck, wedged in by his own weight and tied in place by his own protective gear. The tank from the breathing apparatus was jammed tightly into the floor. Smoke ascended in ghostly fashion around him.

At first, Nick felt nothing. He was thankful he had not fallen all the way through. Glancing about, he looked for his radio. He saw it about four feet away, a foot out of reach. He could not call for help. He looked at the little boy, who was now shrieking at the top of his lungs.

It took only moments for the superheated air and fire now freshly charged with oxygen from the hole in the floor to efficiently burn away the firefighter's boots and pants. Soon the sound of Nick's screams resonated with that of the injured boy.

It had taken months in the hospital and sixteen surgeries to save Nick's legs. He had lived through the fire, but now he must live with the pain and disfigurement of the burns he received.

The department gave him a citation for bravery. The mayor called him a hero. Then he was put out to pasture on medical disability. The department had tried to find a new place of service for Nick. They gave him office work and even asked him to teach in the fire academy, but he could not stand to see other men do the job for which he had been born. Every uniform was a reminder of his loss, of his former glory—a glory that had burned to nothing.

The fire had burned more than his legs; it had burned his mind. The jovial spirit and even temper that had made him one of the favorite captains in the department had been scraped away with each layer of skin that had been removed by doctors and nurses to allow for new, albeit scarred, skin.

Nick was now a bitter man. People soon came to loathe his quick temper and his eternal self-pity. Nick came to loathe it too, but he was helpless to stop it. It was this same ill-temper that became too much for his wife to bear. At their wedding she had promised to love him in sickness and in health, but not in abuse and mental torment. A year after the accident she was gone. The sad thing was, Nick didn't care.

The lights were gone now, as were the sirens. Nothing more to see. Nick ambled back to his chair and sat down heavily. He couldn't change the past and he didn't care about the future. He picked up his magazine. It was the latest issue of *Time*. He seldom read the articles, but he enjoyed leafing through the pages. It was fairly mindless and passed the time. And that was all Nick had left, time. Career was gone. Family was gone. Now there was just time.

The worst part of it all was not the injury to his legs, but the damage done to his manhood. He had found his identity and purpose in his work, but that had been pirated away from him. Now he was just a shell of a man—a scarred, damaged, mutilated shell.

Nick flipped the pages of his magazine, gazing down at them through unseeing eyes. Then something caught his eye. Something had moved. He knew that couldn't be true, but it had certainly looked as if something on the page had moved. He flipped back the pages until he came to an ad for a . . . well, he didn't know what the ad was for. It was a color picture of the interior of a restaurant. People were seated at tables. Everyone was smiling, laughing, and pointing at a waiter who was positioned in the center of the photo. It was a happy scene and suddenly Nick wanted to be happy. He wanted to laugh and fellowship with other people. He wanted to be in that restaurant.

Then it happened again. Movement.

The waiter smiled. Not at the others, but at Nick. Then he winked. Nick quickly dropped the magazine on his lap and closed his eyes.

A moment later he opened them and picked up the *Time*. Now all the people were moving; some dusted themselves off, others were righting fallen chairs. It was as though the act of dropping the magazine had actually jarred the restaurant.

"I've been locked up in this room too long," Nick said to himself. "I'm losing it." He looked back at the picture, and the waiter was staring at him and waving his finger the way a mother scolds a child. But the waiter wasn't angry, in fact, his grin was enormous. Now he made another gesture with his hand—a "come here" gesture. The man was inviting Nick to join them.

"This is too Twilight Zone for me. I need to get some help." He started to close the magazine, but found that he couldn't. He wanted one more peek at the bizarre photo.

Nick Stern stared intently at the advertisement as if he were looking at one of those computer-generated pictures that look like nothing but colored squiggly lines but turn into three-dimensional images if gazed upon long enough. The waiter smiled, motioned again, a behavior that was soon repeated by everyone in the restaurant.

Nick let himself relax. The picture was enticing, filled with cheerful people who seemed glad to be together. Wouldn't it be wonderful if there really were such a place? Wouldn't it be exceptional to be a part of that group? "If only I could be there," Nick said. "I could use a little company."

Nick was there, surrounded by joyful folk who seemed genuinely glad to see him. Nick's apartment was gone and somehow he knew he wasn't in Fort Worth, Texas, anymore.

The waiter walked up to Nick and put his arm around his shoulders. "I'm glad you're here, Nick. Real glad. Sit down, let me get you something to eat, then we can talk."

Two hours later, Nick was back in his tiny run-down apartment. The flat was the same, but it was a different Nick, still scarred on his body, but no longer on his soul. Suddenly Nick felt whole and useful.

That day, Nick found a purpose in life.

Five

San Diego, California

Adam shivered as he sat in a high-backed, mustard-yellow, vinyl chair. He watched as nurses entered and left the small glass cubicle that was Rachel's ICU room. They seemed warm enough, yet Adam felt cold. He knew he was responding to the shock of finding his wife unconscious on the floor, the subsequent ride in the ambulance, and the fear of the unknown. He shuddered again and rubbed his arms.

He had been in this very room several times over the last few years, but always as a pastor paying a visit to an ailing church member. He had held their hands, prayed with them, and offered words of comfort. Now it was his wife in the bed, wired to monitors and connected to IV bags. Now he was the one sitting in the ugly and uncomfortable chair, waiting and fighting back fear.

The room was quiet despite the monitors. Lights flashed, a heart monitor digitally displayed Rachel's heart rate and graphically displayed her heart's rhythm. There was a small television in the room, but Adam couldn't bring himself to turn it on. There was a far larger drama being played out in his head.

Adam had never been "lucky" with women. He had been engaged twice, once in college and once to a woman in his first church. Each engagement had ended badly, with the first fiancée moving away to attend college on the East Coast and leaving behind her former life as well as Adam; the second had simply been unfaithful. Both events had shaken Adam and he responded by throwing himself into his work and resolving himself to the fact that he would never marry.

When he had met Rachel he had done so under the worst possible conditions. An appendicitis attack had landed him in the hospital. He had ignored all the early warning signs. Finally the pain could be ignored no longer. Adam collapsed to the floor on a Sunday morning while standing behind the pulpit.

His surgeon was Dr. Rachel Tremaine, acerbic, self-absorbed, and antireligion. Adam represented everything that Rachel resented: faith, hope, optimism. Adam found her obstinate, cold, and recalcitrant. He was also attracted to her. It had made no sense, it was unwise, but he found himself being drawn to her professional passion and keen mind.

Physically, she was not impressive: a little shorter than most women, thin, with extremely short black hair. She wore no makeup and no jewelry. But that was all right with Adam. None of those things mattered. What did matter was the woman hidden within the doctor's shell. Events that ultimately put both their lives at risk helped that woman emerge.

Adam chortled. He was remembering the time, months after his surgery and several social interactions with Rachel, she had attempted to seduce him and he had to call upon every fiber of his faith to resist. That's when he discovered her temper. But time healed that rift.

Over the months, Adam and Rachel grew closer and she became more open: open to him and open to spiritual ideals. Slowly, painfully slow from Adam's perspective, she came to understand the principles of belief and faith. One of the most rapturous moments in Adam's life was when he baptized her. A few months later they were married.

Each new day brought out a previously unseen facet of his wife.

She grew in faith, but also in the way she viewed the world. The former bitterness had melted away and was being replaced with optimism and joy. She laughed, told jokes, praised other people when they did something special, and learned to give herself to Adam in love. She was a new creature.

If so much could go right then, why is so much going wrong now? Adam wondered. He felt tears welling up in his eyes. "I will not lose you, Rachel," he said softly. "I will not surrender you." He reached over and took her hand. It felt soft, weak; not at all like the hand he held so often.

A sigh, deep and heavy, fell from Adam's lips. He wished Dick could have stayed, but the nursing staff insisted that only family could visit. Family. Adam realized that he should call Rachel's family. They would want to know. It was a call he was dreading.

Warm sunshine coated her face. She could feel it touch her nose and neck and arms. It felt good, satisfying, salubrious. She lay still, fearing that any movement might deprive her of the profound sensory pleasure she was experiencing.

Peace.

Joy.

The soft sound of surf caressing the shore provided a natural music that far surpassed anything written by mortals. The tide was coming in, slowly, deliberately, tenderly. The satiny foam lace at the edge of the water fondled the heels of her feet and cuddled lightly along her bare toes.

Exhilaration.

Tranquillity.

She was lying on her back. That much she knew. And although she hadn't opened her eyes the sounds and sensations around her told her that she was on a beach, a distant, quiet, peaceful shore. A place she had never been. Without knowing why, she felt that she was the first person to ever touch this place.

Curiosity.

Wonder.

Reclining forever with her eyes closed appealed to Rachel. Sensing the sunshine, hearing the melodious movement of the nearby water had brought more peace to Rachel than anything she had ever experienced. But if such peace could be found through sound and touch alone, then what greater serenity awaited her eyes?

Slowly she rose, eyes still closed, until she was seated on the sand, her legs drawn up and her arms cradling her knees. Slowly, compelled by anticipation but fearful of disappointment, Rachel opened her eyes.

Had anyone been there to observe her they would have seen a woman immobile, silent, statuesque. At first there was no expression, no response, no sound. A moment later, Rachel smiled, then giggled in a way she hadn't done since she was girl on the edge of adolescence.

Above her was a sky of green—a perfectly natural green for this world. Before her was an ocean of the purest azure highlighted by wispy, gossamer foam. Around her was sand, fine, almost powdery and hued the perfect neutral gray. Behind her, she saw after slowly turning, was a deep wooded grove forged by tall, thick trees.

Verdant.

Perfection.

Rachel inhaled deeply and sensed aroma she had never experienced. All her senses seemed more acute. Everything seemed without blemish. She was alone without a hint of loneliness. I could sit here forever, she reasoned. Sit here and never move. I would be happy. I would be complete. Rachel wasn't sure where she was, but one thing she knew: she never wanted to leave.

Six

Ojai, California

The canvas was blank.

"So what's the problem, Picasso? What's the matter with me?" The orange tabby cat looked casually at his mistress but didn't offer a response. "No ideas, huh? What about you, Rembrandt? Do you have an opinion to offer?" The powder gray feline neither budged from its comfortable location on the file cabinet across the room nor paused in its self-administered bathing ritual. It had spent a full ten minutes on the front left paw and couldn't be bothered with anything else. "You guys are no help."

"You don't get out enough, that's what I think." The unexpected voice came from the studio's doorway. The voice's owner was a stout woman of sixty-five, dark hair with its share of gray, and an overbearing demeanor. She walked into the room uninvited. "You sit in this art studio too many hours if you ask me." No one had. "I know this is how you make your living, but you really should get out and inhale some of that beautiful air. It's a lovely day."

"Oh, hello Mother," Katrin Coeur said evenly. "I didn't see you there."

"And the way you talk to those cats, I swear. If someone saw you, he would think you were some kind of a nut instead of a famous artist."

"I am some kind of a nut, Mother."

"Nonsense, you're a lovely girl admired by many."

"No, Mother, my paintings are admired by many, not me. There's a difference, you know."

"All you need is some companionship—male companionship. And you're not going to find it sitting around this dusty old studio."

"My studio isn't dusty, Mother."

"Thirty-six years old and still unmarried." Katrin's mother shook her head dismally.

"Guys aren't interested in me. I'm not their type." Katrin fiddled with her long, straight fawn hair, alternatingly wrapping strands around her finger and unwrapping them. She glanced over at a small canvas leaning against a wall. It was a self-portrait she had painted while in college a decade and a half ago. Aside from a few creases around the eyes the image she saw in the mirror this morning was not very different from the one she saw on the canvas. Painting that image, a requirement for a class, was a painful experience then; thinking about it now was just as distressing. The painting showed the same long, straight brown hair, blue eyes, and pouting lips. The girl in the portrait didn't smile. It was an accurate portrayal.

"Nonsense. Come on, let's go down to the mall in Ventura. We can have lunch and take in a movie."

"I can't, Mother, I'm busy. The studios want some more paintings."

"So, they can wait a little. My baby girl needs some away time."

"I'm not a little girl, Mother. Besides, these paintings help us live quite well."

"That's because you are one of the most sought-after painters living today. You are the best. Your paintings are the best. And you are also a recluse. Come see a movie with me."

"Another time, Mother. You go. Eat some popcorn for me."

Katrin heard her mother sigh heavily. "Oh, all right. But you're missing a beautiful day. I'll be back by dinnertime. OK?"

Katrin swiveled her stool back to face the blank canvas. Her mother walked over and kissed her on top of the head. "Sure you won't change your mind, baby?"

"I'm sure, but thanks for the offer."

Mother sighed loudly again and left.

The canvas was primed and ready for the artist's hand. It was blank, waiting for genius to pour forth and create upon its surface an enchanting image made with oil paint that was dabbed, stroked, pulled, and spread in various combinations until the scene was visible to all, eliciting praise and wonderment.

But the canvas was still blank. It was as blank now as it had been the hour before and the hour before that. Not one dollop of paint, not one stroke of pencil to create an outline. Just plain, prepped canvas and nothing more. Katrin had run out of ideas. The ceaseless images that played through her mind day after day, year after year, had evaporated.

This was a new experience for Katrin Coeur. She had been touted in the art journals as a rare talent, the kind that comes around once a decade, maybe once a lifetime. Her paintings sold well and they sold high. She made enough money from her first show to allow her to quit her job as a technical illustrator for a Santa Barbara book company and take up her passion full time. That was a decade ago. Now she was wealthy, famous, admired, and lonely.

"Perhaps I should have gone with Mother, Rembrandt. I don't seem to be getting much done here."

Meow.

"Ah, so you do have an opinion." Katrin laughed lightly and then raised her pencil to begin sketching the light outline that would later guide her brush. She stopped. She had planned to lay out a simple scene: a mother buying a prom dress for her teenage daughter. Katrin had never worn a prom dress, never been to a school dance. She had spent much of her time alone with only a few girls for friends. Painting such scenes often made her feel sad, but she knew that emotion came across in the painting. It was that passion and emotive quality that made Katrin's paintings so sought after. Today, however, she could not seem to get started.

Standing for a moment, she stretched, then repositioned the canvas and easel to better pick up the soft afternoon light. Outside her window she could see the branches of the oak trees moving rhythmically with the breeze. Mother had been right: it was a lovely day. Sitting again, she stared at the empty canvas that now seemed to be mocking her.

"Maybe I need another subject," she said to the cats and the empty room. "Maybe I'm not meant to do that picture right now. But if not that, then what?"

Closing her eyes, Katrin wished for something to paint. Something impressive. Something worthwhile. She took a deep breath and opened her eyes. What she saw caused her to gasp, dropping her brushes on the floor.

But she hadn't been holding brushes. She had been holding a sketching pencil. She looked at the paint-laden brushes strewn at her feet, splatters of color cast from their ends. How did they come to have paint on them? She noticed she was squinting. The light was nearly gone. When she had closed her eyes the sun was still high in the afternoon sky, but now it was nearly dark. Where had the time gone? Had she fallen asleep?

"What is this?" she asked aloud. Before her was the canvas, which was no longer blank. Instead it was filled with color and images—disturbing and frightening images.

"Katrin, I'm home," came her mother's voice as she walked down the hall. "You missed a good movie. Have you had dinner yet? If not I can . . ." As her mother crossed the threshold into the studio from the hall she stopped short. "That's . . . that's . . . interesting," she stammered. "Not your best work, but it certainly is captivating. What does it all mean?"

Katrin looked at the image on the canvas, an image she had no recollection of painting, and replied, "I'm really not sure."

Across the room, Rembrandt and Picasso, two cats so independent and individualistic that they had little to do with each other, sat huddled together under an old wooden desk, watching Katrin suspiciously. Propped next to the desk was another painting that Katrin didn't recognize. It was similar to the one on the easel, yet significantly different.

Rembrandt mewed a quiet, frightened meow and moved farther back under the desk, never taking his eyes from Katrin.

Seven

London, England

Inhalation. Slowly, smoothly, Lindsay Blair drew in a long breath and then released it in a silent flow that passed her slightly puckered lips. She inhaled again, this time deeper. She felt her heart slow, her muscles relax.

Inhalation. Cool air. Elixir.

Exhalation. Slow, purposeful release.

Cautiously she extended her arm, moving her hand millimeter by millimeter toward its destination. She was in no hurry; the hard part had been done. Every contingency had been considered, every precaution taken. Even hanging upside down from the aluminum scaffolding she had erected, she knew that her plan was flawless. Her plans were always flawless.

Under the knit mask that covered her head and face a smile emerged. She had been four months in the planning of this heist. Four months of detailed analysis, physical training, and mental preparations. Just like her father had taught her. "Details make all the difference," he used to say. "Overlook the smallest thing and it can come back to haunt you."

Lindsay never overlooked details—she couldn't afford to in her line of work. She had taken care of everything. The four video cameras trained on the object that was just a few centimeters away from her hand concerned her not at all. The two guards who watched the monitors were fast asleep, thanks to the drugs she had injected in them through the air-powered tranquilizer gun she had brought. Actually she had brought two such guns, one for each guard. Since the specialized pistols could hold only one drug-laced dart each, and since—despite weeks of practice—it took twenty seconds to reload and fire, Lindsay had opted for two weapons. That had taken care of the video.

Lindsay had taken a different approach with the guard who had been circulating through the museum, checking doors and halls. She stood at the end of the hall crying. When the guard saw her, he had stopped and stared, wary at first then irresistibly drawn to her. She had seen the response in men before. They saw her waist-length raven-black hair, her eyes of dazzling green, and her smooth, unblemished pale skin and they became transfixed.

She had often been mistaken for a model, an image she fostered. A dazzling beauty as a child, Lindsay had grown more elegant with each year. Now at the age of twenty-nine she was envied by women and longed for by men. But she had no interest in men. Her love was saved for two things: rare art and the thrill of theft.

The guard had approached her, beguiled by her beauty and unsettled by her soft weeping. "Are you all right?" he asked kindly. Lindsay slowly dropped her hands from her face and fixed a tender gaze on the Good Samaritan. She then snapped into motion, quickly bringing her right hand up with unexpected speed and planting an open hand blow on the tip of the man's chin. He grunted and staggered backward. Lindsay spun on her left leg and delivered a powerful kick to his abdomen. She watched as his eyes widened at the blow, and she could hear the air rush from his lungs. He would not be able to breath for a minute or more as his temporarily paralyzed solar plexus struggled to regain sufficient control to be able to draw air.

There was more than enough time for Lindsay to approach the doubled-over man, grab him by the hair on the back of his head, and slam her knee into his face. He fell in an unconscious heap to the floor. A few strips of duct tape rendered him bound and gagged.

She looked at the dart gun in her hand and asked herself why she hadn't used it instead of risking failure by a physical confrontation. The only answer she could come to was entertainment. What was the purpose if one could not enjoy one's work?

Now her hand hovered over a gold Peruvian bust the size of a grapefruit. The piece was a marvel of craftsmanship and more than five centuries old. It was a one-of-a-kind find discovered only three years ago by an archeologist on a dig in the green mountains of Peru. Most scholars believed it to be a likeness of a previously unknown god. Lindsay saw it not only as a beautiful artifact, but also as a two million dollar fee.

With her gloved hand lingering over the object, she imagined she could feel the coolness of the metal and the substantial weight of the gold. In her planning she had even determined the best and most efficient way to place her fingers so as not to risk dropping the priceless piece.

It never bothered her that she was a thief. She was no common criminal skulking furtively in the shadows of big cities mugging pedestrians for pocket change or carjacking expensive automobiles in broad daylight to demonstrate some misguided hubris. Those people were the dregs of society who lacked imagination and purpose. Petty was the only word that could describe their efforts. They were valueless as people.

She, on the other hand, was a highly trained professional who pirated inestimable and cherished items that lesser thieves didn't know existed. And she did so with élan. It wasn't enough to steal the most precious gems, works of art, and industrial secrets; it had to be done in a way that even the police would admire. Intrigue, wealth, and adventure were the triplets of her philosophy, a philosophy she adopted from her father.

Nigel Blair had learn the art of burglary from his father as did his father before him. Three generations of Blairs had increased the family fortunes through the art of theft. Like Lindsay they had focused on only the best items. "If one is going to risk imprisonment," her father used to say through his thick British accent, "one should do so only for the rarest and best items. It wouldn't do to be jailed over some bauble or some businessman's wallet."

So the training began. First she attended the finest schools, ones that emphasized art and history, as well as the basics. Lindsay excelled in school. She had been blessed with a fast mind and a keen memory. While others slaved to master terms, history lines, and chemical formulas, Lindsay simply read the text once and could recall everything. Some of her female classmates hated her for her skill and beauty. The boys did not share that hatred.

After school, while others played sports or hung out with friends, Lindsay was still studying. Her late afternoon courses were vastly different from the ones the instructors taught. Instead of grammar she learned security systems; in lieu of home economics, Lindsay explored the various ways of persuading a safe to give up its contents. All under the tutelage of her father.

Lindsay loved her father more than she had been able to express. While other teenage girls rebelled against their parents, Lindsay's admiration for her father grew. This was partly due to the absence of her mother, who died in an auto accident when Lindsay was three, and to the indulgent nature of her father.

Lindsay had just turned twenty when her father died from an erupted aneurysm on his descending aorta. She was crushed. Gone was the only person in the world she had ever loved. Since Lindsay was an only child the estate, which was considerable, passed to her without contest. She had more money than she could spend, but it wasn't enough. There was a family tradition to carry on, and Lindsay was determined to continue the trade that had brought the initial wealth.

Her first heist was a night burglary of a small but well-to-do art dealership in London. She was less interested in stealing something than in proving she could defeat the security system and testing her mettle. The task she set for herself went so smoothly that she felt cheated. She needed a bigger challenge. Soon she had purloined goods from jewelry stores, museums, and private residences.

Six months later she was planning larger and more complex jobs. It was then that she noticed a change in herself: she no longer stole out of obligation to her father's memory, but because she enjoyed the act so very much. She had become addicted to the craft just as her father and grandfather before him. It was in the blood.

Blinking back the memories, Lindsay prepared to lift the bust from its resting place. That act would trigger a security alarm that was meant to alert the guards and activate an automatic dialer that would call the police with a recorded message.

The guards were taken care of and Lindsay would be three miles from the scene before the first bobby crossed the threshold. She could have taken care of the alarm with a computerized signal generator set to interrupt the electronic alert, but Lindsay had grown fond of the image of police racing to a place she had left minutes before. Adventure required some risk even if Lindsay had to introduce the risk herself.

The time had come. She took one more deep breath and then let it trickle from her lips. She closed her eyes, mentally playing out the escape route she had charted, then opened them again. With a slight drop of her shoulder Lindsay seized the bust, feeling the roundness of the garish head in her hand and . . .

FLASH.

Light. Stabbing bright. Eyes hurt. Dizzy. Spinning. Tunnel of light. Falling. Free fall. Fast descent. Tunnel walls moving, churning, pulsating.

Above her Lindsay could see a bright light, a light from which she was quickly falling away. With each passing second the light became more removed. Instinctively she knew that the light was her world, a world she had somehow just left. Below her, at the end of the tunnel was a void of liquid blackness. Around her the walls of the tunnel moved as if alive, as if she had been swallowed by some gigantic creature and she was now passing down its gullet. It was more than mere movement, more than simple biological undulation.

Still shocked by the sudden change, she had yet to feel fear, just confusion. Looking closely at the wall that raced past her, she saw something that shattered her stunned mind, releasing a tide of terror that she had not only never experienced but also could never have imagined. The wall was not a solid mass of material but was instead composed of faces—human, screaming, terrified faces. And each face was screaming her name.

Lindsay joined the screaming. Her voice echoed loudly and the more she screamed the more the choir of shrieks increased until there was a crescendo of horror-laced chaos.

Each face in the wall was as human as could be. Each had skin pulled taut over a bony skull, a mouth open in perpetual anguished cries, eyes wide and unblinking. Lindsay attempted to control her fall, to move away from the tortured faces, but every effort she made caused her to spin all the more wildly, bouncing into the walls, her hands touching the cold flesh of flared nostrils, furrowed brows, and trembling lips. Skin cold as ice water yet covered in despair-driven perspiration.

Falling. Screaming. Falling. Weeping.

Terror unmitigated. Fright undiminished.

Falling. Accelerating. Tumbling.

Seconds poured into minutes in a deluge of time. Each second took her further from the warm light above and closer to the inky blackness of night below her.

There was only a moment's relief when Lindsay dropped head-long into the darkness, relieved that she could not see the faces any longer. The respite was only momentary, for the blackness that engulfed her was absolute and carried the stench of evil—a profound evil.

Nothingness . . .

Blackness . . .

Void . . .

Vacuum . . .

Lindsay was still falling. This was something she felt, something she knew apart from sensory input because she could see nothing, feel nothing. It was as if she were being sucked to the bottom of an ocean of ink by a riptide bent on drowning her in blackness.

Flailing, swimming, struggling, kicking, reaching. Lindsay had been holding her breath, not wanting to inhale the liquid blackness that had enveloped her, but the burning of her lungs soon forced her to involuntarily open her mouth in a desperate effort to breathe. The void was vile, the blackness bitter. Lindsay gagged and retched. Despite her body's reflexive attempt to purge the thick, syrupy blackness, it invaded her anyway, even oozing its way into her pores.

The blackness was alive! It crawled on her skin like ants on a fallen piece of ripe watermelon. It moved, undulated, caressed, scratched, pulled, pushed, flowed, ebbed. Each involuntary breath that Lindsay took filled her mouth and throat with the infested darkness.

There were no thoughts in Lindsay's disciplined mind, no logical questions, no attempt to reason. She had degenerated into an instinctive animal fighting back against an overwhelming foe that she did not understand. She was no more successful than a baby mastodon in the La Brea tar pits. They were sucked to their deaths by viscous tar. Lindsay was being pulled down by the sticky, tenacious power of blackness.

Lindsay Blair was helpless and she wished for death, but she knew that even death couldn't help her.

The syrupy blackness changed. Lindsay was no longer falling, no longer sucked through darkness. She was on the ground. She didn't remember falling to the earth. She didn't remember an impact or any tactile sensation that she had touched down on the surface of wherever she was.

She was still surrounded by blackness, but this darkness was different. It didn't move, it wasn't thick, and, to her surprise, she could see. There was no light, no sun, moon, or stars, no source of illumination, but still she could see. It was as if she were in a place of perpetual twilight. Seeing in darkness made no sense, for she felt the darkness was as black as any moonless night, but reasonable or not, her eyes worked.

She was looking up at her outstretched hand that was raised high above her head as if she were reaching for a lightbulb. It occurred to her that she was on her knees. That's when Lindsay understood. She was in the same position she was in before the nightmare began, except she wasn't upside down. Before, she had been suspended on an aluminum scaffolding that allowed her to hang by her knees and hover over the gold bust, but now she was kneeling in the dirt, reaching toward a sky that wasn't there.

Slowly, she lowered her hand, stood to her feet, and looked around her. The absolute blackness surrendered a modicum of sight. What she saw brought her no comfort. The terrain was composed of a ground of gray mottled with black. Leafless plants sprouted from the earth like thin black coral, a skeleton of what once might have been a verdant growth. There was no sky; there was no horizon. Even the starkest desert would have seemed lush and verdant compared to the bleak nothingness of this place.

A sound, mournful and high pitched, was carried by a wind that wasn't there. There was no direction to the sound, no discernible origin. The sound grew, and Lindsay recognized it immediately. It was the sound of tormented life, of people in anguish and pain. It was the sound uttered by a community ravaged by earthquake, leveled by monsoon, burned by volcanic eruption. It was the sound of people being destroyed without end. The sound grew in intensity.

It was a chorus of angst and abysmal pain. It was a concert of hope-lessness and utter despair. It was a melody of madness set to coun-terpoint with anguish. If terror and wretchedness had a sound this was it.

It was the saddest thing Lindsay had ever heard. She felt tears run from her eyes. She raised a hand to wipe away the trickle of tears when she froze in place. Her hand! Her hand was wrong, it was, it was . . .

Lindsay added her voice to the choir of sorrow. She stared dis-believingly at the skin of her hand and arm. It bubbled. It moved. It looked as if she were baking in a gigantic oven that had been set too high. Her skin was burning right before her eyes. She raised the other hand and saw the same thing. Slowly she touched her face and felt the pockets of skin rise and fall. She knew that her face was a boiling caldron of flesh.

What she saw on her long naked legs rocketed her panic to an even higher level. Her feet were covered in a teeming, undulating mass of foot-long worms. A moment later the worms changed into spiders as large as coins. The spiders transformed into large black scorpions that picked at her pink flesh with vicious pinchers and then pierced her with their large poison-laden stingers. She could feel each creature and each sting. The scorpions transmuted into a bundle of snakes that slowly worked their way up her unmoving legs. Worms to spiders to scorpions to snakes to bees and hornets and back to worms. It was as if someone or something was testing to see what would terrify her most.

It was then that she felt the heat—unimaginable, inexplicable heat. Burning. Searing. Scorching. She was immersed in flame. Flame that could not be seen, but could be felt. It was a flame that would-n't diminish, couldn't burn out. It was fire with a purpose, malev-olent heat, that seemed to enjoy the act of burning.

Lindsay was screaming incessantly now, adding her ululation to the ever-present backdrop of anguished cries.

So this was death. So this was hell.

A movement in the darker shadows of the shadow world caught Lindsay's eye. Someone was approaching. Someone who clearly knew this domain. She was not alone. No matter how bad it is, this place might be bearable if there is someone to share it with me, she thought.

She was wrong.

It took only moments for the creature to approach. Creature was the only term Lindsay could think of, for what she saw was not human by half. It had a head, two arms, and two legs, but that didn't make it human. Its hideous head was elongated and reptilian. Its eyes glowed yellow with flashing speckles of red like glowing drops of blood. Sauntering as it approached, just a rugged, glimmering hide that changed in shades of gray that matched this colorless world.

The creature stopped four feet from Lindsay. It, the It, was taller than Lindsay by three feet or more. She could smell its putrid breath that wafted over a row of sharp teeth. The beast smiled and with the smile communicated a palpable evil. Lindsay wanted to run, to flee the outrageous, terrifying specter before her, but she could not turn, could not move. She was paralyzed.

"Hello, Ms. Blair," the creature said. Its voice was strangely melodious yet still harsh and coarse like an old scratched phonograph record. "I'm so glad you could join us."

Lindsay screamed.

"What kind of greeting is that?" the It hissed. "I want us to be friends." Lindsay said nothing but simply shook in terror. As she watched, the creature's skin began to change. On its left chest the flesh bubbled, metamorphosed, and became the screaming, crying face of a man. The creature plucked it off and threw it to the ground. Lindsay watched in terror as the face continued to scream. "Must have been someone I ate," the It said, then laughed a grating, grinding, rusty iron gate laugh.

The creature raised his arm and gently cradled her chin in his hand. His skin was painfully hot. "It's a shame I can't keep you right now. We could have so much . . . fun together. Unfortunately, I'm here just to deliver a message." His voice had turned bitter and hate filled. "As if I'm some human errand boy."

Lindsay stood transfixed by the horror before her. She could think of no words to say; her mind held no thoughts, just abject, cold fear.

"Well, let's get this over," the It said. "I have nations and people to terrorize. But before we talk, there's someone I'd like you to meet." The It slowly motioned to his right. Lindsay reluctantly turned her gaze to where the It was pointing.

A short distance away stood a man—a man only vaguely familiar at first, but then easily recognized. He was in abysmal pain and screamed ceaselessly. His skin boiled and bubbled, his face was tortured. Like Lindsay's, his body was covered with worms and other insects. He extended his arms out and cried with a terror that went far beyond his own need. "Lindsay! Help me, Lindsay!"

For the first time since her descent, Lindsay spoke: "Daddy! Daaaaaaad-dyyyy!"

"Oh," the It said glibly. "You two know each other." The It laughed loudly enough to overpower the ever-present moans and screams. "Hell is such a small place these days."

Eight

San Diego, California

Adam awoke with a start. He felt a rush of confusion. His heart pounded. For a moment he was lost, confused about time and place. Quickly he glanced around and took in his surroundings. The motion caused pain to shoot through his neck and down his back.

He saw the pale white walls of the ICU cubicle, the IV bags with their tentacles of clear plastic tubes dangling down. The cardiac monitor still flashed the rhythmic beats of his wife's heart.

Adam took a deep breath and calmed himself. It was clear to him now: he had fallen asleep in the high-back chair, which accounted for his stiff neck and aching back. He had been in the hospital room all night but he knew he hadn't slept long. The clock on the wall said six-thirty and Adam remembered being awake at two that morning. At most he had slept four, maybe four and a half-hours.

Rising from his chair he approached the still figure in the bed. He looked at the instruments attached to Rachel. He was not a medical expert, but as a pastor he had been in hospitals enough to know some of the basics. The IV bags were about half full, which meant a nurse had quietly come in while he was sleeping and changed them.

The digital display on the IV pump indicated that it was faithfully doing its job. The heart monitor showed a steady rhythm and the red LED numbers indicated a pulse rate of sixty. He watched the blood pressure cuff wrapped around her thin arm begin to inflate as if by magic. It would automatically take her blood pressure and record the results for the medical staff to review later. Everything seemed right and in place. The only thing wrong was his comatose wife.

Adam had spoken to the doctors shortly before ten last night, but they still knew nothing. They were, by their own admission, baffled.

Leaning over the still figure in the bed, Adam kissed her forehead. "Good morning, kiddo," he said softly. "If you'll get up, I'll take you to breakfast." There was no answer. There was no movement. "I'll even pay." He brushed her black bangs back and watched as Rachel's eyes moved rapidly back and forth. She was dreaming.

Something was going on in Rachel's head. Adam was sure of that. But he didn't know what, nor did he know what he could do about it.

The air smelled of tangerines still ripe on the tree and Rachel inhaled it deeply. As a doctor she knew the weakest of human senses was the olfactory. The sense of smell could easily tire and become ineffective. But here things were different. No matter how much or how often she inhaled the fragrant atmosphere of this strange world the bouquet neither changed nor diminished. It was redolent with the perfume of life. She could smell the forest behind her, the ocean before her, and the space above.

The incense of existence blended perfectly with the sights and sounds around her, serving up a banquet of sensory delight. Even the touch of the sand on the bottoms of her feet and the caress of the breeze on her smooth cheeks was delightfully rich, intense without being acute.

She was strolling along a shoreline that looked untouched, unpolluted by human existence. Rachel had a profound sense that she and she alone had walked this shore and that her feet had been the only ones to leave the imprint of existence pressed into the powdery sand.

The ocean gently, tenderly pushed its water forward in a diaphanous fuzz that fondled her toes, gracing them lightly with its touch as if it were worshiping her presence.

Rachel had no idea how far she had walked or how long she had been on the shoreline. Oddly, it didn't seem to matter, as if time were on holiday in this place.

She stopped and raised her face skyward, feeling the warmth of the yellow sunshine as it poured through the jade green sky. Then, placing her hands behind her back, she resumed her walk with no idea of where she was or where she was going.

That lack of knowledge made her feel all the more relaxed and blissful. Not having a place to go seemed more than permissible; it seemed right, correct, fitting the plan of the universe—whatever and wherever this universe was.

"Not hungry, huh?"

Adam looked up from the tray of unappetizing food before him and saw the stout figure of Dick Slay.

"You're going to have to pray real hard to make that stuff look good."

Adam smiled. "I'm surprised the nurses let you in here."

"I didn't ask their permission. If you don't ask, they can't say no." Dick walked slowly into the room, crossing over to the bed upon which Rachel lay. He took her hand and stood motionless. Adam could tell he was praying. A moment later Dick asked, "You been here all night?"

"I couldn't bring myself to go home," he replied, setting aside the untouched breakfast. "She hasn't changed. It's as if she's in a dream world. Her eyes keep darting about. I wonder what she's seeing."

"You're going to have to go home sometime, my friend," Dick said softly. "It's no good you staying here all the time."

"I don't think I can."

"You can." Dick's voice was firm but kind. "If you don't take care of yourself, you can't take care of her. It's the same advice I've heard you give others."

"True, but . . ."

"No buts, Pastor. I think you should go home and get some rest. Sleep in your own bed tonight."

"I don't want her to be alone. What if something happens? What if she wakes up?"

"I've got it all taken care of. She won't be alone." Dick reached into his pocket and pulled out a small black plastic box that Adam recognized immediately. "I got you a pager. We'll leave the number with the nurses. They can get hold of you immediately if anything changes."

"I appreciate this, Dick, but I don't feel comfortable leaving just yet."

"No one is asking you to leave this minute, but you need some rest, some real sleep, and you're not going to get it sitting in that chair."

In his mind, Adam knew Dick was right. Sitting around the hospital seemed the . . . loyal thing to do. But he also knew that spending hours sitting in the hospital room would only increase his frustration over his helplessness and lead to further depression. Adam rubbed the stubble on his unshaven chin.

"You know I'm right about this, Adam," Dick said firmly.

"I know, I know."

"So then it's settled." Dick placed his strong stubby hand on Adam's shoulder. "Let's go to the cafeteria for some coffee, then you can come back and visit some more. Later I'll bring Chloe with me and she can sit with Rachel. You know how close those two are."

That was true. No two women could be more different. Rachel was slight in frame, just a little over five feet tall with shiny black hair. Chloe was ten years older, taller than most men, heavy, and had a full head of prematurely gray hair. She blamed the hair on living with Dick and rearing three mischievous boys. She was also one of the sweetest women Adam knew.

Adam nodded in silence, surrendering to the wisdom of his friend. He exhaled noisily and stepped to the bedside of his love. "I'm going to get some coffee with Dick," he said softly and stroked her pale cheek. "I'll be back soon."

There was no response.

"I love you so very, very much," he uttered breathlessly. "Please come back."

Dick Slay stepped to the side of his pastor and friend, put his arm around his shoulder, and made no comment at all about the tears streaking down both their cheeks.

She was not tired, she was not winded from her walk, but she nonetheless wanted to rest, to sit upon the ground, to close her eyes. Rachel had left the shore and began a slow stroll into the lush forest before her. The woods proved as pleasing to the senses as the beach. The plants were similar but still foreign to her. The leaves, each broad and velvety to the touch, were the deepest green. Under her feet was a lush carpet of grass.

Rachel lay down and gazed peacefully at the emerald sky above her. Leaves of plants she could not name framed a portrait of fleecy white clouds and green sky. No artist could paint this, Rachel thought, no philosopher could imagine it.

She smiled broadly.

She closed her eyes.

She slept.

A universe away, in a sterile white hospital room, the cardiac monitor attached to Rachel's body recorded an alarming slowing of her heart.

Nine

New York, New York

Pruit Bain shifted uneasily and listened as the sanitary paper that separated his seat from the exam table protested the movement. He watched as the man before him studied Pruit's outstretched hand.

"Does this hurt?" the elderly, white-haired Dr. George Hicks asked as he pressed the flesh in the center of Pruit's palm.

"No."

"Then sit still, Pruit. You're fidgeting. Do you know how difficult it is to examine a moving object?"

"Sorry, I guess doctors make me nervous."

Hicks sighed. "It hasn't always been so. How long have I been the family doctor?"

"I'm not sure," Pruit replied slightly chagrined.

"I was your father's physician and I have been your doctor since the day you were born. That's a lot of years, Pruit, a lot of years. Even after your company went with that big uptown HMO, you and your family have been coming to me. Now you tell me that I make you nervous."

"That's not what I meant. It's just this whole thing has me on edge."

"Well, that's understandable considering what you've told me." Dr. Hicks leaned forward and peered closely at the fleshy palm. "I'm afraid that I don't see anything that would explain what you've described. When did you say this happened?"

"Two days ago," Pruit replied. "I was out of state when it happened."

"Two days," Hicks repeated. "If it were an injury I should see some scabbing or other sign, but I don't. You say this just happened without any warning and without any pain."

"Right. I was driving my car back from a meeting when it started," he lied. "Next thing I knew there was blood everywhere."

"And it originated from your hands—just your hands."

Pruit nodded. "It started trickling from my palms first, then the back of my hands." Dr. Hicks turned Pruit's hand over and shook his head. "I don't mind telling you that it scared the daylights out of me."

"I still don't see anything."

"You think I'm lying?" Pruit snapped.

Hicks raised his head and looked Pruit in the eye. "Of course not," he said evenly. "All I said was I don't see anything. What's got you so on edge?"

"Tired, I guess."

"When was the last time you had a complete physical?"

"I don't know. Awhile, I guess."

"Doesn't that fancy HMO encourage annual checkups? I'm just a simple general practitioner but I send out reminders to my patients. Come to think of it, I sent one out to you."

"I got it," Pruit said impatiently. "I've been busy lately."

"Well, I think we ought to run some tests. Blood work, that sort of thing. You're looking a little thin and peaked."

"No," Pruit snapped.

The doctor slowly put his hands into the pockets of his white doctor's coat. In his mid-sixties, Dr. George Hicks had seen everything a doctor could in a practice. People had sat on his examination table and wept, laughed, thanked him, blamed him, and struck out emotionally at him and his staff. He stared in silence at his patient.

"I'm sorry," Pruit said with genuine embarrassment. "Work has been unusually stressful. I didn't need this . . . this . . . event." He looked at his hands. "What do you think it is?"

"I have no idea," Hicks said. After a brief pause the doctor continued. "May I ask you a question without your becoming upset?"

Pruit drew his lips tight then nodded his assent.

Dr. Hicks pulled a small round stool with wheels in front of Pruit then sat down. He folded his arms, bowed his head for a moment in thought, then looked straight at Pruit. "How sure are you that this really happened? Could you have imagined it?"

Pruit chuckled softly then shook his head. "Not a chance, doc. Not a chance."

"How can you be so sure?"

"I have evidence," Pruit retorted quickly. "If it were just my imagination then my imagination left several splatters of blood on my pants as well as on the steering wheel of my car."

"Is the blood still there? On your pants, I mean?"

He didn't answer immediately; instead Pruit frowned. "Not now, no. I washed them in cold water as soon as I could. The stains came right out. Lucky for me too because those were expensive slacks."

"What about the steering wheel? Did you clean that up too?"

"Of course. Wouldn't you?" Pruit said sourly.

Hicks held up his hands. "Easy now, you promised you wouldn't get upset."

"I'm not upset, but this is a stupid line of questioning."

"I'm just trying to get the whole picture, Pruit," Hicks said firmly. "I assume you used a rag or something similar to clean the steering wheel?"

"That's right, a rag. But I threw it away because it was ruined. And don't ask where it is now because the garbage was picked up this morning. The rag is probably somewhere in the municipal dump."

"What about the car seats? Any blood get on those?"

Pruit shook his head. "I know where you're going with this. You think I imagined the whole thing, and since I happen to like things clean and tidy, I can't prove that my hands started bleeding on their own."

Hicks stood up. "I'm not accusing you of being insane, Pruit. I'm just gathering as much information as I can."

"But you think I imagined all this, don't you?"

It was Hicks' turn to shake his head. "No, not really. But understand my position. I see no marks, no evidence of puncture or abrasion, no cuts. Your hands look perfectly normal. There are no wounds."

"That doesn't mean it didn't happen!" Pruit leaped to his feet. "I began to bleed from the palms of my hands. I didn't imagine it."

"Sit down, Pruit," Hicks demanded firmly. "I can't help you unless you are up-front with me. Besides, you don't have to be crazy to imagine things. You said it yourself—you've been under a great deal of pressure."

"I'm in the advertising business," Pruit responded as he began to pace the little exam room. "Pressure is part of the game. You don't make it as far as I have unless you can handle the stress."

Dr. Hicks exhaled noisily. "The mind is a powerful thing, Pruit, powerful. It's also fragile. You are a creative person and that creativity has served you well in your work. Maybe that creativity took over for a little while. Maybe your mind was giving you a warning?"

"A warning about what?" Pruit replied sarcastically.

"You tell me."

"There's nothing to tell."

"OK, fine," he said, exasperated. "Let me ask this: Did anything else happen?"

"What do you mean?"

"Did you see anything else, feel anything, hear anything?"

Pruit averted his eyes for a moment as he thought of the voice he heard in the car. He could remember each word spoken clearly, as he played the conversation over and over in his mind. He heard the words in his dreams; he recalled them vividly during the day. "No," he lied. "Nothing else. What are you getting at anyway?"

"I'm not sure," the doctor replied. "Just probing. I will say this: The mind is a powerful device and shouldn't be underestimated under any circumstance. We're just beginning to understand some of that power."

"So you do think I imagined this?" Pruit said bitterly.

"Not necessarily. Sit down, let me explain." Reluctantly Pruit made his way back to the exam table and sat down. Dr. Hicks sat on his stool. "My point is just the opposite, really. Just because something comes from the mind doesn't mean that it can't manifest itself physically. Some research was done some years ago with patients under hypnosis. The patient would be told that he or she was being touched with a hot iron rod. In reality, they were being brushed with a pencil. Many of them reacted as if they were being burned, but some developed a blister just as if they had been burned."

"You're kidding, right?"

"Not at all. You see, the mind has difficulty distinguishing between reality and fiction. That's why people jump and scream in scary movies. Consciously they know what they're seeing is a fabrication, but subconsciously they can't differentiate the real from the imaginary. They feel fear or sadness or whatever the moviemaker wants them to feel."

"You think my mind caused my hands to start bleeding?" asked Pruit.

"Look, it either happened or didn't . . ."

"It did." Pruit injected.

"If it did happen the way you said it did, then, based on my limited—and I emphasize the word limited—examination, I can only surmise that something out of the norm is happening. People's palms don't start bleeding spontaneously without injury. I see no injury."

"In other words," Pruit said, agitation in his voice, "you have no idea what happened."

"I have no idea whatsoever. Either you dreamed it or something in your mind overcame rational science and caused your hands to bleed. The best thing to do is to run some tests."

"No tests." Pruit was adamant. "I don't need tests; I need a doctor who will believe me!"

"I didn't say I didn't believe you. All I'm saying . . ."

Pruit jumped off the exam table. "I've heard enough. It's clear this is beyond your experience."

"Pruit, wait," Dr. Hicks called out as Pruit exited the room. Pruit Bain neither waited nor responded; he simply marched from the office.

The drive to Madison Avenue passed with tormenting slowness. Traffic was heavy and people impatient, but Pruit Bain paid little attention to his surroundings; his mind was elsewhere. Too upset to head straight for the office, Pruit chose to circle Central Park, allowing himself time to cool down. He felt ashamed over his outburst in Dr. Hicks' office. The man had been a family friend for decades and deserved far more respect than Pruit had given.

Still, that was a small worry when compared with the other problems he faced. And now this whole matter about his hands was making things worse. He should have known that no one would believe him, especially a doctor, but where else could he turn? No, he assured himself, he had made the right decision in approaching Dr. Hicks, even if Hicks couldn't see how real and how terrifying the event had been. Pruit wondered what Hicks would have said if he had been told about the voice Pruit heard.

The words of the voice still resonated through his mind like an echo that never diminished. He would hear the same words uttered in his dreams at night and in his thoughts by day. Not harsh words, not coarse words, but words that were direct, firm, and very serious. Pruit had snapped his head around looking for the owner of the words but found no one.

He was as alone that moment as he had ever been. Still, he hadn't felt alone. Instead he felt a strong and powerful presence with him, around him, through him. It had covered him like a blanket and oozed into his body. Every filament, every nerve pathway, every cell was impregnated with the sensation of the presence.

At first, Pruit thought that he was being possessed by some malevolent force, even though such reasoning went against his beliefs. Pruit had no belief in spiritual matters. There was no God, no angels, no demons. He was too smart to have such beliefs, and he had seen too much evil to believe in a Being of love and power. But there was no mistaking the sensation of a presence.

Perhaps, Pruit reasoned, Dr. Hicks was right. Maybe, just maybe, he had imagined the whole thing. The entire incident could be attributed to stress. Hicks was right about the effects of stress, and Pruit was under more stress than he had ever been before: stress that haunted him, plagued him, pursued him relentlessly day and night. Each day that passed raised the level of anxiety to a higher level. There was no doubt in Pruit's mind that the stress would kill him and it would do so soon. That kind of stress could cause a man to imagine things, strange things. It wasn't unheard of, after all.

The thought only lasted a moment. No, Pruit thought to himself, what happened to me was real and no amount of rationalizing can make it go away. I saw what I saw, and I heard what I heard. The only question, the only really important question: What am I going to do about it?

An hour later, Pruit pulled his car into the underground parking structure beneath the Basil Building and parked in the stall reserved for him. Bain, Lockeridge, and Mullins Advertising occupied the top two floors of the twenty-story structure. Five minutes later, he walked into the large foyer outside his corner office.

"Welcome back," Gina Ritter offered. "Did all go well at the doctor's?"

"Doctors are doctors," Pruit grunted.

"I hope there's nothing wrong," Gina said as she stood behind her secretary's desk, phone messages in hand. She was a tall thin woman with a full head of blond hair. "Nothing serious, I mean."

"Nothing's wrong," Pruit replied as he marched across the deep blue carpet. "Any messages?"

"Several." Gina shuffled through the small stack of paper in her hand. "The Los Angeles office called about the Digabyte account, and London called about the magazine slicks for Lady True cosmetics. There are several others, but nothing of importance."

"Good," he said taking the slips of paper from Gina. "I need some time to myself to finish some work. Hold all my calls."

Pruit didn't see Gina nod as he hastily made his way into his office. Once inside, he locked the door and crossed the ornate office. Setting his briefcase on his cherry-wood desk, he looked around the space where he spent so many hours. It was spacious, with expensive art on the walls, a deep pile carpet, and white leather furniture.

A momentary smile, a rare occurrence in recent days, crossed his face. His office was a source of pride with him. He could recall his early days in advertising, when he shared a space like this with fifteen other "creatives" crammed into tiny cubicles where they dreamed of making it big in the fast-paced world of advertising. That was twenty years ago. Now he was the head of one of the leading agencies in the world. No small achievement in anyone's mind. Still, he was not happy; worse, he was becoming despondent and he felt helpless to change things. He was a man who had lost control. No, he was a man who had surrendered control.

Seating himself in the high-backed, white leather desk chair, he closed his eyes and sighed heavily. Things used to make sense. He had a plan that brought him wealth and admiration. He worked hard to achieve everything he possessed. No one gave him anything. No one helped him. His success came through determination, perseverance, and a never-say-die attitude. Somehow those qualities had abandoned him. They had evaporated slowly and steadily over the last few years like water from the ocean that rises to make clouds.

However, that water always returns in the form of rain to replenish its source. So far, none of the qualities that had slipped from his life had shown any sign of raining back into his life.

Why hadn't he been able to kill himself two days ago when he wanted? The plan seemed flawless. Yes, it was the coward's way out; yes, he would leave a widow and a teenage son, but they would be all the better for his demise. They had plenty of money, a fine home, and the corporation to take care of any unforeseen needs. Killing himself made sense. It would solve all the problems that seemed so unsolvable now.

Still, it hadn't happened. His car wouldn't move, his hands started bleeding, and the disembodied voice spoke to him. None of it made any sense.

Perhaps it was the stress. Or perhaps it was something else—something that he hated; something that owned him. Slowly, Pruit opened his briefcase and looked at its contents. Anyone looking inside would see items carried by many CEOs: a laptop computer, several pens, and a Daytimer. But Pruit knew that the small brown case held more. Removing the loose items in the case and setting them on the desk, Pruit took a small pocketknife from his trousers and pried out the false bottom.

In the bottom of the case were several tiny ziplock bags filled with small white nodules. His heart quickened as he gazed at the cocaine and his mouth was dry with anticipation. It had been his secret companion for years. No one knew he used the drug. No one suspected that he danced with the devil on a daily basis. He had come to depend on its chemically induced euphoria. As far as he was concerned, it helped him concentrate, helped him work, helped him feel alive. A deeply sequestered part of his mind would occasionally succeed in surfacing to remind him that those were all lies; that the drug not only didn't help him in his work, it was killing him and everything he loved. But the draw of the drug and the power of rationalization always pushed his conscience back into the dark hole that was its prison.

Cautiously he withdrew one of the bags, closed the briefcase, and set the bag on its lid. Glancing at his office door, he checked the doorknob to be sure he had locked it. Satisfied that no one could walk in unexpectedly, Pruit opened the bag, reached in with thumb and index finger, removed a small coagulated lump, and set it on top of the bag.

Pruit stared at the little powder rock. He studied it, taking in each nook, each tiny crevice. He examined it as a jeweler might examine a gem for defects. Like a jeweler, Pruit was admiring the item before him. He should have felt guilt; he should have been overwhelmed with shame, and years ago he would have been. But he had come too far now. He had been seduced by an evil seductress that now controlled him. Although he would never admit it, the white pebble before him owned not only Pruit, but also everything Pruit had: his family, his business, his future. Such thoughts no longer brought angst or regret. Pruit was possessed.

Reflection time was over. The stress of the last few days had become unbearable. The fact that the doctor had dismissed his account as some psychological fiction had only increased the anxiety that Pruit felt. He needed help. He needed relief. And that little bundle of white dust held all the help he needed.

It was then that Pruit realized that he had forgotten the small two-inch square mirror in the briefcase. It would be an easy matter to move the bag and cocaine to the desk, open the case, and retrieve the mirror, but Pruit was impatient. All he needed was a smooth, nonporous surface like glass. Quickly, he scanned his desk and found just what he needed—a metal-framed picture of his wife and son. The glass in the frame would work perfectly.

Snatching the picture from the desk, he laid it flat on the case. Taped on the picture was a postcard with his wife's handwriting. Gina must have placed it there so that he wouldn't overlook it. Quickly he tore the postcard away and tossed in on the desk unread.

Tenderly he took the lump of cocaine and set it on the glass that covered the family portrait; then, with the small pocketknife that was still in his hand, he methodically and meticulously began to chop the nodule into a fine powder, being careful with each stroke of the knife not to spill any of the drug. Every grain was valuable to him.

Once Pruit had diced the rock into powder he divided the tiny pile into several lines. Only one thing remained: forming a tube from a bill in his wallet and snorting his prize. Removing the first bill in his wallet, a twenty, he quickly and expertly rolled the paper into a thin tube. As he did this he rested his elbows on the desk, allowing his hands to hover over the cocaine.

Plop.

Pruit paused for a moment at the barely perceptible sound. Then he heard it again.

Plop. Plop.

Looking down he saw the source of the sound. Something red had splattered on the picture and the cocaine. As he watched, another red drop fell and landed on one of the lines of powder. Before him now was the picture of his family covered in cocaine and blood from the palms of his hands.

He watched as another drop fell on the face of his wife and then one on the face of his son. The drops of blood spread across the glass and mingled with the snow-white cocaine.

Looking at the discarded postcard, he read the note that had been written in the fine script of his wife: "We love you and miss you very much. Wish you were here."

A cloud moved over Pruit's wounded soul—a dark, ominous, overshadowing cloud that threatened to sponge up what meager light remained in his life.

Pruit Bain buried his face in his bloody hands and began to weep.

Ten

London, England

No one had been in Lindsay Blair's home since the death of her father more than ten years ago. In fact, no one other than landscapers had even been inside the high wrought-iron fence that surrounded the ten acres of lush green land forty minutes outside London.

Consequently, no one had seen the opulence with which Lindsay surrounded herself. Paintings, many invaluable and illegally taken, graced the heavily paneled walls. Statues, both classical and modern, stood like silent sentries throughout the twenty-two-room Tudor mansion. No one had seen the workroom where Lindsay built the specialized instruments she needed for her life's work. No one had seen the state-of-the-art gym where Lindsay trained.

Now, no one could see the huddled figure of Lindsay Blair shaking in the corner of her bedroom. The window shades had been drawn, the lights had been turned off, and only a haze of sunlight that struggled through the expensive cloth draperies enabled Lindsay to know that day had finally arrived.

Still she did not move. Still she did not speak.

Grendel, a two-year-old Irish setter, lay at Lindsay's feet, breathing noisily. The dog, which Lindsay bought to celebrate the successful theft and sale of an ancient manuscript of *Beowulf*, had greeted his mistress' return with a wildly wagging tail, several barks, and much prancing. Lindsay did not respond. She simply made her way to the corner of her bedroom, slumped to the floor, and did something she had not done since she was ten years old: she cried. Grendel had given up trying to gain Lindsay's attention; instead, he patiently wait-ed for her to move—something she had not done for more than six hours.

Lindsay was not asleep. Both physically and emotionally exhaust-ed from the events of the night, she struggled to keep her eyes open, preferring the shadowy images of her room to the soul-renting visions of her dreams.

Lindsay had never before been frightened, but now she could not stop shaking. She had seen what no living person had ever seen. She had experienced what no breathing person had ever experienced. She saw things she could not describe and would not if she could. She just wanted it to go away, but she could still see, still hear, still feel all that hell was. She saw her father, and most frightening of all, she could see and smell the It that had tormented her and brought her the message she did not understand.

The phone rang. It sounded shrill and piercing. Lindsay did not move. She remained huddled on the floor, her face streaked with mascara. The phone rang again, and then again, before the answer-ing machine picked up.

"I'm not available; leave a message," Lindsay's recorded voice said.

"Lindsay? Pick up if you're there." Lindsay recognized the voice, despite the tinny quality of the answering machine. There was noth-ing in the voice to compel her to rise from her corner of solitude. "What's the matter with you anyway? The buyer has gone absolute-ly ballistic and he's not a man to be messed with. How could you blow it so badly? It's all over the news. You had better call me and call me quick." The words were ended by a loud bang. The caller had slammed the phone down.

The call didn't frighten her, but her memory of last night did. Her hands shook, her breathing was ragged, and sweat oozed from every pore. "Oh, God," she cried aloud. "Oh, God; oh, God."

Grendel exhaled loudly, wagged his tail once, and rolled over.

Eleven

San Diego, California

When Adam returned from the hospital cafeteria with Dick he felt somewhat refreshed. Dick had insisted that he eat something and brought a plate of eggs and bacon to the table. The food was far more appetizing than that which had been served him in Rachel's room, but Adam still didn't feel hungry and said as much. He ate the food anyway after Dick had threatened to feed it to him like one would feed a baby.

During breakfast Dick had struggled to keep the conversation light but consistent. He had even been successful in making Adam smile a few times. Now as they exited the elevator and passed through the large double metal doors that led to the ICU area, Adam was feeling close to human. His confidence level was a little higher and his emotions were on a more even keel. All of this, no doubt, helped in part by the consumption of several cups of strong coffee.

However, no breakfast and no amount of coffee could counter the fear he felt when he stepped into the ICU's hall just in time to see a nurse run into Rachel's room, followed closely by another nurse pushing a small handcart loaded with esoteric medical equipment.

Adam sprinted down the short hall, followed closely by Dick. In the ICU cubicle that was Rachel's room was a doctor and three nurses moving with precise and practiced motions. The terse and intense expressions on their faces caused pains of anxiety to raggedly pierce Adam's stomach.

"What's going on?" Adam asked. His mouth was dry and his heart was pounding like a kettledrum. No one answered.

"BP?" the doctor asked firmly. Adam didn't recognize the squat man in the white coat and reasoned that he must have been the closest physician at hand when the emergency started.

"One hundred over forty and dropping," a nurse said. "Pulse is forty-five and respiration's ten; both are dropping."

The doctor swore. "OK, let's give her an amp of epinephrine IV, draw some blood, and let's have a chem-seven, electrolytes, and the rest. You know the drill. Let's do this stat."

"Will someone tell me what's going on!" Adam said loudly.

The doctor glanced over his shoulder for only a moment. "Who are you?"

"I'm her husband."

"Your wife's vitals are dropping precariously and we don't know why yet. We're doing everything we can. It would be better if you waited outside."

"What's wrong?" Adam asked in desperation. "What's causing this?"

A strong hand was placed on Adam's shoulder. Adam turned to see Dick standing beside him. "Let's wait outside the door," Dick said.

"I want to stay here!"

"Let the professionals do their work," Dick said quietly. "They can work better if they don't have to worry about us."

Adam looked back at the doctor, who was barking out orders. "Call cardiology; we may need to put a wire in her if her heart rate continues to drop. Let's get respiratory here too. I prefer to have them intubate, but we better be ready to do it ourselves. I want a six-point-five tube ready and sixty succinylcholine ready."

"BP has dropped another ten," one of the nurses said matter-of-factly.

The doctor swore. "All right, let's give her another amp of epi and an amp of bicarb." He paused for a moment then continued,

"Let's also give her an amp of calcium. Let's look alive, people."

Slowly, Dick turned Adam from the horrific scene before him and walked him to the door. "Let's go, buddy. We're in the way." Adam's walk was stilted, every step made with reluctance. Outside the room, Adam leaned against the wall, covered his face with his hands, and then slowly slid down until he was seated on the floor. He didn't see the cardiologist and respiratory therapist enter the ICU. All Adam could see was the image of his wife dying on a cold hospital bed.

Slowly, Rachel opened her eyes. She was still lying on the soft matted grass. Above her was the green sky with white clouds framed by the branches of trees. She inhaled deeply and smiled. Her sleep had been deep and rich, yet something had awakened her, but what? She had sensed a presence and instinctively knew that she was no longer alone.

Turning her head slightly to the right, she saw the source of that sensation, that presence. Seated next to where she lay was a man, but not a man. At least no man that Rachel had ever seen. His legs were crossed in front of him and his hands were folded on his lap. His face was strong but very different. It was human in every way except it seemed to lack the subtle detail that made a face a face. The man had eyes that were the deepest green; not green a person's eyes might be green; no, his eyes were green like grass is green or jade is green.

He tilted his head to one side as if studying her, curious about the creature that had been sleeping on the grass. Slowly, he pulled his lips back in an effort to smile. Rachel had the sense that smiling was not normal for him. He looked like an android attempting to mimic a grin for the first time. It was a clumsy effort, but a sincere one.

"Blessed Woman," the man said. His voice was unlike anything Rachel had ever heard. As a doctor she had encountered people who had suffered trauma to their throats that left their speech impaired, but this was different. The words flowed on notes an octave apart, as if it were really two people speaking simultaneously.

"Who are you?" Rachel asked. It occurred to her that she should be afraid. After all, a peculiar-looking stranger with an unusual voice was seated next to her. But she felt no fear, no apprehension.

Such emotions seemed foreign and unwelcome here, as if they did not, could not, belong in such a place.

The creature tilted his head again, made another valiant attempt at smiling, and then repeated, "Blessed Woman."

Rachel stood up without taking her eyes off the one before her. There was a simple majesty about him and an unmistakable notion of power. "Who are you? Where am I?"

Without putting his hands to the ground, the stranger arose to his full height. He towered over Rachel. Not being especially tall, Rachel had grown accustomed to dealing with men taller than she, but this stranger, this creature, was far taller than anyone Rachel had ever met. She estimated his height at better than nine feet.

He was oddly proportioned. His shoulders and arms were massive but blocky, lacking the smooth contours of the human form. At first Rachel thought he was deformed, but she soon realized that such was not the case—he was merely different. He wore no clothes, but surprisingly, did not appear naked. He just simply was.

Yet the oddest thing about the man who loomed over Rachel was not his size, bulk, or lack of dress (if indeed he was unclothed), but the slight white glow that surrounded him. It was as if he were emitting a light all his own.

He extended his hand: "Come, I have much to show you."

"Where are we going?" Rachel took his hand without reluctance. It felt cool and firm. His fingers were long, graceful, and powerful. For a moment, she thought she felt a tingle of exchanged energy.

"Come, Blessed Woman. There is much to see." Rachel nodded lightly and let the strange man lead her deeper into the woods.

The cardiologist stood ready to insert a wire through the carotid artery of Rachel's neck. The wire, which would be guided down to her heart, would be attached to an external pacemaker that would keep her heart beating.

"OK," the cardiologist said. "Let's begin . . ."

"Hold it," one of the nurses interjected. "I think she's improving." There was a pause as she and everyone else in the room looked at the EKG strip as it fed out of the monitor. "Her pulse is up to sixty and rising a little. It's a strong beat too."

Another nurse chimed in: "BP is rising; one-ten over sixty.

Looks like she's breathing easier."

Just outside the room, Adam heard their words and sprang to his feet, racing into the room. Dick followed behind. "Is she going to be OK?" Adam asked with desperation. "Is she going to be all right?"

The doctor looked at Adam, his face revealing the puzzlement he felt. "I didn't think so, but she seems to be rebounding nicely. But we better keep a close eye on her."

"Is she waking up?" Adam asked as he pushed his way to Rachel's bedside.

The doctor leaned over the bed and spoke. "Rachel? Rachel? Can you hear me?" There was no response. Placing his fingers in her limp hand, he said, "If you can hear me, Rachel, squeeze my hand."

Adam watched intently, wishing with all his might that she would move her fingers. Even the slightest movement would be a reason to rejoice.

He saw nothing.

"She's still in the coma," the doctor said, shaking his head. Then to one of the nurses he issued a set of terse commands. "I want constant vigilance on her telemetry over the next few hours. Call her doctor and tell him what happened. If he has questions he can page me. In the meantime, let's clear the room."

Nurses quickly began reorganizing the equipment they brought and moved out into the hall. Both the cardiologist and therapist left without a word. This was routine for them.

Soon only Adam, Dick, and one nurse remained. The nurse straightened Rachel's bedsheets and flimsy blue hospital gown. She then turned to Adam, "She seems comfortable for now. We'll be monitoring her at the nurse's station. As you know, we receive a constant readout of her vitals. That's how we discovered the problem in the first place."

Adam nodded absently as he stood by the bed, holding Rachel's hand.

"I assume you will be staying for a while, Mr. Bridger."

"I'm not leaving again," Adam replied firmly.

The nurse nodded and then turned to Dick. "I think we need to give them some time. I must ask that you leave."

Dick's eyes were focused on Rachel as he shook his head. "I'm staying with my pastor."

"I'm afraid that's not possible," the nurse responded quickly. "Hospital policy limits visits to family."

"I'm staying."

"Please, sir, don't make me call security," the nurse replied resolutely, her hands placed on her hips.

Dick took his eyes from Rachel for a moment and stared at the woman before him. "Lady," he said quietly, "you don't have enough security to make me leave this room."

The fire in Dick's eyes was not lost on the nurse. She had dealt with difficult people before, but there was something in Dick's tone, in his stare, that made her realize that she was fighting an uphill battle. Without another word, she retreated from the room.

A heavy, anguished silence filled the room as if it were being poured in through a spout in the ceiling. Neither man spoke, for there was nothing to say. There was, however, much to be felt.

Twelve

Fort Worth, Texas

A strange and foreign sound reverberated through Nick Stern's apartment, a sound that had long been absent. In nearly any other home the sound would not be unusual, but Nick's home had not been normal since the accident. Today, however, was different.

Nick was the source of the unusual noise: he was humming a tune.

It had been a long time since Nick had been happy enough to spontaneously generate music. When the sun rose this morning, pouring its effulgence through the dirty apartment window, it shone on a different man. Nick was still scarred by the fire that rendered his flesh stiff and coarse, but he was a changed man nonetheless. The morning sun greeted him with warmth and light and he returned the greeting with delight.

As he showered, the sight of his scarred legs, which normally initiated the cycle of depression and despair that had haunted him over the years, bothered him not at all. Instead, he took no notice of them. He had, in the space of one night, instigated by one vision, substituted joy for bitterness.

At the root of his joy lay a bedrock of purpose, something he had lacked since that awful night. Purpose. Life-enhancing purpose. He no longer felt useless, no longer felt a cripple. He had something to do. He was part of something magnificent. He knew that to be true even though he did not possess any details. But the details didn't matter. What did matter was that he had been selected. That someone or something still found in him a person of value.

The moment of this epiphany was played over and over in his mind. The magazine picture that came to life, his inclusion in the vision, and the message he heard had opened the rusty cage of his existence.

He had tried to repeat the vision several times last night, holding the magazine in his lap and staring at the picture of the restaurant. He gazed minute after long minute until his eyes watered, his neck stiffened, and his head hurt. The vision never returned, but that didn't mean the first occurrence hadn't happened; it just made the original that much more precious.

Nick was packing. He had decided not to waste any time. He had been given his direction, his orders, and he fully intended to carry them out quickly and completely. An old yellow suitcase lay on his unmade bed, filled with underwear, shirts, pants, socks, and bathroom paraphernalia. The last item Nick packed was the *Time* magazine that had changed his life the night before.

Looking at his watch, Nick rehearsed his upcoming schedule. It was now 11 A.M., he would pack a few more things, heat up a can of chicken noodle soup for lunch, and then make his way down to the street in front of his apartment at precisely 1 P.M. The taxi would arrive soon after that and carry him to the Dallas-Fort Worth airport. A few hours later he would arrive in California.

He had no idea where he would stay, but all of that could be figured out later. He had access to his somewhat anemic checking account through ATMs. He wasn't a wealthy man by the stretch of anyone's imagination, but he did have enough money to last him for a few days. Early next week his disability and retirement checks would be automatically deposited in his account so he knew that he wouldn't starve in San Diego. All he had to do was find a cheap hotel and eat simply from inexpensive restaurants.

Nick began humming again. Life was starting to make sense. He didn't quite know how, but he was certain of the truth. Whatever happened in San Diego would change him forever.

Thirteen

Ojai, California

"Are you still looking at those paintings?" Katrin's mother entered the studio with a plate of cookies and a tall glass of tea.

"I can't figure it out," Katrin replied without looking up from the painting on the easel. A similar painting was on the floor, leaning against the easel's leg. "It's all so odd."

"I still think you should see a doctor," her mother said in her quick nasal way. "Blacking out like that can't be a good thing."

"I'm OK, Mother. If I had really blacked out I would have fallen off my stool. I didn't. I just can't remember painting these."

"Not remembering is not good either, you know. Mrs. Woodring's daughter passed out once and they found out she had a brain tumor . . ."

"Mother, please!" Katrin interjected forcefully. "I don't have a brain tumor, but I will have a nervous breakdown if you don't stop hovering over me."

Mother looked shocked. "No need to snap at me, young lady. I'm just trying to help!"

"I know," Katrin said in much softer tones. "I'm just irritated about these paintings. They must mean something."

"They look like a comic book to me."

Katrin studied the paintings. Mother was right. Both paintings had been divided into an amalgamation of different-sized squares like the page of a comic book. In each square was a small yet detailed painted image. "Yeah, but what does it mean?"

"I know what that one means," Katrin's mother said, pointing at the uppermost left square. "That's you."

"Me?"

"Sure. Don't you think I would know my own daughter? That's you sitting at your easel painting. I've watched you do that hundreds of times. That's what it looks like."

Leaning forward, Katrin squinted at the image. It could be her. It was certainly a painter sitting at an easel. Behind the painter was a window with a large oak tree outside, just like Katrin's window.

"OK," Katrin agreed, "but what does the next panel mean?"

"I have no idea. It looks like a skyline or something."

Katrin nodded in agreement. "Yeah, but which skyline?"

"Beats me; now eat your cookies. I'll be done packing your things soon."

"I could have packed my own suitcase, Mother."

"Well, now you don't have to. How long will you be in San Diego?"

"Not long. The art show runs for several weeks, but I'm just making an appearance. I should be back in a couple of days."

"Take longer. San Diego is beautiful and you could use some time off. Who knows, maybe you'll meet someone special. That Kevin Wilson seems nice."

"Mother, stop trying to marry me off," Katrin responded with exasperation. "Besides Mr. Wilson is fifteen years older than me. He's an art dealer who carries my work and nothing more."

"Pity. Still . . ."

"No, Mother, there is no 'still' and probably never will be. I've come to terms with that and so should you."

"I don't give up so easily."

"I'm not giving up. I just have different expectations than you do. Now please give it a rest."

Silence separated the two for a moment before Katrin broke the hush. "Did Raul get the van loaded?"

"Yes, dear," Mother responded coolly. "He has put all the paintings in the van and checked the list twice."

"That's good," Katrin said. "I think I'll ask him to put these two in also. Maybe Mr. Wilson will have some ideas about what all this means."

"Whatever you say, dear," Mother offered with a noticeable tone of hurt in her voice. "I'll just go finish packing your bags."

Katrin watched as her mother attempted a melodramatic exit. Katrin could only shake her head and sigh. Mother meant well but she possessed no concept of who Katrin really was deep inside. For that matter, neither did Katrin.

Fourteen

London, England

Lindsay Blair eased herself down into the wide, deeply padded, leather seat, thankful that she didn't have to sit with the masses who were crammed like sardines in the coach section. First class was the only way Lindsay had ever flown and she saw no reason to change now.

She watched as others meandered up the steep boarding ramp, their hands filled with bags, carry-on luggage, and other bundles of their lives. Some looked with envy at the first-class compartment through which they were forced to walk. Some just looked ahead, frustrated over how frequently the line of humanity was forced to stop while some traveler placed his or her bag in the overhead compartment or took five minutes to situate his or her seating area before exiting the narrow, thinly carpeted aisle of the Boeing 747.

Many of the passengers, however, stared at Lindsay. Her raven black hair, crystalline eyes, and exquisite face frequently attracted the attention of both men and women: men with desire, women with envy.

Lindsay had learned long ago to avoid eye contact with those with whom she didn't want to speak. The cost of her beauty included being approached by men who felt compelled to know her. Fortunately, most lacked the bravado to approach uninvited. Some, however, had no reservations about taking such initiative. Of those some found their courage more readily available when their minds were lubricated with alcohol. They would come close, reeking of scotch, bourbon, or beer, confusing their uncertain swaying with swagger.

She had dealt with all of these and had done so successfully. Usually she could dissuade them quietly with a lie: "I'm married," and, indeed, she did wear a ring on her finger to heighten the illusion. In those few cases in which a marital bond held no value to a would-be suitor, Lindsay would respond with a strong and practiced phrase: "I don't date outside my species." And should that fail to do the trick, Lindsay had not been above driving her point home with a volley of punches and kicks. An unconscious man was no longer a problem.

Although several unaccompanied men were seated in first class—and each of these filled his eyes with Lindsay's form—none approached. Lindsay felt lucky for a moment, but then she realized why she was on the plane in the first place.

As the sun had crawled higher in the sky (as evidenced by the changing light that forced its way through her bedroom drapes) Lindsay became convinced that she could not stay huddled in the corner of the room until she starved to death. After all, if she saw what she thought she saw, then death was no solution at all. She toyed with the idea of ignoring the vision, writing it off as a trick of the brain, but she knew better. That had been no dream. Fleeting images fluttered through her mind like malicious, bloodthirsty bats, bouncing from one side of her mind to the other. No thought was free from their presence. Even as she sat in the plane remembering the last few hours the thoughts plagued her.

Doing nothing was not an option for Lindsay; the creature had made that clear. Unaccustomed as Lindsay was to fear, the mere thought of returning to the infested caldron of hell rattled her soul, strained the fibers of her mind, and caused her body to tremble.

It took every grain of determination for Lindsay to rise from the dark corner of her room. Numbly she walked to the bath and showered, washing her body several times as if she could scrub away the memory and rinse away the pain and fear. She washed her waist-long hair even though she knew it would take nearly an hour to dry. Perhaps, she thought, the task would allow her attention to be focused elsewhere.

After the shower she put on fresh makeup, dressed, and began packing. A call to Pampered Pups brought a van around to take Grendel to a kennel for dogs with wealthy masters. She would have to unspoil the dog when she got back—if she got back.

With Grendel nestled safely away, Lindsay called for a hansom to take her round to Heathrow Airport, on the west side of the city, where she bought a one-way ticket to the States. Her plan was simple: go where the It had told her to go, deliver the message the It told her to deliver, and then check into a nice hotel by the beach and try to forget the unforgettable.

None of this made sense to Lindsay. Not the vision, not the destination, and not the message. Nor did she understand her role in the matter. Why her? Of the nearly 6 billion people who populate the world, why had she been recruited?

Clearly, however, her understanding was not required, and neither was her consent. Lindsay was unaccustomed to taking orders from anyone. The only person she ever allowed to command her in any fashion had been her father.

The thought of her father immediately made her heart race, her stomach tighten, and tears well up in her eyes. She could see him so clearly: the bubbling skin, his wide-eyed terror, his mouth stretched open releasing a scream of undiluted horror . . .

Shock waves shuddered through her, making waste of her emotions and thoughts like a tsunami over a tiny island. She raised a trembling hand to her now-perspiring brow.

"Are you all right, miss?" a heavily accented voice asked.

Manchester, Lindsay thought, she's from Manchester in the north. Looking up, Lindsay saw a pert blond woman in a blue stewardess' uniform. She was smiling sincerely.

"Not afraid of flying, are we?" the stewardess asked kindly. "Safer than bathing in your own tub, you know."

"I'll be fine," Lindsay replied as she returned the smile. "I'll be better once we're in the air."

"Right you are," the young lady answered cheerfully. "We will be leaving soon and then you'll feel right as rain. Once we're in the air I'll bring drinks round; perhaps that will help."

"That would be nice." Lindsay struggled to reflect the woman's glib optimism. She didn't like chronically cheerful people, especially women. They annoyed her deeply.

An electronic tone sounded.

"That would be the flight crew," the stewardess offered. "Probably want to tell me how to make the coffee. Men! Such demanding things, don't you agree?"

"Oh, yes, quite," Lindsay replied, widening her smile and feeling thankful that the stewardess was needed elsewhere. Laying her head back against the headrest of the high-backed seat, she drew in a long deep breath and then slowly released it. She repeated the act while mentally uttering "Relax." Soon the rhythmic breathing and silent mantra slowed her pounding heart and eased her tense muscles.

Mental discipline was more than a science with Lindsay; it was a life-saving requirement in her business. Anxiety and fear made for mistakes. Only steel-cold rational thought could be trusted.

The pervasive question that wormed its way through every layer of her thoughts was, Could steel-cold rational thought save her from losing her mind?

The answer, she knew, awaited her in California.

Fifteen

New York, New York

Fortunately for Pruit Bain a private bathroom adjoined his office. It was ornate and reflected the expensive design sense of one of New York's top interior decorators. Pruit, however, took no notice of the gold-plated faucet, designer tile wainscot, or even the imported Italian toilet. Instead he gave his undivided attention to the clean-up operation that occupied him.

Using the soft, cobalt blue hand towel that hung near the sink, he slowly, tenderly dried the framed photo of his wife and son. He had taken great pains to clean the glass of the macabre combination of snow-white cocaine, red blood, and clear tears. Already the blood was exchanging its crimson color for one of dark rust.

By lightly moistening a wad of toilet paper, Pruit was able to wipe the glass clean without having to hold the frame under a stream of water from the faucet. Always a cautious man, Pruit took extra care not to spill any of the cocaine on the rug, himself, or anything else, where it might leave a residue that could be used against him. The toilet paper wipe, now laden with blood and cocaine, was flushed down the toilet. He repeated the process several times until he was certain that there were no remains on the glass or frame.

Pruit paused to gaze at the photographic image he held in his hand. The words from the postcard clamored in his head. Slowly he touched the face of his wife then of his son. He did miss them very much, although he never said so.

Meredith Bain was a fashion-plate wife. Her youthful figure, wavy fawn hair, blue eyes, and easy laugh made her one of the most popular guests at any business party. A former Junior Miss winner in her home state of Arizona, she went on to study at NYU, where she made the cheerleading squad and, between social events, picked up a degree in business administration. It was there that she met Pruit.

Pruit was working hard on a marketing degree when, as luck would have it, he bumped, quite literally, into Meredith while he was carrying a trayful of cafeteria food. He immediately fell in love with her. She, with her blouse stained with gravy and a Salisbury steak stuck to the top of her shoe, took longer to develop feelings for him. Yet, after unceasing apologies and several bouquets of flowers, he was successful in winning her.

They were married right out of college. Two weeks later, Pruit was hired as a copywriter for a major ad agency on Madison Avenue. It was there that his obsession began. Success became his god, advancement his only goal. Meredith played her part faithfully: always supportive, always available, never complaining.

When Michael came along, Meredith threw her heart into being a mother. Over the years she did it all for her son. She went to the PTA, the shows, the Little League games. She went to all the places and did all the things that Pruit had been too busy to do. And she never complained.

A sadness inundated him and he felt his eyes begin to burn with tears again. How could he have gone so wrong? He had what every man dreamed of: love, family, position, money. There wasn't one in ten thousand males who wouldn't trade places with him, yet he hadn't been able to see it. There was always something else to reach for: a major client to steal from a competitor, a new office to open, another award to win.

Being a winner was what life was all about, or so Pruit thought. He won at everything he did, and the few times he did lose, he made sure it never happened again. Winning. It was his goal, his life, his purpose for existence. Now, looking at the picture he held in his hand, he was coming to realize that in his great pursuit to be a winner, he had become the biggest loser of all. He was close to losing his business, his pride, his family, and his life.

He stroked the image of his wife's cheek and wished he was feeling her soft skin instead of cold unyielding glass. He looked at his son, now a college student, and wished that he had taken time to see his son slide into second or swim in the ocean.

An urge welled up in him, an impulse to bolt from the bathroom, race through the lobby, hop in his car, and drive to the airport to take the first jet to Europe and join his family. But he couldn't. The voice in the car had told him his task and Pruit instinctively knew that he must obey. He couldn't turn back the clock to make things right, but he could stop doing things wrong. Perhaps there was still some hope after all.

Looking at his hands, Pruit was relieved to see that the openings from which blood had steadily trickled an hour before were now nothing more than faded pink spots. Soon there would be no evidence of his strange affliction.

Checking the bathroom once again to be certain that nothing remained that might raise questions, Pruit re-entered his office and sat at his desk. He pushed the intercom button on his phone.

"Yes, Mr. Bain," Gina's voice floated out of the speaker.

"Gina, I'm taking another trip. Please have the jet ready and arrange to have my car picked up at the airport after I'm gone."

"Yes, Mr. Bain. Where shall I tell the pilot you're going?"

"Have him file a flight plan for San Diego. Oh, I'll also need a rental car. Something nice. You know what I like."

"Will you be gone long?"

Pruit thought for a moment. He had no idea how long he would be gone. "I'm not sure. Better tell the pilot to plan to return as soon as possible. One of the partners may need the jet. I can send for him when I'm ready."

"Then I'll need to make hotel reservations for you too."

"Right. I'd like to leave tonight if possible."

"OK, but let me check something." Pruit could hear the clicking of Gina's keyboard. "The jet is not scheduled to be used at all this week, so the pilot should be available. Except . . ."

"Except what?" Pruit asked quickly.

"There's a note in the computer that he's asked for the night off.

It's his kid's birthday."

Too bad, Pruit thought, I guess he'll just have to miss the little tyke's party. After all, I've had to give up a lot of things to get where I am . . . Pruit stopped midthought. Yes, he had given up a lot to get where he was. In fact, he had given up too much.

"I'll tell you what," Pruit offered. "I'm checked out to fly that bird. Why don't I just fly myself? It'll be fun. I paid a lot of money for those lessons and I haven't flown in a month."

Flying was one of Pruit's great joys. His business required that he fly to many of the major cities in the country and some overseas. That meant he spent many hours in the air waiting to get from one place to another, which Pruit viewed as "down time." Why not learn to fly? he had asked himself. I'm in the air anyway. So, Bob Tome, a former airline pilot and now the pilot for Bain, Lockeridge, and Mullins, began to tutor Pruit, who quickly demonstrated an innate talent. It had taken several years for Pruit to pass the various written and practical tests that took him through single engine, multi-engine, and finally jet qualifications.

It took scores of hours for him to achieve his pilot's license, and now Pruit wondered how he had made the time for that endeavor when he had never bothered to make time to spend with his family. Another pang of guilt pierced him.

"Are you sure, Mr. Bain? California is a long way to fly."

"Not in a Gulfstream V jet, it isn't. Don't you remember? I flew myself to Washington, D.C. last month and I didn't get a single dent or scratch the paint."

"Yes, sir, I remember." Gina chuckled, which was a rare occurrence.

"Oh, Gina, I would like you to do me a favor. Take off early this afternoon—say, a couple of hours—and pick up a birthday gift for Bob's son."

"Daughter, sir."

"Oh," Pruit replied, embarrassed about not knowing some of those little details about his key employees. It was one thing in a firm with over 200 employees to not know all their children, but Pruit had flown with Bob so many times—often sitting in the copilot's seat—that he felt he should have known that he had a daughter. "Pick up a card too."

"Very well, sir. What shall I do about your meetings?"

Pruit rubbed his forehead. This was entirely too complex. All he wanted to do was get out of town. He turned to his computer screen and called up his personal schedule, knowing that Gina was looking at the same thing on her monitor. "I'll make some calls canceling what I can and rescheduling the others."

"Would you like me to do that, sir?"

"No, Gina," Pruit replied. "It would be better if it came from me. Here's another little change. I want you to pick up my car at the airport. You can drive it while I'm gone. I'd rather have it on the road than in my garage or at the airport."

"That would be nice, sir. Thank you."

Pruit knew that Gina loved his late model Jaguar. As his administrative assistant she made good money, but not enough to afford a luxury car like his.

"Just don't get any tickets or get it towed, but drive it as much as you like. Take a trip this weekend if you want."

Gina was taken aback. "That's very kind of you, sir."

"It's nothing," he replied. "I'd better get on these calls." With that Pruit pressed the button that disconnected the intercom, picked up the phone, and began dialing.

Sixteen

San Diego, California

The sun had passed its zenith an hour ago just as it had done yesterday and the day before and for eons before that. It never changed. The universe continued running like a clock that never misses a tick. Such immutability was reserved for things cosmic; things earthly changed constantly. Rachel Tremaine was proof of that.

Dick Slay sat in the yellow chair with the high back, watching his pastor, his friend, hover over his wife. Here was the saddest picture Dick had ever seen, and as a former marine with two tours in Vietnam he had seen a great deal. He had seen others suffer, but in most cases he didn't know them as he knew the shaken man who stood next to the hospital bed. These people he knew and he loved them both.

Dick was neither a demonstrative man, nor one who made lasting attachments. In fact, he could count the number of people he labeled friend on one hand. Of those, the one he was closest to was Adam Bridger.

It was an odd pairing in many ways, for the two had little in common. Dick was a stocky man with a thick chest, thick muscular arms, and limited formal education. Adam was slender and scholarly. Dick loved television, Adam favored books. Dick was a man with deep spiritual convictions but could quickly lose his temper, an affair frightening to see. Adam was a thinker who responded to almost all situations with measured action.

Despite their differences no two men could have held more admiration for each other. Despite Dick's limited education, he was street smart. Very few things got past his attention and very few people could deceive him. It was such practical knowledge that on several occasions caused Adam to seek Dick's advice. He had even sought Dick's guidance about his growing interest in Rachel.

It was Dick who stood by Adam's side as best man during the wedding. "If this doesn't work out," Adam had said, "I need someone to blame."

"If this doesn't work out," Dick had replied, "it will be your own fault. I plan on taking Rachel's side in everything."

When, what seemed ages ago but was less than a decade, Adam was being considered for the pastor's position at Maple Street Community Church the congregation was asked to vote. Only Dick voted no. A year later the church would hear Dick say, "That is the only time I've ever been glad to be proved wrong."

There was no doubt that Dick would give his life for Adam and Rachel. If it were in his power he would exchange places with Rachel and let her be the one watching him lie motionless in the hospital bed. But such was not in his power. In fact, nothing was in his power.

It was this sense of powerlessness that bothered him most. There should be something that could be done—someone to call, some action to take—but Dick knew of none.

So he prayed. He prayed silently and he prayed often. He bargained with God, cajoled the Almighty, and made promises. When words failed him, he simply sat and silently repeated the words "Please God, please God."

Once an hour, Dick would leave the ICU to make phone calls to his wife, Chloe; the manager of his trucking business; and Fannie the church secretary. Each time they would ask how Rachel was doing, and each time he delivered the same grim message: "No change. No change at all."

Something attracted Dick's attention—a sound. It was difficult to hear at first and impossible to make out initially. Cocking his head, he listened more closely. The sound rose in volume only slightly but it was enough. Dick recognized it. He was hearing a song, a familiar song often sung in church. But the chorus, which was normally a song of joy, was being intoned with mournful slowness. Adam was singing quietly what Dick knew to be Rachel's favorite church song: Hallelujah.

Hallelujah, hallelujah.

Hallelujah, hallelujah.

It was just one word sung over and over and over. Dick watched as Adam rocked back and forth, back and forth, in deliberate tempo as if in slow motion. It was clear to Dick what was happening: Adam had run out of words to pray and was thus left with a simple song to be offered as a supplication of the soul. And he sang the word in a baritone resonance that had clearly filtered through the greatest pain, the deepest fear, and a tenacious hope before quietly erupting in the world.

Dick watched but wished he didn't have to see, as Adam held Rachel's limp hand close to his chest as he rocked, as he sang, as he rocked, and as he sang.

It occurred to Dick that watching his dearest friend in such agony was the hardest thing he had ever had to do.

Rachel and the creature had walked "a ways." That was the only term Rachel found useful. If asked she could tell neither the distance they had walked, nor the duration they had traveled. Both time and space seemed different here. They could have been hiking for hours over many miles or just beginning their journey. Such spatial confusion should seem unnatural yet it felt normal.

They walked in silence, the man-thing leading with Rachel following close behind. He walked with ease and a regal bearing. It was clear he knew his destination well.

"Do you have a name?" Rachel asked, breaking the silence.

"Yes," the creature answered but offered nothing more.

Rachel decided on a different approach. "Is this heaven?"

The creature stopped and turned to face Rachel. After a moment he spread an awkward smile across his face and made a noise that Rachel took to be a chuckle—although it sounded more crackle than chortle.

"No," the man offered, "heaven is . . ." he seemed to be struggling for the right words ". . . better." He then turned and began walking again.

Despite the lack of information she possessed, Rachel felt no sense of frustration. That in itself was unusual, for she was not a patient person by nature. She had improved greatly over the time she had been married to Adam, but she was still more likely to lose patience than keep it. But all that seemed like a long time ago and the fiber of her being and thinking had clearly changed.

Somehow Rachel knew that the one before her was merely a facilitator of something greater. She had no idea of what that greater thing might be, but she felt that she would know soon enough. If the creature did not wish to talk, Rachel decided, then so be it.

They continued their hike through the lush forest with its broad green leaves. From time to time Rachel would see exquisitely beautiful flowers with large white petals augmented with veins of red. They were unlike anything Rachel had ever seen.

The flowers reminded her of the beauty of the world that now surrounded her. It was all so different yet still familiar. How could anyplace be more beautiful, more serene, than this world?

A few moments later the forest seemed to part, giving way to a vast, circular clearing. In the clearing there were no trees or shrubs. All foliage was gone and in their place was a tall mound of reddish rock that Rachel estimated to be forty to fifty feet high.

"Look, Blessed Woman," the creature said, pointing at the mound. "Look and remember."

The words struck Rachel as strange for there was so little to see, just a large rock outcropping. No, that wasn't right. What she was seeing wasn't a pile of rocks but a single bell-shaped rock that loomed over the surrounding earth.

"Come with me," the creature said as he left the fringe of the forest and began scaling the mound. Rachel followed closely. The slope was steep but not so much as to make the ascent difficult. The man-thing reached the top first, and Rachel could see him staring down at the middle of the mound. When Rachel crested the slope she quickly saw what had captured his interest.

The rock knoll was hollowed out—at least partially hollowed out. Someone had carved away the stone from its top to its base, leaving a structure in the middle. The result was a cross-shaped building hewed from solid rock. On the roof had been carved a large cross within a larger hollow cross.

The building could be seen only from the top edge of the rock mound or from the air. Anyone stationed at the forest edge would see only the red rock mound and nothing more.

Surrounding the cross-shaped structure was an excavated trench as narrow as twenty feet in some spots and widening to large grottoes and courtyards in others. Rachel felt a moment of vertigo as she peered down the four-story moat-like furrow.

"Incredible," Rachel exclaimed. She studied the building closely. She saw no joints, no mortar, no blocks, just a massive monolithic building chiseled out of a hill of stone. The structure was complete with windows and doors.

"This way," the creature intoned as he turned toward one of the trenches.

Rachel followed without question and soon came upon a stairway of stone that led from the brim of the hill down to the floor of one of the grottoes. Without a word the man-thing descended the ancient stone steps. Rachel stayed close behind.

There was an eerie silence in the trench, a hush broken only by the quiet footfalls of the creature and Rachel. There were no other human sounds, no voices, no music.

Rachel estimated that the stairway was eight, maybe ten, feet across. The steps looked worn and polished as if hundreds of thousands of feet had ascended and descended their treads. Touching one of the stone walls, Rachel felt a coolness that was almost damp. Like the structure, the walls on the side of the staircase were of a single unit, carved from the solid mass of stone.

The foot of the stairs opened into a large bay that Rachel judged to be roughly the size of a small house. Looking up gave Rachel an overpowering sense of being at the bottom of a deep and dry well. The high walls obscured the view of everything but the jade green sky above.

She then turned her attention to the stone building in front of her. From its base it appeared to tower into the sky. The stone of the building was the same as the stone of the trench: red, tooled smooth, and cool.

"What is this place?" Rachel asked in hushed tones.

The creature stood near a large, heavy-looking door, turned, and gazed quizzically at Rachel. "Why, it is a church."

"A church?" Rachel replied. "I've never seen a church like this before."

"There are many like this," he replied casually. "Follow me."

With a turn in direction and the push of his hand the creature opened the large wooden door. It swung open silently. Rachel had expected a tooth-jarring squeak, for the door, like the steps, looked very old and very worn. But it emitted no sound and swung easily on its hinges. The creature stepped inside.

Rachel hesitated. Not in fear, for that emotion was out of place in this world. Her reluctance was rooted in amazement. Her mind had become a sponge that was soaking up every last detail that she could see, smell, and touch. She wanted to miss nothing, forget nothing.

The creature reappeared through the doorway and looked at her. "Please, Blessed Woman." He beckoned with a long finger for her to follow him. Rachel quickly complied.

Blessed Woman? Why did he keep calling her that? Rachel wondered. She was tempted to ask but was certain that she would receive only a cryptic reply.

Once inside the structure, Rachel froze. The first thing she noticed was a tall man standing just inside the doorway. Unlike the creature that Rachel had been following, this man looked as natural and as human as any man she had ever seen. He was thin in frame with dark chestnut skin that was scarred with what Rachel judged to be marks from a severe case of chickenpox. He wore a long white robe with a band of red near the feet. On his head he wore a turbanlike white hat. His chin was graced with a short, black, curly beard accented with an abundance of gray. The man appeared very, very old.

"Oh, hello," Rachel said, slightly startled at seeing another human. The man smiled lightly, offered a slight bow, but said nothing.

Venturing farther into the strange church, Rachel was immediately taken aback by the massive vaulted domes of the ceiling that towered above her. It was clear that these too had been hewed out of the indigenous rock. The entire structure, inside and out, had been cleaved from a single massive boulder. It seemed an impossible task, but the impossible seemed normal here.

Each vaulted dome was painted in bands of color, ribbons of red and blue that caressed each curve and cornice of the ceiling. At the apex of each dome there was painted a white cross similar to the one Rachel had seen on top of the building, yet slightly more elaborate. The crosses looked more like plus signs. Each arm of the cross was wider at its end than it was at the intersection.

Walking slowly, Rachel did her best to take in everything she saw. Her mind was filled with questions. Where was she? What was this place? Who built it and why? But she held her silence. For the moment, questions seemed inappropriate.

"Look here," the creature said, pointing at a large pole in the center of the building. Rachel approached and studied the column but discovered that there was little to see. The pillar was covered in a thick purple drape that was wrapped in spiral fashion from top to bottom. Nothing could be seen of the pole itself.

"I don't understand," Rachel said quietly. Despite the softness of her voice, her words rattled around in the stone structure. "All I see is this cloth."

"Watch," the creature said, his already strange voice being augmented by the rock walls.

A moment later, Rachel saw the purple drape begin to unwind from the top of the column down, slowly unwrapping and falling as if in slow motion. It dropped with a gossamer frailty that belied its apparent thickness. It fell in a languid, airborne dance until it piled itself softly at the base of the pillar.

The column now stood unrobed, its every side bare for observation. Rachel approached and looked closely at the tall pillar. It, like the building, was made of a single piece of stone. It was obvious that this column had not been milled elsewhere and transported here, but that it was an indivisible part of the whole structure. The column had not been erected, but rather the stone around it had been chiseled away until just the pillar was left.

· But the monolithic nature of the support was not all that made it unique and captivating. Unlike the other columns in the building, this one had carefully etched pictographs engraved on its surface. While Rachel felt that the column, and indeed the whole structure, was very old, the pictographs showed no signs of wear or aging.

The detail astonished Rachel. The artist must have been a master craftsman, for each image was clear and without distortion. The stark realism of each representation, each figure, made comprehending them easy. These images were not stylized as some ancient art that Rachel had seen; these were more like photographs etched in stone.

Cautiously Rachel reached out and touched one of the images, running her fingers along the sharp edges that formed the pictograph.

"It's a face," Rachel said more to herself than to the creature. She touched the face's eyes and nose. "They're all faces." Before her, and wrapped around the column, were four distinct portraits: two men and two women. Under each face was a name sculpted into the reddish stone. She read them aloud: "Pruit Bain, Nick Stern, Katrin Coeur, Lindsay Blair." The faces and names were repeated in alternating bands that began at the pillar's base and continued to the ceiling.

The strange harmonic voice of the creature snatched Rachel back from the depths of her thoughts. "Through their eyes the world will see."

"I don't understand," Rachel said, slowly shaking her head. "Who are these people? What do they have to do with me?"

"Through their eyes the world will see," the creature repeated. "And through yours."

"Mine?"

The creature nodded and smiled.

Rachel let the words marinate in her mind. Although she understood the words, she could not grasp the content. "See what?" Rachel asked. "What will the world see?"

"Look, see, remember, Blessed Woman."

A sigh fell from Rachel's lips. "I am looking, I am seeing, and I'll do my best to remember, but I still don't understand. I don't understand the building, this church. I don't understand the pole or the people whose faces are inscribed on it."

"You will," the creature intoned. "All will be made clear."

"I take it you're an angel," Rachel blurted out, surprising herself.

The man-thing nodded.

"Somehow you're not what I expected."

The angel tilted his head to the side, grinned broadly, and replied, "You're not what I expected."

Rachel chuckled.

Adam, whose eyes had been closed as he stood by Rachel's hospital bed still holding tightly to her hand, snapped his head up. "What was that?" he asked, concern saturating his voice.

"I don't know," Dick said as he sprang from his chair and quickly made his way to the bedside. "It sounded like a . . . a giggle."

As if on cue a small noise issued from Rachel's lips. It was the sound of muted laughter, constrained humor.

"It sure sounds like a giggle," Dick said. "Should I call one of the nurses?"

"I don't know," Adam said. "I don't know."

Rachel held a hand to her mouth. "I'm sorry," she said. "That struck me as funny."

The angel practiced his smile. It was getting better, Rachel thought.

"There is one more thing for you to see, Blessed Woman." The angel turned from the pole and walked to a large pair of wooden doors. Rachel followed behind. The angel paused at the doors to allow his charge the opportunity to study the massive gateway. The doors reached from floor to ceiling and were brightly painted. On each door was a mural depicting people in various activities. She gazed at these images for a few moments before the angel swung the doors open.

Stepping over the threshold, Rachel entered the room. What she saw took her breath away.

Seventeen

San Diego, California

"What is this, some kind of test?" Kevin Wilson asked as he peered at the paintings before him. "These are interesting, but they are not what people normally think of when they hear the name Katrin Couer. Still, I know a couple of abstract art lovers that might have their interest piqued by these."

"I didn't bring these to sell, Kevin. I just needed your help with something."

"All paintings are meant to be sold," Kevin said jovially. "That is the art dealers' motto." He was a portly man who kept his body "toned" with twice yearly trips to the gym. His hair was dark and pulled back into a fashionable ponytail. A clotheshorse, Kevin always wore the trendiest clothing, especially those outfits that con-tributed to his cultivated air of art expert. Everyone who knew him was aware that Kevin Wilson had a more exalted image of himself than others held of him. He was, without a doubt, a legend in his own mind. But he knew art and he knew how to sell it.

"We artists have a motto too," Katrin replied. "Never tolerate uppity dealers."

"Oh, you are a sensitive bunch," Kevin replied with a laugh. He genuinely liked Katrin. He found her mousy appearance and demeanor endearing. Still, he had decided, if she were going to share any of his world, he would have to invest some time and money in getting her appearance made over. He had a flashy image that needed to be protected and Katrin just didn't fit, and, judging by the graceful way she snubbed his advances, she didn't want to fit.

"Do any of the images mean anything to you?" Katrin asked.

"You mean you don't know what they are? You did paint these, didn't you? That is what you said after all."

"Yes, that's what I said," Katrin replied. "Consider this as experimental art and tell me what you think you see."

Kevin raised his hand to his chin and struck a thoughtful pose. "Well," he said, "I can't recognize anything on the second painting, but this one starts off fairly easy. The first frame is a clear representation of you sitting at your easel. The next frame is the San Diego skyline . . ."

"San Diego?" Katrin interrupted. "Are you sure?"

"Oh, come on, don't play with me. Of course I'm sure. I live here, remember? The skyline is easy to recognize." Kevin stepped closer to the painting and began pointing with one of his well-manicured fingers. "That's the Hope Building and that's the Coronado Bay Bridge. Those two landmarks are a dead giveaway."

"What about the next frame?" Katrin inquired excitedly.

"Patience," Kevin replied with a mock British accent. "You can't rush genius, you know." He struck his thinking man pose again. Katrin couldn't help but think how pretentious this man was.

After moving his head back and forth, approaching the painting and stepping back, and uttering several grunts and sighs to show the effort of his thinking, Kevin finally spoke: "It's a building."

"It's a building?" Katrin said stupefied. "Of course it's a building. Anyone can see that."

"Ah," Kevin replied with upheld finger. "But can just anyone tell you which building it is?"

"You know?"

"Why, of course. It's elementary. That is the Kingston Memorial Hospital."

"How can you be so sure?"

"As I've already said, I live in this town. Besides, I had my arm put in a cast there last year. Rollerblading accident, you know."

Katrin tried to picture a man in his late forties with Kevin's ample physique on rollerblades and then struggled to suppress a burgeoning smile as well as a pressing need to chuckle.

"That's Kingston Memorial all right," Kevin continued oblivious to Katrin's struggle with her emotions. "Not all that far from here. It's up in Kearny Mesa. Top-notch hospital."

"Can you give me directions there?" Katrin asked.

"Of course."

"What about the rest of the painting? Does any more of it make sense to you?"

Kevin restudied the paintings then shook his head. "It seems to me that there is a radical departure from the first few frames. I see a few more people and some pretty exotic-looking places but they mean nothing to me."

"I see."

"All right, now it's time for you to open up," Kevin said, turning his attention to Katrin. "What's up with you and these paintings? You're not giving up on your usual approach, are you?"

"No, not at all," Katrin replied quickly. "This is just a fluke."

"So what's it mean?"

Katrin didn't respond right away. She wasn't sure how to answer the question. The paintings were a mystery to her. Not only did she not know their meaning, she couldn't even remember painting them, but she didn't want to admit that to Kevin. She could simply state the truth, but there was the danger that Kevin would think her crazy. She didn't need that in her life.

"Well?" Kevin prompted.

"I think I'm going to exercise my womanly right to be mysterious, Kevin, and keep my own counsel on this."

"Ah, come on. Don't keep me in the dark. This is Kevin you're talking to. I'm your art broker and friend. You can trust me."

"It's not a matter of trust, Kevin. Really, it's not."

"Then what is it? Did you plagiarize these or what?"

"Of course not!" Katrin interjected. "You know better than that. It's just . . . well, I'm not ready to talk about them yet. I'm not sure what I think or feel about them."

"I still think I could sell them," Kevin offered. "Not to the usual crowd, but I know a few people who might . . ."

"No thanks," she interrupted. "I don't think the world is ready for this . . ." she struggled for the right word ". . . treatment."

"Whatever you say," Kevin said with resignation. "Whatever you say. You did bring me other paintings, didn't you? The regular kind of stuff, I mean."

"I brought four new paintings. They're out in the van."

"Well, let's not keep them waiting. I'll get Roger to start unloading. In the meantime I'll draw a little map for you so that you can find the hospital."

"Thank you," Katrin replied. Maybe I should see if they have a psycho ward while I'm there, she thought. Perhaps they could tell me what's going on in my head. An artist that paints while unconscious isn't normal.

Eighteen

San Diego, California

Rachel stood frozen by the sight before her. Slowly she dropped her hand from her mouth and looked around. She was in a room that was approximately thirty feet square and thirty feet from floor to ceiling. The walls were covered in gold and inscribed with the images of majestic angels, their wings outstretched.

Opposite the doors and to Rachel's left was a large statue of an angel that she estimated stood fifteen feet high. It had two outstretched wings that reached from its place near the back wall to twenty feet out. The statue, like the room, was plated in bright shimmering gold.

In rapt attention, Rachel watched as her guide walked across the room and stood in the unoccupied right corner near the back wall. He pointed to a bundle of purple linen draped over some unseen object. "Uncover," the angel said. "Uncover the Holy, Blessed Woman. The world will see through your eyes and theirs. Uncover."

With that the angel began to transform. He grew rapidly until his height matched that of the sculptured angel in the room. Wings appeared from his back, wings that he spread forward until the left wing touched the gold wall and his right wing touched the outstretched wing of the statue.

Standing in front of the covered object, Rachel looked up at the two pairs of wings that overshadowed her like a canopy. The angel who had been her guide looked down at her and said, with a much more realistic smile, "Is this what you expected?"

Before she could answer, the angel turned his face toward the opening through which they had come and then became rigid. Gold began to cover him from foot to head until he was the identical image of the other angel statue.

Rachel could not move; she merely stood fixed in place, blinking wildly as she attempted to take in the impossible thing she had just witnessed. She looked away for a moment then back at the two gigantic statues before her. She had no words, just confused thoughts.

The words of the angel rang in her mind: "Uncover, Blessed Woman, uncover." He had been pointing at the pile of thick purple cloth that shrouded something. Gently, timidly, Rachel began to pull the cloth away, allowing it to fall to the ground. A moment later, pulled by its own weight, the entire covering fell to the gold-covered floor.

Once again Rachel was reduced to blinking only. What she saw amazed her more than anything she had yet seen. For before her was the most magnificent, the most beautiful, object her eyes had ever beheld.

In shape it was little more than a box the size of a hope chest except this chest was made purely of, or at least covered in, brilliant gold. There was no color but gold. On top of the box rested the image of two angels, very much like the large gold statues that stood at the back wall. These angels, however, were facing each other and in a kneeling position, their heads bowed low. Their wings stretched up and forward until just the tips touched in a light caress.

"What is this?" Rachel asked aloud.

It seemed vaguely familiar, as if she should recognize it immediately, but she did not. Slowly she circled the object, taking in every corner of it, every sparkle and glimmer, every detail. It had about it a mysterious glow, as if the box itself were giving off a pale golden light powered by some unknown and unending source.

It was majestic.

It was beautiful.

It was radiant and powerful and captivating; charming, appealing, delightful, irresistible, and fascinating. It enchanted the mind and moved the heart. It occurred to Rachel that there were not enough adjectives in the world to describe the object of her attention.

There was another quality about the chest that occurred to Rachel: it was also magnetic. Not in the sense that a piece of metal can be magnetic so as to attract another piece of metal. This was a different type of magnetism, one that worked on the heart and mind. The object was calling her, beckoning her to approach.

Drawing near, Rachel felt a sense of awe wash through her. At first she thought it to be fear, but then realized that the emotion had little to do with fear at all. She was feeling wonder and that wonder warmed her, excited her, tickled her.

She giggled, then giggled again, then laughed. Her glee resonated in the gold-encased room and returned to her in reverberated echo. The angel was right—she was a Blessed Woman. She was blessed to be allowed to see this magnificent room, to be surrounded by glorious angels, and to gaze upon the most beautiful object in creation. In her rapture she felt that she stood at the center of the universe, that the whole cosmos circled in obedient orbit around this most splendid work of art.

It took only a moment for Rachel to realize that what she gazed upon was more than art. The chest, the gold box, had a significance that went beyond the scope of art. The box was . . . she struggled for just the right word: Mystical? Supernatural? Spiritual? All those things to be sure, but there was more, something with deeper meaning than those terms could convey.

Holy! That was the best term. The chest was holy. It was imbued with godliness; it radiated purity. It had about it the very nature of God. Rachel knew that no object could hold or confine or ever define God, but like someone who has been in a smoke-filled room carries the scent of that smoke on them, so this device had been touched by the holiness and glory of God.

Rachel dropped to her knees, suddenly aware of the Almighty as she had never been aware of Him before. As a Christian, albeit a new believer, she had sensed the indwelling Christ, the indwelling God. She had experienced that supernatural peace that comes from being a part of the family of faith. But what she felt here went beyond anything previously experienced. It was as though a pure and clean wave had washed over her and through her, carrying away any hint of sin, any spot of evil, any speck of wrong.

There was something that Rachel wanted, and she desired it more than anything in her life. She longed to touch the box, to feel its cool, smooth gold surface, and in the touching be touched by the power of God.

Hesitancy sprang up in her mind. Who was she to touch something so holy and pure? Would she by the very caress of her fingers spoil and degrade the relic? Would her inadequacy diminish its beauty? Could she by her very touch taint the purity of the chest or sully its perfect beauty?

Still.

Still she was the Blessed Woman. The angel had said so. And wasn't that why she was here in the first place? If not to absorb and to appreciate the relic, then why was she brought here?

With the greatest care, with the slowest of movements, Rachel pushed her hand forward in a tortuous approach until the very ends of her delicate fingers were a hairbreadth away, lingering, waiting for that last tiny command to be issued by the brain that would close the microscopic air space that separated flesh from gold.

Touch.

Surge!

Power!

Flash!

White, green, black. Spinning, falling. Stars and darkness. Sun and light. Warmth and cold. Movement, faster and faster.

Like a rocket, Rachel felt herself compelled skyward. She watched as the room disappeared, then as the stone church diminished in the distance. Soon there was just the green forest and the gray sand and the azure ocean receding from her, and then those diminished until there was only the large green orb hung in space. She watched as it grew smaller and smaller and as the distance between them grew.

"No," Rachel said feeling an overwhelming sense of sadness. "I'm sorry. Let me come back."

The orb continued to move away or Rachel was moving from it. In any case the place of peace and beauty was leaving her.

Darkness. Abject blackness.

Now stars, now moon.

Flash.

White.

Adam was clutching Rachel's hand and praying as he had never prayed before. He had heard her giggle, he was sure of it. Even Dick had heard it. He hadn't called the nurses or the doctors for he was afraid that they would tell him that spontaneous noises were typical and not to get his hopes up. But he wanted his hopes up. He wanted to believe that everything was going to be fine and that this was just a momentary condition.

His Rachel would be back. He had to believe that. He couldn't, wouldn't let go—not now, not ever.

Dick stood beside him, his hand firmly on Adam's shoulder. Adam was thankful that Dick was there. He needed his strength and his ability to believe the impossible.

Rachel sat up in bed.

She did so with such explosive speed that both Adam and Dick leaped back, startled beyond words. Rachel fluttered her eyelids, looked down at the bed on which she lay, then quickly looked around the room. Her eyes fell on her husband and she smiled.

"Is this the best place you could think of to take me to dinner?"

Adam's eyes burned as his tear ducts unleashed a flood that coursed unhindered down his cheeks. Without hesitation he stepped to the side of the bed, took Rachel in his arms and held her tight, burying his face in the crook of her neck, and began to sob uncontrollably. Rachel returned the embrace and gently stroked his hair.

"It's all right, I'm back."

Stunned silence, an attribute rarely associated with Dick, gave way to a shout of joy and a spontaneous jig. "Yes!" Dick shouted and pumped his arm in the air. "Yes, yes, yes!"

Rachel turned to Dick and watched as the normally subdued man pranced about. She couldn't help but laugh and Adam, hearing his wife laughing, raised his head to watch the impromptu show. Wiping the tears from his face, Adam joined in the laughter.

Suddenly Dick stopped and a puzzled look crossed his face. "Doctors," he said loudly. "The doctors and nurses need to know!" With that he raced from the small room into the ICU nurses' area, slipping on the highly polished floors and nearly falling. "Come, come look," he shouted at the nurses then raced back into the room.

In seconds a stream of nurses bolted into the room, expecting to see the worst. Instead they saw Rachel sitting up in bed, Adam standing next to her still weeping, and the squat Dick bouncing on the balls of his feet in unbridled enthusiasm. For a moment no one spoke or moved. Then Dick, still unable to constrain his excitement began hugging the nurses, not even pausing when he came to the one who had threatened to call security.

Rachel returned her attention to Adam, whose face was radiating both joy and relief.

Stroking Rachel's hair, Adam said, "I was afraid I was going to lose you."

"I'm back," she said tenderly, "and, boy, do I have a story to tell you."

Nineteen

San Diego, California

Pruit banked the sleek white Gulfstream V sharply as he approached Lindbergh Field. Through the window he could see the sparkling lights of the nation's seventh-largest city. Slowly he throttled down the twin jet engines to slow his approach for landing. The 38-million-dollar aircraft handled like a dream. Although the jet had a top speed of 593 miles an hour, Pruit had opted for a more leisurely pace, never allowing the craft to exceed 400 miles an hour. While this would save on fuel, Pruit's motivation was something other than frugality. Pruit had wanted to think.

Something strange was going on in Pruit's life—something that he couldn't explain and didn't understand. Time and time again, he would take his hands from the aircraft's controls and stare at them. Once again they looked normal. No cuts, bruises, or scabs to indicate that blood had spontaneously issued from his palms. They looked like normal hands, but Pruit knew better.

As the jet slowly dropped in altitude to begin its landing approach, he felt compelled to look at his hands one more time. Only the discipline of a pilot prevented him from doing so. That discipline, however, could keep neither the image of his bleeding hands nor the haunting words he had heard from elbowing their way to the front of his mind. Why him? he kept asking himself, but no answers presented themselves during the seven-hour trip. He was as much in the dark now as he had ever been.

During the trip he applied as much logic as he could to the situation. He reviewed in detail everything that had happened. So far the only conclusion he could come to seemed beyond the realm of his belief. Each occurrence of the bleeding had come at a time when he was planning to harm himself: the suicide attempt when he had been poised to drive off a cliff and when he was about to snort a large amount of cocaine. There would have been a time when he would have argued that the cocaine was not harming him, but he had been possessed by the drug long enough now to know the truth of the matter.

Perhaps that was the key, Pruit thought. Maybe there's some subconscious force at work here to keep me from hurting myself. Maybe it's a self-defense mechanism. Pruit chuckled at the play on words. Self-defense! Normally, the phrase meant to protect oneself from someone else. In his case, he was having to defend himself from himself. What would that be? Self-self-defense?

It was time to push those thoughts aside. It wouldn't do to destroy such a fine aircraft with its gold fittings, satellite communications, and onboard office simply because he had been daydreaming instead of paying attention. Bringing the wings level once again, Pruit continued his descent toward the runway the control tower had assigned to him. Quickly he scanned the sky for other craft that might be on a collision course. This he did out of habit, a habit he picked up when he first learned to fly. He had initially been trained on an old Cessna that lacked the sophisticated radar and collision-alert system possessed by the Gulfstream. Had any traffic been too close both the tower and the onboard radar would have warned him. Still, he checked. Then he activated the switch that would lower the landing gear. He immediately felt the plane slow as the lowered gear increased the jet's drag.

Raising the flaps that would further the craft's drag, Pruit began the rapid drop toward the concrete runway. Those who flew only in large commercial jets seldom understood how fast a plane's descent was. In the much smaller Gulfstream which could seat only nineteen people instead of several hundred, the descent was very noticeable.

Pruit felt his pulse quicken. Landing always filled his system with adrenaline. If anything was going to go wrong, it would most likely happen on landing. His anxiety, although well controlled, was heightened by the knowledge that he had not flown in the last thirty days or so. That shouldn't matter, considering the many hours of flight experience he had, but the thought was still there.

The sense of speed increased dramatically the closer to the ground Pruit came. He passed over a busy street with cars rushing to their destination. Soon he was over the runway, and he lowered the craft slowly, waiting to hear the telltale roar of rubber tires on coarse concrete that would signal touchdown. He was rewarded a moment later. Immediately he moved the engine levers to their neutral position and then into reverse. The reverse thrust of the engines slowed the plane dramatically. When his ground speed was sufficiently slow, Pruit pressed the metal foot pedals that applied the brakes. It was a perfect landing.

All that remained was securing the business jet on the tarmac, picking up his rental car, and making his way to the Wharfside Hotel. Tomorrow he would do what the voice in his head had told him to do. Then, maybe then, he could put all this behind him.

Twenty

San Diego, California

"Ow! Can't you smooth this out a little?" Nick asked forcefully. "You're killing me back here."

"Sorry," the driver said, his words heavy with a Middle Eastern accent. "The company makes me drive this old car. It needs shocks bad."

"You're right about that." Nick leaned back in the cab and tried to make himself comfortable. The flight he had just taken on Pacific West Airlines had left him stiff. The coach section had been cramped and uncomfortable. That, coupled with the walk down the ramp, through Lindbergh Field's east terminal, lugging his old suitcase, had been more physical exertion than Nick had experienced since he left therapy. His back and legs were a churning caldron of agony.

"You OK?" the driver asked. "You don't look so good."

"I'll be fine once you get me to the motel and I can get out of this back seat."

"That motel is like this cab, old and cramped," the driver said with a laugh. "I know of better places. You want me to take you there?"

"No, I want the Sleepy Hollow Motel. It's near where I want to go."

"Yes, yes. The hospital, right?"

"Exactly."

"They treat you there?"

"No, I'm going to see someone and I don't want to be too far away."

"Family member?"

Nick rubbed his eyes in frustration with the driver's questions. It was none of his business where Nick was going, where he stayed, and who he was visiting in the hospital. Then again, Nick had only partial answers to those questions himself: just a name and a place.

"Not a family member," Nick finally said. "And I'm not in the mood to talk. I just want to get there soon."

"Ten minutes, tops," the driver promised with a huge grin. "Ten minutes and then you'll be there."

Nick nodded thankfully. He desperately wanted to be someplace where he could lie down and stretch out all the kinks in his body. He needed rest for he knew that tomorrow was going to be a big day.

Where Nick's trip from the airport had been fraught with bumps, cramped conditions, and uncomfortable seats, Lindsay's was far more luxurious. The first-class accommodations gave her more than enough space to stretch and nap. The service by the flight personnel had been flawless, and now as she seated herself in the back of the limousine she had little to do but wait until the driver had loaded her luggage in the back.

Once inside, the driver lowered the privacy glass that separated the front seat from the passenger compartment and asked, "Where would we like to go tonight?"

Lindsay studied the man for a moment. He was young with short blond hair. Most likely a college student. If he was struck with her beauty he didn't let it show, at least not initially.

Lindsay contemplated a note she brought with her. She had committed its entire contents to memory, but she consulted the list just the same. "Hotel Circle in Mission Valley. I'm staying at the Radisson."

"You're not from around here, are you, ma'am? You know how I know that?"

"The accent, I assume," Lindsay deadpanned.

"That's right," he offered a large smile. "I'll bet you're from . . . don't tell me, I'm good at this sort of thing . . . Australia. Right? Sydney to be specific."

"You'd lose your bet. I'm from London," she said and then thought: only a moron would confuse a Brit with an Aussie.

"Are you sure?"

"Quite," Lindsay replied with a patience she didn't feel. She had been traveling a long time and had lost more than one night's sleep. The catnaps she had taken on the plane did little to relieve her weariness. "Now may we go?"

Twenty-One

A parade of emotions rambled through Katrin Couer's mind. She was standing in front of the eight-story Kingston Memorial Hospital debating whether or not to pass through the automatic doors into the lobby. She felt at once silly, embarrassed, and apprehensive.

Once inside, whom would she ask for? She had no name, no person in mind, only the image of the hospital that appeared mysteriously on one of two paintings she apparently created while in a trance. Kevin had been right, Kingston Memorial was the hospital in her painting, but that knowledge couldn't provide direction for her next action.

She knew she should be here, but didn't know how she knew. The whole thing was too mystical for her: trances, mysterious paintings, time and memory loss. Yet she had to know, had to follow through. To not do so would leave a gaping hole in her life. She would always wonder what might have come from the mystery.

Taking a deep breath, Katrin moved forward toward the lobby. The automatic doors swung open before her, then promptly closed, shutting out the cool San Diego evening. She glanced around, looking for direction, a way of gaining her bearing, and, more importantly, a clue about what she should do next.

The lobby was expansive with blue padded chairs filling the space. Individuals sat alone, pretending to read old magazines; groups huddled together talking softly. Katrin realized that a large portion of the lobby was used as a waiting room. The people here were those who were forced to suspend their lives and emotions for a time while they waited on news about loved ones who were at that moment under the knife of a surgeon or being treated for some emergency.

On the north side of the lobby was a small, brightly lit room filled with flowers and get well cards. A small bunch of silver Mylar balloons in the display window heralded the words "Get Well Soon" in bright colors of red, blue, and green.

Turning from the gift shop, Katrin let her eyes trace the rest of the lobby. A donut-shaped simulated oak counter was in the center of the room and standing in its middle was a matronly woman wearing a pink frock. A pink lady, Katrin thought. One of those retired ladies who pass part of their day doing volunteer work in hospitals. Maybe she could help, if I only knew what help to ask for.

On the back wall was a series of portraits. Most were of men in dark suits or white doctor's coats. Slowly, Katrin let her eyes absorb each photograph. Each picture was set in an oak frame and hung in its place to form a straight line. It was the last picture that caught Katrin's attention: a woman in her thirties with shoulder-length black hair. She, like several of the men in the gallery, wore a doctor's coat.

Katrin wasted no time in walking to the picture for a closer look. It was her all right. She had seen this woman before. More accurately, she had painted this woman's likeness before. Katrin could see one of her mystery paintings clearly in her mind. In one of the many frames was this woman's face.

Looking at the wooden frame that surrounded the portrait, Katrin saw a small brass plaque with the words "Rachel Tremaine, MD. Physician of the Month." Now Katrin had a name to go with the face. Rachel Tremaine.

Emboldened, Katrin turned, quickly walked to the lady in pink and waited to be noticed.

"May I help you?" the pink lady asked pleasantly enough, but without a smile.

"I'm looking for Dr. Rachel Tremaine," Katrin asked meekly. "Do you know how I can find her?"

The woman pursed her lips for a moment then said, "You and everyone else."

"Excuse me?"

"Dr. Tremaine seems to be quite popular of late," the woman said quickly. "Room 512. Down the hall. Elevators on the left."

Katrin was puzzled and wondered how the woman could know what room a doctor would be in at any given time. Perhaps she had meant office 512. "Is she on duty right now?" Katrin asked.

"On duty?" The woman surrendered a gutteral chuckle. "Hardly. Dr. Tremaine is a patient at the moment."

The news startled Katrin. "A patient?"

"Yes, ma'am," the aide replied, letting slip a little sarcasm. "Doctors get sick too you know."

"Um . . . thank you," Katrin stammered. "Room 512, you say."

"That's right, room 512."

Katrin turned and slowly walked to the elevators. As she did, she struggled to find the words she would use when meeting Dr. Tremaine. Nothing seemed right. "Hi, my name is Katrin Coeur and I had a blackout recently in which I painted two paintings, and your face appeared in one of them. Who are you and what are you doing on my canvas?"

That sounds sufficiently psychotic, Katrin said to herself. She's liable to have security toss me out on my ear.

During the short elevator ride to the fifth floor, Katrin rehearsed different approaches. It didn't take long for her to notice that each speech she considered began, "Hi, I'm not crazy . . ." or "I really am normal, but . . ." Katrin wondered sadly if all that was true. Was she sane? Was she really normal? Or had she truly begun to lose her mind?

The normally innocuous sound of the elevator chime sounding out its message that it had arrived at the fifth floor filled Katrin with dread. She wanted to stay onboard the lift, ride it down to the lobby, walk as fast as possible back to her car, and drive to her hotel. There, amidst the warm water of a bath, she would make every effort to forget the whole thing.

Instead, she stepped from the elevator.

The little foyer off the elevator was brightly lit, and the walls were graced with watercolor prints. To Katrin's left was a wide hall and a nurse's station. People moved up and down the hall. Some, judging by their dress, were medical personnel, others were "civilians" like her. As she stepped into the hall she could see doorways evenly spaced down the wall. Next to each doorway was a blue plastic plaque with a three-digit number on it. The first plaque read 501 while the room directly opposite it was numbered 502. South side will be rooms with odd numbers, Katrin reasoned, and the north side will be even numbered.

No one took notice of her as she strolled slowly down the corridor, reading each blue sign. Moments later she stood near the door of room 512. She could hear voices. Maybe I should come back later, Katrin thought, not wanting to interrupt. No. It's now or never.

Taking a deep breath and without any idea of what she would say, Katrin crossed the threshold.

The room was full of people, most of whom stood quietly near the walls; one was seated. There was a bed with a woman in a hospital gown reclining on it. Katrin recognized the woman immediately as the one in her painting. Standing next to the bed and holding the woman's hand was a man with dark hair, thick glasses, and a slight stoop in his posture.

The mix of people was remarkable. There was a tall woman of exquisite beauty, long black hair, and a serious, almost pained expression on her face. Standing next to her was an imperial looking man with sharp facial features and dressed in an expensive looking suit. He too looked troubled. The only seated person was a man who grinned constantly and looked as if he were about to bubble over like a pot of water left too long on a stove.

As she entered all eyes in the room turned toward her. There was silence. Katrin tried to speak but words failed her. She felt foolish and her skin turned hot with embarrassment. There had been enough anxiety at the thought of speaking to Dr. Tremaine and relating the strange story about the paintings, but to do so before a group was just too much.

"I'm . . . I'm . . . uh," Katrin offered, her words faltering. She struggled to form a single cogent stream of thought. "What I mean is . . ."

"Hi, Katrin," the woman in the bed uttered with a quick and genuine smile. "We've been waiting for you."

"You . . . you have?"

"Absolutely," Rachel replied, effervescing with enthusiasm. "We knew you would be here soon. Come on in and meet the others. We have a lot to talk about."

Katrin could only nod in agreement.

Part 2
Around Faith's Corner

Now faith is the assurance of things hoped for, the conviction of things not seen. For by it the men of old gained approval.
— Hebrews 11:1-2

That the proof of your faith, being more precious than gold which is perishable, even though tested by fire, may be found to result in praise and glory and honor at the revelation of Jesus Christ.
— 1 Peter 1:7

Twenty-Two

Rachel and Adam watched as the man in the white coat walked from the hospital room into the corridor.

"Dr. Snell didn't look all that happy," Adam said returning his gaze to his wife, who was sitting up in bed.

"No doctor likes loose ends," Rachel offered, "especially neurologists. There's too much at stake."

"But he said that all the tests, the EEG, the new CAT scan, the MRI, blood work, everything, were just fine—like nothing had happened."

"Exactly," Rachel replied, swinging her legs over the edge of the bed. She was dressed in her blue jogging suit. "In his mind something did happen and not only can he not explain it, he can't even see that there ever was a problem. That's hard for a doctor to reconcile."

"Does he think it will happen again?"

"I'm sure that thought has crossed his mind, but we know better, don't we?"

Adam sighed heavily. "I don't know what to believe. Everything is so bizarre. Everything you told me is just too amazing."

"Too amazing to believe?" Rachel asked suspiciously.

"It's not that I don't believe you," Adam said smoothly. "I just

126

don't know what to make of all this. I'm not sure how all this fits together and what we are supposed to do about it."

"I bet that's how Dr. Snell feels," Rachel said with a grin. "I know that's how I would feel if I were in his shoes. But I saw what I saw, and I know that it was real. You've got to believe that what I experienced was not the result of an overactive imagination."

"I believe you, Rachel, but what does it mean?"

"I don't know. I do know that it's significant, though, and that we have something very important to do."

Adam nodded slowly then asked, "Why didn't you tell Dr. Snell what you experienced?"

"It would have only confused him. I know that I'm fine and that what I saw was real, but I can't prove it. Telling him would only run the risk of me being diagnosed as delusional."

Adam said nothing.

"What?" Rachel asked quickly. "You don't think I'm delusional, do you?"

"Of course not," Adam replied, shaking his head. "Just two days ago we had a room full of people from all over the world here, and each one to see you."

"I can't wait to hear their stories. I bet something similar has happened to them."

"I don't know," Adam offered softly. "There's something unusual going on here. A couple of them didn't look all that happy about being here in the first place."

"True," Rachel acknowledged then smiled broadly, "but I'm glad to be a part of it all. It's so exciting . . . No! It's more than exciting, it's exhilarating."

"Perhaps, but I don't think they all share that exhilaration with you."

"You know, Adam," Rachel said playfully, "you're being a real wet blanket."

Adam chuckled. "I suppose I am." He crossed over to her and took her in his arms. "I was really scared. I was afraid you were going to die and I would be left all alone. Even now the thought makes me shudder."

Rachel returned the embrace. "I'm just fine now, Adam. All this happened for a purpose. It's a good thing, really it is."

"But what purpose?" Adam asked as he took a step back. "What does it all mean? What are we supposed to do next?"

"Well, we need to hear what the others have to say. What little we heard makes me think that each of them experienced something unusual. We need to know what. Maybe when we have all the stories, we'll know more."

"Maybe," Adam agreed.

"But the first thing we do is get out of here." Rachel jumped from the bed. "I've had all of this room I can take."

"You don't think you need to stay another day . . . just in case, I mean?"

"Stop worrying, Adam. Dr. Snell has released me to go home. Let's let some sick person have this bed."

"OK," Adam conceded, "but I'm bringing you back at the first sign of trouble."

Twenty-Three

Walking through the doors of the education building of Maple Street Community church gave Adam Bridger a strong sense of normalcy, something he welcomed eagerly. The first door off the hall led to the church offices.

"Hi, Pastor," Fannie Meyers said exuberantly. "How's Rachel?"

"She's fine, Fannie," Adam replied with a smile. "Thanks for asking."

"I have some messages for you here," she said rising from her seat behind a large metal desk. Fannie Meyers had been the church secretary when Adam became pastor ten years before. She was a gregarious woman, quick to smile, and possessed a genuine Christian spirit. She was also fiercely loyal to her pastor. Perpetually cheerful, a needed quality in her job, Fannie was a slightly rotund woman in her fifties. Her coal-black hair had been softened by a mild intrusion of gray.

"Anything important or pressing?" Adam asked.

Fannie shook her head as she rounded the desk while reading the pink message slips she held in her hand. "Three were salespeople—I asked them to call back next week; one was from the Lutheran pastor down the street—he had heard about Rachel and wanted to see if you needed anything."

"That was nice of him," Adam replied.

"Yes, it was. All the rest of the messages are along the same line. Do you want me to call them for you?"

"No, but you could put together a few thank-you cards for me to sign. I'll put a little note in each one. It's good to know that people were praying and thinking of us."

"There was plenty of that going around," Fannie said. "We rang heaven's phones off their hooks."

The mental picture of thousands of phones in heaven all ringing at the same time made Adam snicker. "Well, the prayers worked."

"So Rachel is at home taking it easy?"

"I wish," Adam answered. "When I left she was cleaning house. Some people are coming over tonight."

"Shouldn't she be resting?" Fannie asked with surprise. "I would have thought you would have confined her to bed."

"Fannie," Adam said steadily, "you know Rachel. Do you really think I could confine her to bed? In fact, do you know anyone who could?"

Fannie laughed lightly. "I suppose you're right. She does have a mind of her own."

"That's what I love about her."

The smile on Fannie's face broadened. No one in the church had been happier for Adam than Fannie. She knew what only a few people did, that her pastor had been unlucky in love, having been engaged twice before only to be rejected. Fannie had feared that Adam had given up any hope of marrying. She had even made several attempts at matchmaking herself, but Adam had quickly put an end to that.

"Anything special you need from me today?" Fannie inquired.

"Not really. I plan on catching up on some research."

"Good. I need to get the newsletter out and that's going to take most of the day."

Adam nodded and then crossed Fannie's office to his own and shut the door. The office was like every other occupied by ministers across the country. It was adorned simply with inexpensive paintings on the wall, a thin carpet on the floor, and two walls covered in books.

It was a comfortable place for Adam. He enjoyed the hours he

spent in the room writing sermons and Bible studies, counseling parish-
ioners, and handling the administrative business of the midsize church.
The office represented something to him: it was a special place where
the work of God was conducted.

Seating himself behind his desk he turned on his laptop computer
and waited while it booted up. Then he took a chrome-colored plastic disk and inserted it in the CD-ROM drive. Adam was computer
literate and enjoyed the extra productivity the computer brought
him. He especially loved the Bible program that he used almost daily.
It gave him the ability to do word and topic searches much faster
than turning pages in a book.

For Adam, though, the computer would never replace the book.
Computers were faster, but there was something more intimate in
the holding and reading of a book. Adam was a true bibliophile. Even
as a child he had surrounded himself with books. While some
children could not sleep without a particular blanket or teddy
bear in bed with them, Adam had preferred a book. Reading in bed
was a practice that had continued into adult life.

The disk that Adam had just placed in his computer contained
the complete text of more than dozen reference books and Bible trans-
lations, and he could search through them in a matter of seconds.
Which was good, for Adam had much research to do.

After listening to Rachel's account of her vision, and after she
answered his many questions, Adam had decided to do some inves-
tigating. He had no doubts about what Rachel had seen, although
a part of him wanted to attribute the vision to stress or the mental trauma of her mysterious coma. Such a conclusion might have
been easier to believe if four strangers had not almost simultaneously shown up at the hospital, each knowing Rachel's name and
location.

There were many questions floating in the tide of Adam's
mind—far more questions than answers.

When looking for answers Adam always turned first to his
Bible. In doing so he always found wisdom, guidance, and comfort,
even if he couldn't find a specific answer to a particular question.

"All right," Adam mumbled quietly to himself, "Rachel thinks
she had a vision." He paused. "No," he corrected himself, "she did
have a vision. But what does it mean?"

During the drive from his home to the office, Adam had confessed to himself that he knew very little about dreams and visions. Oh, he knew that they occurred from time to time in the Bible and that some of the greatest biblical heroes—Daniel, Isaiah, Paul, Peter, and others—had been the recipients of such spiritual communications. But that was just about all he knew. So, he decided, it was time for him to learn more.

The Bible program on his computer had a topical index. With it, he could search all the scriptural references on almost any subject. He started with the word "vision." It took a few moments for the computer to scan every verse in the Bible for the chosen term. Adam waited patiently, knowing that if he were doing this search by hand it would take weeks.

Less than a minute later, Adam was staring at a long list of Bible verses. A quick count revealed about eighty references. He then tried the term "dream" and soon discovered that the word was used more than seventy times. Between them there were more than 150 Bible verses on the screen. Adam chose to print the list.

The laser printer near his desk spewed out two pages containing the references. Pulling his favorite study Bible down from the shelf behind his desk, Adam began sampling the listed Bible texts. He could have done this through the computer, but for Adam, some things were done better the old-fashioned way. Besides, his study Bible contained notes that he had penned over the years. One of those notes might prove useful.

Hours passed without notice. Adam was one of those individuals who could lose himself in thought for long periods of time. Sitting quietly at his desk, poring over his Bible, making notes in the computer, pulling down reference texts and commentaries might look tedious and boring to some, but to Adam it was as exhilarating as an amusement park.

Adam was a scholar by nature and by training. Before the day was finished, he would have a deep grasp of the subject before him— and maybe even some answers.

Twenty-Four

"Sorry I'm late," Adam said as he burst into the living room of his home. "I lost track of the time."

"You're not that late," Rachel said easily. "Actually, everyone just arrived."

"The front of the house looks like a used car lot," Adam joked. "I hope everyone found the place easily enough." There was some head nodding and a few grunts.

"I've just made coffee," Rachel offered. "Anybody want some?" The head nodding and grunts returned.

Adam surveyed the group of strangers sitting in his living room. The two women sat on the couch but not close; Nick Stern sat in the leather easy chair with his feet up, and the tall man sat alone on the love seat.

Rachel carried a tray with a coffee urn, mugs, and cream and sugar from the kitchen into the living room and set it on the wooden coffee table.

"I'll let you serve yourselves," she said cheerfully and then sat down on the love seat.

"Let me put my stuff down," Adam said, raising the briefcase he had in hand. "I'll be right back." He disappeared into the bedroom and returned a moment later with a folding chair. He set the chair down in the middle of the room so that he could face everyone. "Well, I'm not sure where we should begin. Perhaps I should start by saying thank you for coming here tonight."

Everyone nodded, but no one spoke. It was clear that they were waiting for someone else to take the lead.

"OK," Adam said. "Let's start off by acknowledging that something strange is happening. I think we can all agree on that."

"Do you know what's going on?" Katrin asked.

Adam shook his head. "No, not really, but I think we will know soon."

"How?" Pruit asked bluntly. "This is beyond my experience, and frankly I find it all very unnerving."

"Unnerving is a good word for it," Katrin agreed.

"I think we're in agreement with that," Adam offered. "But uncomfortable as it is, we must press on. I don't think we can or should ignore this. Unless I miss my guess, at least some of you have attempted to ignore the whole thing but to no avail. Am I right?"

"I haven't," Nick said. "I think it's great."

"That makes one of us," Lindsay voiced bitterly.

"OK, OK," Adam said soothingly. "Let's see where we are first; then we can see where we need to go. Here's what I understand so far. A few days ago my wife fell unconscious while she was alone in the house. I came home and found her in our walk-in closet. At the hospital they told me that she was in a deep coma. During that time each of you received some kind of direction to leave your homes in Fort Worth, New York, Ojai, and London to come here to San Diego and contact Rachel. Have I got this right so far?"

They all nodded.

"All right then, why don't each of you tell your story and let's see if we can start piecing together the puzzle. Fair enough?"

"I'll start," Nick said eagerly. "I'm Nick Stern—you already know that because I told you that in the hospital. You also know that I'm from Fort Worth. What you don't know is that I used to be a firefighter. While doing a rescue in a building, I fell through the floor and became trapped with my feet dangling in the burning apartment below. It burned my legs severely. I lived through a lot of pain and spent a lot of days in the burn ward. The good news is that I got to keep both legs. The bad news is that I can't work anymore and I'm nearly crippled. I can walk around some, but it hurts an awful lot.

"But the fire burned more than my skin," Nick continued. "It burned my self-esteem. When I couldn't go back to work, I got depressed. I lost my will to live. My wife left me and I became so bitter that my friends stopped coming round. Anyway, I was in one of my blue funks when it all happened."

Taking a deep breath, Nick proceeded. "Now I need to tell you right up front that this is going to sound really off the wall, but I swear to you that it's true. All I ask is that you hear me out. OK?"

"OK," Adam replied for the others.

"I was readin' this magazine, see—*Time* magazine—thinking about how unfair life was and how horrible my life turned out. Anyway, I'm readin' this magazine when I come across this advertisement for some restaurant. Maybe it wasn't about the restaurant but it was some kinda ad anyway. I start looking at this ad when—I swear this is the truth—the people started movin'.'"

"The people in the advertisement?" Rachel asked quietly.

"Yeah, the people in the picture. Just like they were real. And the waiter, he looks at me and then motions for me to join 'em—right there in the magazine.

"Well," Nick said, throwing his hands in the air, "it scared the tar outta me. I dropped the magazine on my lap and rubbed my eyes some. When I picked it up, the people were still moving. They were laughing and having a good ol' time. I wanted to laugh and have a good time too. I guess I was wishing for that when the picture came to life.

"Anyway, the next thing I know, I was in the picture—right there in the restaurant in the ad. Except now I could hear everything and smell everything. It's like I dropped in on some party. Pretty soon people are gathered around me, slapping me on the back, and treatin' me like I'm some kinda movie star or somethin'.'"

Pruit Bain leaned forward and listened intently. "You mean to say that you were transported into the picture? Literally? And there were people in there?"

"That's exactly what I mean," Nick answered firmly. "Sounds crazy, doesn't it?"

Nodding sharply Pruit replied, "I thought my story was strange."

"It gets better," Nick said with a grin. "While I'm sitting there the waiter—the guy who motioned for me to join 'em—brings this big plate of food. It smelled great. I'd been living off frozen dinners for months, so this stuff looked real good. Except it's not like any food I've ever seen before."

"How do you mean?" Adam inquired.

"Well, it kinda looked like pasta. I mean it had the color of pasta, but it was more like bread. I tasted it and it was great! Kinda sweet but not too much. You know what I mean? Anyway I ate everything on the plate, but wanted more. So the waiter brings this big metal jar and sets it on the table. Now here's the kicker. This jar is made outta gold. Real, honest-to-goodness gold. He takes the lid off and dishes up some more of the stuff. Then he begins to dish it out to all the other people, but no matter how much he gives out the gold jar remained full. It was the weirdest thing I had ever seen."

"This gold jar," Adam began, "how big was it?"

Nick thought for a moment. "Pretty big, but not real big." He thought for another moment. "I'd say it was about two feet tall and about that round," he held his hands about eighteen inches apart.

"Then what happened?" Katrin asked.

"Well, I'm enjoyin' the food, and the music, and the people. I was feeling better than I had ever felt before when the waiter comes back over and hands me the bill."

"The bill?" Rachel exclaimed. "You're kidding."

"Not a bit," Nick said with a smile. "I start thinkin' that I'm in big trouble, because I've got next to no money. So I turn the bill over and instead of a dollar amount I find a note: Rachel Tremaine, San Diego, Kingston Memorial Hospital. And at the bottom of the bill there's this picture of you." Nick pointed at Rachel. "Pretty good likeness too.

"So I ask the waiter, 'What's this?' and he says, 'Just remember.' Well, I go to stand up—which is hard for me with these bum legs—and when I do I notice that there's no pain. I feel my legs with my hands and they feel normal. No stiff skin, no stiff joints. My legs are like they used to be.

"The next thing I know, I'm back in my chair in my apartment, holdin' the magazine, except the picture doesn't move anymore, and my legs are still the old damaged ones."

Katrin gasped involuntarily. "That must have been awful."

Nick shook his head. "That's the strangest part of all. It didn't matter to me. I felt as good then as I did in the restaurant, and I have continued to feel good. I should be bummed out, but I'm not. I've never felt better."

Adam glanced around the room, looking each person in the eye, expecting at any moment that one of them would leap to his or her feet and shout, "That's the most ridiculous thing I ever heard!" What he saw in their eyes was not suspicion but relief. They were learning that they were not alone. This is going to be an interesting night, Adam thought.

Katrin was next to offer her story. She did so willingly, but Adam immediately sensed the stress that the emotional exposure caused. Clearly, Katrin was an introvert who was most uncomfortable talking to a group of strangers. Adam couldn't help but feel sorry for her.

"I'm a painter," Katrin said softly. "I have a studio in Ojai, which is just a few miles inland of Ventura. It's a lovely town, quiet and filled with oak trees. It's the perfect place for me to paint. The other day I was in my studio alone. I was starting a new painting, but couldn't get a clear image in my mind, so I just sat there looking at a blank canvas. That was in the morning. The next thing I knew, it was afternoon and there was a freshly painted work on my easel—actually two works: one on the easel and one propped next to my desk."

Katrin looked meekly at the others for a moment before continuing. "I don't know how they got there," she said softly. "I had brushes in my hand and there was paint on them—paint that matched that which was on the canvas. But I don't remember painting the pictures. I don't remember anything that happened during that time." Katrin bit her lower lip and lowered her head. "It makes me feel as if I'm going crazy."

"You're not going crazy," Rachel said soothingly. "The rest of us are testimony to that."

"That's true," Adam said. "Do you know how long you were . . ." He hesitated. "I'm not sure what term to use. Can you tell how long you were . . . out?"

"Not exactly," Katrin answered, "maybe four or five hours."

"That's a long time to be sitting on a stool unconscious," Pruit said.

"She wasn't really unconscious if she was painting, was she?" Lindsay declared.

The room fell silent for a moment, then Adam asked, "Did you bring the paintings with you?"

Nodding, Katrin replied, "Yes, they're in my van outside."

"May we see them?"

Again, Katrin answered with a nod. "I'll go get them."

"Let me help," Adam offered.

"No, that's OK," Katrin said. "They're not heavy, and it will only take a second." With that, she rose from the sofa and went outside.

"I think I'll have some more of that coffee," Pruit said, wanting something stronger.

Rachel poured a cup for Nick, who couldn't reach the pot from his chair. He hadn't asked and Rachel knew that he was too proud to do so. Rather than making him lower the footrest on the recliner and get up—an easy task for anyone else, but painful for Nick—Rachel took the initiative. Others, with the exception of Lindsay, helped themselves.

It took only a few moments for Katrin to retrieve the paintings. They were rather large but she carried them easily. She propped them up against one of the nearby walls. Both paintings were covered with white cloth.

"I can't say that this is my best work," Katrin began, "I can't even say that they are my work, but here they are." Removing the coverings, Katrin displayed the paintings, stepping back so that the others could see. She raised a hand to her mouth and began to chew on a fingernail.

Both Adam and Rachel picked up on her body language and exchanged knowing glances. Showing these paintings was not easy for Katrin. They brought back a disturbing and confusing memory. Their very existence was a physical reminder that something strange and frightening had happened to her.

Everyone leaned forward to study the canvases.

"My mother says they look like pages out of a comic book."

"More like a storyboard," Pruit said, his eyes fixed on the artwork.

"How's that?" Adam asked.

"I'm in advertising," Pruit replied. "When we create a television commercial one of the first things we do is make a storyboard. They're simple, really. Generally an artist makes a sketch on a piece of paper of what the viewer is going to see on television. Underneath the drawing is an area for the audio; that's what the viewer is going to hear. By making storyboards we can help the client get a feel for not only what a television commercial is going to say, but also what it's going to look like. Movie directors do the same thing except on a much larger scale."

"And you say these look like a storyboard?" Adam inquired, pointing at the paintings.

"Sort of," Pruit replied. "There's no audio line, but it looks like a series of pictures designed to convey a message."

"You mean these paintings are some sort of communication device?" Rachel asked.

"I suppose you can call it that," Pruit answered, "although I wouldn't use the word 'device.' Think of it as a script without words. See here," he said pointing to the top left image of the first painting, "that's San Diego, isn't it? And the next: that's your hospital, right? The place we were all directed to."

Rachel nodded. "I guess it is."

"Now look at the next frame," Pruit continued, "that's you."

Everyone focused on the painting. In the third frame was a small portrait of Rachel. Now it was Rachel's turn to raise a hand to her mouth.

"That's how I found you," Katrin said. "I recognized your picture in the lobby as being the same as the one I painted."

"Amazing" was all Adam could offer.

"Let's keep going," Pruit said. "I can't tell you what it all means, but every one of us appears in one or the other of the paintings. And not only that, but places appear too. San Diego is self-evident, but the others are not—at least not to me."

"But who are the other people?" Nick inquired. "I don't recognize any of them."

"Their skin is dark," Adam said. "African-Americans? Or maybe just Africans. That part of the painting looks familiar to me."

"You've seen this before?" Katrin asked.

"More like something similar, but I can't remember when or what."

"And what about the other painting?" Rachel asked. "Does anyone recognize anything?"

"Ocean," Katrin said. "And the people are different."

"Look closer," Pruit encouraged. "There are fewer of us in that painting. In fact, I can see only Nick, Lindsay, and you, Katrin."

"But why wouldn't we all be in the painting?" Katrin said.

"Hard to tell," Pruit said. "Maybe it means we split up."

Lindsay chimed in: "Or maybe it means some of us die."

Silence.

All eyes turned toward Lindsay.

"Why would you say a thing like that?" Rachel asked somberly.

"Why not?" Lindsay replied coldly. "No one lives forever. Maybe some of us get killed."

"Since I'm not in the second painting," Pruit said, "I can't say I like that idea."

Lindsay only shrugged.

"This is going to take some study," Adam said. "Perhaps a lot of study."

Rachel turned her attention to Katrin. "Have you had anymore blackouts since this painting?"

"None. That was the only time, and I'm not sure that I blacked out. I just don't remember painting these."

Adam wanted desperately to focus on the paintings, taking each frame and analyzing it in the greatest detail, but first he needed the overall story and there were still several accounts to hear.

"Pruit," Adam said, "what about your situation? What happened to you?"

Picking up his coffee cup and leaning back on the love seat, Pruit took a slow purposeful sip. Adam knew he was gathering his thoughts or, perhaps, even stalling for time.

"Mine's different," he began. "And I don't mind telling you that I don't like talking about it. In fact, when I first arrived tonight I wasn't sure that I was going to talk, but hearing what I've heard . . . well, maybe you'll believe me."

"We'll believe you," Adam said quickly.

Pruit took a deep breath and let it out slowly. "My hands bleed," he said plainly. "My hands bleed and I hear voices."

Again a shroud of silence descended on the gathering as each person pictured what he or she was hearing.

"What do you mean, your hands bleed?" Rachel asked seriously.

"They just start bleeding all by themselves," Pruit stated evenly. "Makes a terrible mess too."

"Have you seen your doctor?" Rachel inquired.

"Of course I've seen my doctor," Pruit snapped. "It scared me to death when it first happened." Pruit calmed himself and then said, "He thought it was all in my head, that I imagined the whole thing. Rather insulting, if you ask me."

"May I see your hands?" Rachel asked. "I promise not to accuse you of being a hypochondriac."

Pruit eyed Rachel for a moment then said, "Go ahead, but you won't find anything. It never leaves a mark." He held out his hand to her.

Taking his outstretched hand, Rachel examined it closely, looking at both his palm and the back of his hand. She palpated the fleshy palm and pulled the skin tight, looking for any perforations.

"No bruises, contusions, or punctures," Rachel said, never taking her eyes from his hand. "No sign of any present or past trauma." Then to Pruit she said, "Where exactly does the bleeding originate?"

Pointing one of his long fingers at the center of his palm, he replied, "Right there."

"Does it hurt when it happens?"

"No, not really. It burns somewhat."

Rachel continued her examination. "How much blood would you say issues from your hand?"

"Not much," Pruit answered, "but enough to have dripped on my pants the first time it happened."

"First time?" Adam said. "How often has this happened?"

"Twice" was all Pruit said.

Looking up from Pruit's hand, Rachel asked, "What were you doing when this happened?"

There was a short pause before Pruit answered. "Driving my car the first time. Sitting at my desk in my office the second time."

Adam had a strong sense that Pruit was lying, or at very least, concealing some information.

Shaking her head, Rachel said, "I don't see anything, nor have I ever heard of this happening."

"I have," Adam said firmly. "It's called stigmata."

"Stigmata?" Pruit said, surprised that there was a precedent. "What's stigmata?"

"It means a mark," Adam replied. "We get our words *stigma* and *stigmatize* from the original term. Today it means to mark someone as a disgrace. But there is a religious background to the word."

Everyone had turned his or her attention to Adam. "Most

scholars attribute the first incident to Francis of Assisi, who was on his knees praying. It was August 15 and many Christians in those days held special worship services for what they called Holy Cross day. Francis was praying and imagining what it must have been like for Jesus on the cross. During this deep prayer his hands and his feet began to bleed. It seems he was bearing the marks of crucifixion.

"Since then," Adam explained, "there have been many accounts of people who bear the marks—the stigmata—of Christ. Some have been shown to be frauds, others are just mysteries."

"I wasn't praying when this happened," Pruit explained. "I can assure you of that."

"What were you doing?" Adam asked pointedly.

"I've already told you, I was driving my car."

"Well, whatever the reason it appears that you have joined the unique ranks of stigmatics."

"I was never one for joining groups," Pruit replied sourly. "How do I get out?"

Adam ignored the question but posed one of his own: "You said you heard voices; what did you hear?"

Shaking his head and frowning, Pruit said, "One voice actually. Not much, really." Pruit picked up his coffee cup again and took another sip. "I was told to come to San Diego and find Rachel."

"Anything else?" Katrin inquired.

Pruit's hesitation was evident. "Just one line: The world will see through your eyes."

Rachel gasped. "That's what I was told!"

"What is your story?" Lindsay asked sharply, "what have you got to do with all of this? What makes you so important?"

Tilting her head, Rachel looked at Lindsay puzzled. "Important? I'm not sure that it has anything to do with importance. I'm as confused as the rest of you."

"Maybe now would be a good time for you to share your experiences, Rachel," Adam said, regaining control of the group.

"OK," Rachel said as she took a deep breath. "As you know, I was in a coma for a couple of days. During that time I traveled, or was taken, or was transported . . . I don't what happened, but I ended up on a strange . . . planet, I guess. It was a different world, anyway. The sky was green instead of blue. There was an ocean and a forest. It was lovely—the most beautiful place I have ever been. I didn't want to leave."

Lindsay pulled her mouth tight and looked away. Her eyes narrowed and Adam saw her jaw tighten.

"It was so peaceful there," Rachel continued. "Warm and serene and quiet." Rachel's eyes brimmed with tears. "I walked on the beach for a while—I can't say how long since time didn't seem to matter. Later, I walked into the forest and found a place to rest. I fell asleep, and when I awoke there was this . . . man. Except he didn't quite look like a man. He was different."

"How was he different?" Nick wondered aloud.

"His face wasn't quite human," Rachel responded. "It was like it was a face he borrowed or created but wasn't really his. Anyway, he led me through the forest until we came to a clearing. In the clearing was a big stone mound. We walked to the top and then I saw the most incredible thing: The hill of stone had been hollowed out and a building—a church, I was told—was in the middle. It was huge and carved out of a single stone."

"A church!" Pruit exclaimed. "You mean with a steeple and stained-glass windows?"

Rachel shook her head. "No, it was nothing like that. There was no steeple or anything that we would normally associate with a church building. The structure itself was cross-shaped and was forty or fifty feet tall from its base to the roof. Of course we were on top of the mound looking down at it, but we did walk down some old and worn stone steps to the base of the building."

"Did you go inside?" Nick asked.

"Yes, and that's when things got really strange. Inside was a tall, elderly man who stood by one of the doors. He said nothing, just smiled and bowed a little. The creature showed me a pillar in the middle of the church. Like the building, it had been carved out of the stone. At first the column was covered but the drape around it dropped and fell to the floor. On the column were etched four faces—your faces." Rachel looked at her guests.

"Our faces?" Katrin said.

"That's right," Rachel responded. "Under each face was your name. That's how I knew who you were when you showed up at the hospital. He, the man, then led me to a pair of huge wooden doors with pictures on them . . ."

"What kind of pictures?" Katrin interrupted.

"Well . . ." Rachel paused and a troubled expression crossed her face. "I didn't realize it until just now, but they were like your paintings. Come to think of it, they were identical to your paintings!"

The ramifications of that truth settled heavily in the minds of everyone. Katrin had painted what Rachel had seen.

"Go on," Pruit prompted. "I want to hear the rest of this."

"OK," Rachel said. "The wooden doors opened and the man led me into a room about the size of a racquetball court. It was incredible. It was beyond incredible. The room was covered in gold from floor to ceiling and etched into the gold were images of angels. In the middle of the room was a large object covered in purple cloth. Near the opposite wall was a huge statue of an angel."

"An angel?" Lindsay interrupted. "You mean like Cupid?"

"No," Adam interjected. "The little chubby baby with wings is an image that came out of Renaissance art. Biblical angels are powerful and majestic creatures with high intelligence."

"That description fits this guy to a tee," Rachel said. "He was no baby, that's for sure."

"OK," Katrin said, "so you saw this statue of an angel. Then what happened?"

"Well, the statue was in one corner and it had its wings, which were at least twenty feet long, stretched out in front of it. My guide walked to the other corner near the statue, looked at me, then pointed at the object with the purple cloth on it and said: 'Uncover. Uncover the Holy, Blessed Woman. The world will see through your eyes and theirs. Uncover.' Then, right before my eyes he began to change, metamorphosing into a statue identical to the other one in the room.

"I stood there for a few minutes trying to absorb what I had just seen," Rachel continued. "It wasn't that I couldn't believe it; I just didn't want to forget it. A short time later, I did as the angel said; I uncovered the object. It was the most beautiful thing I have ever seen." Rachel stopped and stared into the distance, reliving in her mind the majesty of the event.

"Come on," Nick exclaimed excitedly, "don't leave us hanging."

Rachel's voice softened reverently: "It was a chest made of gold, or covered in gold—I don't know which. On top of the chest was a lid with two angels kneeling in prayer, their wings stretched up and in front of them. I couldn't believe my eyes. Of all the things I had seen, this was by far the most impressive. I had to touch it."

Rachel's eyes brimmed with tears as she mentally relived the event. "It was so very pretty, so attractive. It drew my hand to it. When I touched it, I immediately began to be drawn away, up into the air." She swallowed hard. "Next thing I knew, I was in the hospital and Adam was standing over me."

"Whew," Nick said, pretending to wipe his brow. "That one takes the prize."

"But what does it all mean?" Katrin asked, frustration in her voice.

"I can help on this one," Adam voiced. "At least a little. I know what the chest is, but I don't understand the stone church, the wooden doors, or the pillar."

"You know what the gold box is?" Pruit asked, surprised.

Adam nodded his head. "Yes. It's described in the Bible as is the gold room that Rachel was in. The object is the ark of the covenant and the room is the holy of holies. The ark was, or perhaps I should say is, the most mysterious and powerful artifact in the Bible. Great power was attributed to it and God was said to have spoken to Moses from between the two cherubim—the angels on the lid. It was a holy object that was to never be touched. Whoever would touch it would die."

"But Rachel did touch it," Katrin said, "and she didn't die. Why?"

"I don't know," Adam admitted. "Probably because she was having a vision and wasn't touching the real thing."

"It looked real enough to me," Rachel said.

"Well, this is great," Lindsay said, her words bathed in sarcasm. "I wish I had your travel agent instead of mine. Your little vacation spot was much better."

"I don't understand," Rachel replied defensively. "Why are you so upset?"

"Why? Why?" Lindsay shot up from the sofa and began pacing the room. "I'll tell you why! Because I didn't get to go to heaven or paradise or wherever you went. And I didn't get invited to some party like our friend over here." She pointed to Nick. "Oh, no! I don't get to take a four-hour nap and paint some pictures, or have a little bleeding and hear voices."

"Settle down, Lindsay," Adam said forcefully. "This isn't helping anything."

Lindsay spun quickly to face Adam. "Shut up, preacher. I don't need you or anyone else to tell me what is or isn't helpful. You didn't experience what I did. From what I can tell, you didn't experience anything like the five of us. In my book, that makes you an outsider."

"Lindsay . . ." Rachel began.

"No! No, Dr. Tremaine," Lindsay said viciously. "I don't want to hear from you either."

A shadow of anger instantly crossed Rachel's face. Adam had seen that look before. Rachel had changed considerably since embracing her faith, but there was still an aspect of her that could be strong, domineering, and explosive. Having been on the receiving end of such an emotional explosion once before, he had no desire to see it again.

"Let's all back up a little here," Adam said, trying to regain control of the situation. "This is all strange and frightening, I know . . ."

"You don't know," Lindsay snapped. "Did you have a vision? Have you heard voices? Were you scarred in a fire? Have you been in a coma? Did you go to hell?"

"Hell?" Katrin gasped. "You went to hell?"

"That's right," Lindsay shouted then turned to Rachel. "No pretty green sky there, Rachel, I can assure you. No warm ocean or lovely forest. No angels. Just hopelessness . . . just ugliness . . . just pain . . . just people who you . . ." Lindsay snatched a coffee cup and threw it forcefully at the front door. It broke into a shower of glass slivers.

No one moved. No one spoke. No one dared interrupt.

"Blessed Woman," Lindsay ranted. "Was that what he called you? Blessed Woman? I didn't have an angel call me blessed anything. Oh no, not me. Instead I get . . . I get . . ."

Lindsay stopped midsentence. Adam could see that she was experiencing the event once again in her mind, something he suspected she did frequently. Her eyes were red, but no tears came.

Softer, Lindsay continued, "I get hell's own hound. I get . . ." Lindsay shivered, then shook her head. "He touched me."

Again Katrin gasped audibly.

"He touched me and drew my face close to his. I wanted to pull away. I wanted to run. I wanted to scream, but I couldn't. I had to stand there and look into his eyes, smell his putrid breath, feel his hot rough hands. So much hate. So much venom." She shook her head to bring herself around.

"I'm sorry about the cup," Lindsay said softly, then shuddered. "I'm normally much more controlled."

"Don't worry about it," Rachel said. "If your vision was as real as mine . . . well, I don't think I could have survived as well as you have."

"It was real enough," Lindsay said firmly. "I'm not sure it was a vision. I think it was real. And as far as surviving all I can say is that this isn't over yet."

Adam repositioned himself on the edge of his chair and leaned forward. "Lindsay," he began evenly, "you're right, I can't possibly know what you went through. I can't even imagine it. But let me say this: Something highly unusual is going on here, and for some reason we've been chosen to be a part of it. Whatever it is, it's bigger than any one of us. Only together can we discover what's going on. That makes us a team, whether we like it or not. That means we have to trust each other."

"I'm not good at trusting," Lindsay blurted in response. "Trusting is dangerous."

"I can't argue that," Adam replied, "but trust has to be a part of all this. We have to feel safe with one another. We all have been unveiling our souls here and we have to feel secure enough to do that."

Lindsay said nothing.

"Without reliving your experience, can you tell us the message you received?"

Lindsay remained mute.

"You did receive a message, didn't you?"

"Yes," Lindsay finally replied, "but it doesn't make any sense."

"So far, none of this does," Pruit added to the conversation.

"The creature," Lindsay began slowly, "the devil, Satan, whoever or whatever he was, seemed upset about having to deliver the message. He tormented me for a while then walked over to a bush, snatched a branch off it, and handed it to me. He said, 'Here, look for this.'"

"What did the branch look like?" Adam inquired.

"Just a branch of the bush, except . . ."

"Except what?"

"Except this had leaves on it. All the other bushes were noth-

147

ing more than dead twisted limbs, but this one was still alive and growing."

"Interesting," Adam said, leaning back in his chair. "Can you think of anything else?"

"No, that's it."

"OK," Adam intoned as he rose from his chair. "We're off to a good start. Did anyone leave anything out?" Adam scanned the room, looking at each person. He had suspicions that one or more had information that they hadn't shared, but he didn't want to pry—not yet. That could be counterproductive. No one spoke.

"All right then," Adam said, "I suggest we all exchange phone numbers and addresses so that we can stay in touch. If anyone has any ideas, then share them. In the meantime, we all need to think about what we've just heard."

Everyone voiced agreement and exchanged information about hotels. As they were leaving Lindsay turned to Adam and said, "Reverend, I don't ever want to go back there." Then she turned and walked into the moonless night. A moment later, he heard her rental car drive away.

Twenty-Five

Standing in the nearly dark room, Adam stared out the window. He could see his ghostly image reflected off the glass. He looked tired. He was tired. The last few days had been an emotional roller-coaster for him. He had been taken from the bliss of lying beside his wife in bed exchanging their love with cute banter to be plunged into abysmal fear upon finding Rachel unconscious later that day. Anxious hour had passed anxious hour with only prayer to support him—prayer and his good friend Dick. Then his emotions skyrocketed to the highest levels of joy when Rachel awoke. That joy remained, but now it was garnished with feelings of confusion and uncertainty.

The scene outside the window offered nothing of interest. Mercury vapor street lamps cast bluish light on the narrow residential road. Opposite the street were houses just like the house in which he and Rachel lived. They were plain stucco exteriors with fiberglass shingle roofs. He knew the only interior qualities that made each house unique were those instilled by the decorative skills of the owners.

Adam wanted to see more. He wanted a view of something beautiful and serene. He wanted a lake or the ocean or tall pine trees. Something, anything that would calm his mind and still his troubled heart.

"Spying on the neighbors again?" Rachel asked as she exited the master bath. "I could buy you a pair of binoculars for your birthday if you want."

Chuckling, Adam turned to look at his wife. She was ready for bed, dressed only in a long San Diego Chargers' football jersey that reached down to her knees. Her hair was loose and disheveled. What little makeup she wore had been washed away. Despite her rather frumpy appearance, Adam thought she was the loveliest vision he had ever seen.

"No need," he replied, turning back to the window. "They must be on to me: all the shades are drawn."

Slowly Rachel approached Adam and wrapped her arms around him, laying her face on his back. "What's wrong?" she asked softly.

"What makes you think that anything's wrong?"

"Let's see," she responded playfully, "I could tell you about my woman's intuition, or my training as a doctor who has been educated in the subtle body language of her patients, or I could reveal that I am really Spiderwoman and my supernatural spider senses have told me that you are troubled."

"I'm allergic to spiders," Adam deadpanned.

Rachel swatted Adam on the fanny. "Come on, what's on your mind? Don't make me hurt you."

"All right, all right, officer," Adam said, raising his hands in the air. "Just don't shoot me."

"No promises."

Adam turned and embraced his wife, first kissing the top of her head then laying his cheek on her hair. "You're right; I guess I am troubled."

"About what?" she asked softly. "About my coma?"

"Partly, but it's really something that Lindsay said."

"She got pretty hot, didn't she?"

"She was scared. Whatever she saw frightened her big time. I think, considering what she told us, that she had good reason to be upset. Clearly, she's had the worst of it."

"True, but I have to tell you that I think she's hiding something from us."

"I think they all are, or at least most of them." Adam broke the embrace and moved to the bed where he sat down. "We don't have the whole story yet."

Rachel sat beside him and took his hand. "I thought Nick was straightforward, and Katrin too."

"That's true, but Lindsay and Pruit, well, I'm not so sure about them."

"Me either."

Looking at Rachel, Adam smiled. "Spider senses again?"

"No," Rachel chortled. "More like your average, everyday suspicion."

The two fell silent for a moment.

"So," Rachel began, "what did the mysterious Lindsay say that has troubled you?"

Adam lowered his head. "She said I was an outsider. That you five have had mysterious dreams and visions and I haven't."

"So?"

"So, I'm afraid she's right."

"Nonsense," Rachel said forcefully. "You're as much a part of this as anyone."

"Why?"

"Why? Because you're my husband and what affects me affects you."

"Pruit's married," Adam countered. "He said so the first night at the hospital when we were all making small talk."

"That's different."

"Is it?" Adam asked. "How is it different? Besides, it goes beyond that. What really puzzles me is a question that keeps coming to my mind: Why didn't I receive a vision? It's not that I think I'm the center of the universe, but why you and not me? I'm the one with the training in Bible and theology."

"I don't know," Rachel responded. "But just so that you don't feel too alone, I've been asking myself why I was chosen. I'm new to the faith and my understanding of the spiritual world is still very immature. Why me?"

"You know, we can apply that question to the others. Why them? Best I can tell, none of them, apart from you, are even believers. Why would God choose unbelievers to be recipients of such special information?"

Rachel shook her head. "There are a lot of unanswered questions."

"There sure are," Adam responded. "I feel like an archeologist

151

who has dug away some sand and found the tip of a great pyramid. I'm delighted with the find but am keenly aware that so much more is hidden underneath the sand."

"Then we had better start digging," Rachel said.

"But that's the whole question, Rachel: Should I even be on the excavation team?"

"Absolutely."

"Why?"

"I don't have all the answers, but I do know this. God has used you as His minister for years. True?"

"True."

"He also involved you when the Healer came to Kingston Memorial Hospital last year. True?"

"Also true."

"Answer this for me: Did every great man and woman of God have visions?"

Adam lay back on the bed and gazed at the ceiling. Rachel leaned back, propping herself up on one elbow.

"Moses had several one-on-one encounters with God, as did Abraham before him. Of course, some of the prophets like Jeremiah and Ezekiel and others had some real mind-benders."

"Were there any whom God used without visions?"

"Of course there were."

"Were they less important? Less useful?"

"All right, I get the point," Adam conceded.

"I'm not done," Rachel said firmly then stroked his cheek gently with her hand. "I was proud of you tonight. The meeting nearly dissolved into anger and resentment several times, but you kept us on course. And that thing about the ark of the covenant, well, I don't think any of us would have understood that, but you recognized it immediately."

"I still don't know what it means, though."

"You will, Adam, you will. That's why I believe that God has called you to this. We've had visions, but we don't have understanding.

Adam remained silent as he absorbed everything Rachel was saying.

"I cite the ark again," Rachel continued. "You recognized it immediately."

"Any student of the Bible would have recognized that. The ark is the most mysterious object in history."

"But we are not students of the Bible. I'm just beginning to under-stand. The others don't have the faith to understand." She paused for a few moments before saying, "If you ask me, Adam, you have already had your vision. It just came over years of study and service. Ours was for a few moments; yours was decades in the making."

Again silence.

"One last thing," Rachel continued, "then I'm going to sleep. You once gave an illustration in a sermon in which a preacher was asked by a newspaper reporter if God spoke to him audibly . . ."

"And," Adam interrupted, "the preacher responded, 'Oh, no. He speaks a whole lot louder than that.'"

"Exactly! Over the years, God has spoken more loudly to you than He has to any of us."

"Amazing," Adam said with a smile. "Just amazing."

"What? That your wife has such keen spiritual insights?"

"No. That you listen to my sermons!"

Adam, blinded by laughter, didn't see the feather pillow Rachel had grabbed with her free hand come plummeting down on his head.

"Hey!"

"You deserve that and more, buddy," Rachel said, then hit him with the pillow again.

Adam fought back, not with a pillow, but with a quiet word: "I love you, Rachel."

Rachel stopped midswing, leaned over, and tenderly kissed her husband.

"I don't deserve you," Adam said softly.

Kissing Adam again, Rachel paused and said, "You're right, you don't, but I think I'll stay for a while longer anyway—at least a life-time."

Twenty-Six

An uncomfortable sense of déjà vu enveloped Adam as he left the classroom on the campus of San Diego Theological Seminary, where he had just finished teaching, and made his way to the administration offices. It was a day like this when Adam left campus to return home only to find Rachel unconscious on the floor. The very act of exiting the classroom brought back the strong and sensitive memories.

This was his second time in the administration offices that day. The first visit was to arrange an appointment with Dr. Julian Newton, president of the seminary. This trip was for the actual meeting.

Over breakfast, Adam and Rachel discussed their next steps. Rachel had suggested using the seminary's expansive library for research, a suggestion with which Adam agreed. The library, which had been underwritten by a wealthy benefactor, was one of the best on the West Coast. It contained not only the latest works but many of the most significant older writings of great theologians.

It was then that Adam had an idea: Why not meet with Dr. Julian Newton? The president of the seminary was a renowned Old Testament scholar and archeologist. Even at the age of sixty-two he still led discovery expeditions into the regions around the Holy

Land. He might be able to shed some light on the subject. The only question was, how much should Adam reveal to Newton? The group members had not discussed secrecy, but Adam did not have their permission to share what were clearly sensitive matters to them.

Rachel had suggested a stepped approach. Show Katrin's paintings to Newton and see if he could decipher them. Adam, however, had reservations about releasing the actual paintings to someone outside the group. He settled on photos taken with a Polaroid.

The paintings were too large to show much detail in a single photograph so Adam took eight shots, one of each quadrant of each canvas.

When Adam stepped through the glass doors that led to the admin offices he was greeted by the receptionist: "Hello, Dr. Bridger. Dr. Newton said for you to go right on in."

"Thank you," Adam replied, taking the few steps necessary to walk down the hall to the first room on the right. A handcrafted wooden sign read "Julian Newton, Ph.D., President." Adam knocked lightly on the door then slowly opened it, peeking around the corner to make sure he wasn't interrupting.

"Come in, Dr. Bridger," Newton said, rising from his seat behind the large cherry-wood desk. "It's good to see you. I hope Rachel is still doing well."

"She's fine," Adam replied, taking Newton's outstretched hand and shaking it. "It's like nothing ever happened."

"I'm glad to hear that. We were all quite concerned."

"I know you were." Adam sat in a leather chair opposite Newton's desk. "We got the card and flowers you sent. Rachel asked me to say thank you."

"It was nothing," Newton offered as he seated himself. "I only wish you and she could have been spared the ordeal."

Adam admired Newton and wished he could get to know him better. Newton was a pleasant-looking man with thin brown hair that was receding, clear blue eyes that still held the twinkle of a younger man, and a disarming smile. Newton was formal in speech and dress. Adam had never seen him wear anything but a suit and tie.

Despite his natural good looks and charm it had been his brain that had made Newton famous. An archeologist with a deep commitment to biblical research, he had authored several significant papers and made two award-winning discoveries. But unlike many in his profession, Newton had time for other pursuits including music. An able pianist, he had composed several pieces that would live long after him.

"Well, Adam, to what do I owe the favor of your visit?" Newton said, dropping the formal academic titles. It was customary for scholars and teachers to greet each other with formal titles then drop them in discussion as soon as possible.

"I'm hoping you can help me unravel a little mystery." Adam pulled the photos from the pocket of his sport coat and offered them to Newton. "This is going to seem strange, but you might enjoy the challenge."

Taking the photos, Newton laid them one by one across the uncluttered top of his desk. As he did, Adam noticed that they were out of order. He started to mention that fact when Newton immediately rearranged them so quickly that Adam was reminded of an adult working a toddler's jigsaw puzzle.

"Interesting," Newton offered. A smile crossed his face.

"A woman I know painted these. They seem to be a storyboard of some fashion."

"I can see that," Newton said enthusiastically. "These were painted recently on two canvases of equal size. The form is basically the same but the story lines are different and contain . . ." Newton reached into his desk drawer and removed a large magnifying glass and resumed his examination of the photos. "And yes, contain different characters. It's an interesting blend of the ancient with the contemporary. Fascinating. A modern painting structured in an ancient story format."

"It looks like something I've seen before," Adam said, "but I'm embarrassed to say that I can't remember what it is."

"Kebra Nagast," Newton interjected.

"Excuse me?"

"Part of this is the Kebra Nagast."

Adam shook his head slightly. "I'm afraid I don't follow."

"The Kebra Nagast is an ancient Ethiopian legend. Paintings similar to these have been done to visually portray the story."

"Ethiopian?"

"Certainly," Newton leaned back in his high-backed chair and steepled his fingers. He closed his eyes for a few moments then continued. "The Kebra Nagast—the name is Ethiopian for 'glory of kings'—

is the story of Solomon and the Queen of Sheba. The biblical account is not very long, but as you know, the Queen of Sheba came to visit King Solomon to test his wisdom. She came with a huge quantity of gifts, including gold, spices, and lumber. Wait a second." Newton pulled open another desk drawer and withdrew a well worn Bible and opened it.

"That story is found in 1 Kings, I think." Newton continued flipping pages. "Here it is, 1 Kings 10:10: 'And she gave the king a hundred and twenty talents of gold.' Let's see, 120 talents would equal about 144,000 ounces. That's about four and a half tons of gold. There were other gifts too, but nearly five tons of gold seems to be the most impressive gift."

"I'm familiar with that account," Adam said. "But what's the connection to Ethiopia?"

"Well, some scholars believe that the Queen of Sheba was from Ethiopia, though most will tell you that she was the queen of Sabea, which would be the southern part of Arabia. It's the country of Yemen now. Of course, other scholars would tell you that she came from India."

"But you think she's from Ethiopia?"

"I didn't say that," Newton corrected. "Most likely her country of origin was on the southern tip of Arabia, but remember, only a narrow straight separates Ethiopia from Yemen. She may well have wielded some influence in Africa. But none of that matters to the present discussion. The point is that the Ethiopians believe the mysterious queen was one of their own and they have a longstanding tradition about it. That tradition is recited in the Kebra Nagast."

"So this legend has a connection to King Solomon."

"Oh, it goes well beyond that." Newton leaned forward over his desk. "Let me tell you the story in a nutshell. The Ethiopians believe that the Queen of Sheba went to visit King Solomon just like the biblical account, but their account continues where the Bible leaves off. Now I'm not saying that any of the Kebra Nagast is true, you understand."

"I understand," Adam acknowledged.

"According to the Kebra Nagast, King Solomon fell in love with, or at least greatly desired, the queen and seduced her. The story at that point is interesting. It seems the queen was interested in

Solomon but made him promise not to take her by force. Solomon agreed as long as the queen would not take anything from him without first asking his permission. She agreed. Later that night the queen became thirsty and took a drink of water. Solomon said she had broken their agreement and therefore, he had the right to take her—and did."

"Over a cup of water?"

"Exactly. Well, it seems the Queen of Sheba returns home. By the way, that's about a 1,200-mile journey. On the way, she discovers that she is pregnant. Back home she gives birth to a child now known as Menelik. As an adult, Menelik discovers who his father is and journeys to see the now much older Solomon. The king is overjoyed to discover he has another son and declares him King of Ethiopia. Later Solomon lavishes Menelik with gifts then sends him home. But here's the interesting twist: Solomon, since he must send his son away, demands that all of his advisers also send an adult son with Menelik. This way Menelik has an educated court to accompany him and get him off on the right foot."

"Fascinating."

"Oh, it's just beginning, Adam. You see, there is a twist in this tale. According to the legend, when Menelik was well on his way home he discovered that some or all of his new entourage had pirated away the ark of the covenant."

Adam sat back in his chair at the revelation. He hadn't mentioned the ark to Newton and to his knowledge the ark didn't appear in the paintings.

"The ark?" inquired Adam.

"Seems strange, doesn't it?" Newton replied. "Menelik had a decision to make at this point. Here he was, hundreds of miles from Jerusalem, with the very ark of God that had been stolen from the holy of holies in the temple. Since they had made it as far as they had, Menelik assumed that it was God's will for him to have the ark."

"But wouldn't it be missed?" Adam asked. "And why would they take it in the first place?"

"Both good questions. The first one is the easiest to answer. It might be missed, but not for a long time. Think about it, Adam. How often was the ark seen?"

"Of course," Adam replied. "Just once a year when the high priest went into the holy of holies to offer sacrifices for the sins of the people. So it could be months before the ark was missed."

"Probably longer than that. Suppose the priests themselves were part of the plot. By simply keeping their mouths shut, no one would know the ark was missing for a good long time, if ever."

"But why steal the artifact in the first place?"

"Remember your biblical history, Adam. Solomon was a great king in the early days, but his desire to expand Jerusalem and build fine structures, including the temple, overtaxed the people. That by itself might not be enough reason to steal away the ark, but Solomon was also becoming less faithful to his God. His many political marriages, that were used to seal agreements between nations exposed him to pagan cultic practices. He soon allowed the worship of other gods. Seeing this, the priests might have felt compelled out of good conscience, or even led by God, to remove the ark to a safer place."

"But this is all too much to believe," Adam said seriously.

"Most serious scholars have strong doubts too. Personally, I find it interesting but not very credible." Newton paused and leaned back in his chair again. He began to scratch his chin. "Of course, it does solve a few problems."

"Like what?"

"The presence of an ancient form of Judaism in Ethiopia for one. The Falasha Jews, sometimes called the Black Jews of Ethiopia, have been present in the land for many centuries. If you adopt the Kebra Nagast legend or one of its many variations, then you have a believable reason for the existence of practicing Jews in Ethiopia."

"Do we know how long they have been there?" Adam inquired.

"No one really knows," Newton responded. "The Falasha themselves believe their lineage extends back to Solomon. Some scholars think the Jewish influence arrived much later, maybe during one of the Roman persecutions, say sometime between the first and sixth centuries A.D."

"There are other legends?" Adam asked.

"A few. Some think the ark traveled first to Egypt, then up the Nile, where it spent some time on the island of Elephantine. Excavations have revealed that a Jewish temple had been built on the island sometime during the sixth century before Christ. That much is fact. The unusual thing about it was that Jews would not build a temple on foreign soil. Just consider the long Babylonian

Captivity. No temple was built in Babylon."

Newton paused and raised a cautioning hand. "I don't want to be misunderstood here. It's possible that the Jews in Ethiopia were there because they were fleeing the wicked King Manasseh. It is true that Manasseh was the king who erected an idol in the temple, but that doesn't mean that Jews fleeing his reign took the ark with them. Of course that would put them in the country 600 years before Christ. That may be too early. It's equally possible, even likely, that some Jews fled the Roman occupation of their land. That would put the time line in the neighborhood of the first century. The truth is, we just don't know."

"It seems odd to think of Jews in Ethiopia," Adam commented.

"Were in Ethiopia," Newton corrected. "Most were airlifted to Israel in the 1970s, a process that continued until the last Falashim left in 1991. But there are many Christians in Ethiopia. In fact, Ethiopia has one of the oldest Christian traditions of any country in the world. I've been there a couple of times. It's a fascinating place full of interesting people and history. It's worth the trip just to see the stone churches."

Adam felt his heart skip. Rachel had seen a stone church in her vision. "Stone churches?"

"Magnificent structures carved out of stone. Some are in hillsides, others formed out of stone mounds. They're crossed-shaped . . . are you all right, Adam? You look a little pale."

"I'm fine," Adam said taking a deep breath.

"Why is it I feel that there's more going on here than these pictures?"

"There is Dr. Newton, but I can't talk about it now." Adam felt silly about keeping secrets from Newton. He was, after all, one of the most respected men in Christian education and research. "I don't have permission to tell you more."

"I quite understand." Newton smiled broadly. "Confidentiality must be maintained at all costs."

"Thank you for your patience," Adam said. "You have been most helpful."

"Well, this is my first love, and when I saw the ark on the paintings here I really became excited."

"I didn't see an ark on the paintings," Adam confessed. "Where is it?"

"Right here." Newton picked up one of the Polaroids and pointed at one of the tiny frames. "This blurry glow in the black frame. It's hard to see, but it has the same basic shape as the ark."

Adam strained to see the tiny image. A moment later he saw it: an indistinct golden smudge, square on all sides but the top, which was symmetrical but uneven.

"I suspect," Newton continued, "that the camera wasn't able to pick up the detail, but if you still have the painting you should see it more clearly. You do have the paintings, don't you?"

Absentmindedly Adam nodded. "I'll look when I get home."

"Well, be sure and let me know what you find. I don't know all that's going on, but it looks exciting. If I can be of any further help, don't hesitate to call."

"Thank you, Dr. Newton, I will consider everything you've said. You've been a big help."

Adam excused himself and exited the office. A moment later Dr. Julian Newton was on the phone.

Twenty-Seven

Seattle, Washington

It was raining in Seattle—again. From his corner office on the twelfth floor of the Datadyne Software building, Gerald T. Quince watched as the bruised sky swelled with dark, rain-rich clouds that seemed to hover over Elliot Bay. It was a spring storm that had dropped in from the northwest to dump its cold water on an already soggy city.

Holding the remote phone to his ear, Quince paced his spacious office, listening intently to the caller. As he walked he stopped at the various ancient artifacts that decorated his suite. Here a spearhead from first century Rome, there a fetish from a secret Mayan dig, here a ritual Aztec knife, and there an immaculate ivory figurine from Central Africa. His office was a tiny, orderly museum. Enough so to make any collector of ancient artifacts salivate.

What only a trusted few knew was that below the Datadyne Software building was an expansive vault with thick, reinforced concrete walls plated with steel and constantly monitored by the finest electronic security system in the world. All of it custom designed to Quince's exacting specifications to protect the largest private collection of antiquities in the world—almost all of it illegally obtained.

That was what Gerald T. Quince did: collect. That and make money. He was rich beyond imagination. *Forbes* magazine listed him as the fifth richest man in the world. "And the other four owe me favors," he was fond of saying.

Still, while all around him exuded expense and wealth, Quince was remarkably casual in appearance, preferring open-necked shirts to ties, and boots to wingtips. He was neither a tall man nor a short one. His hair was brown and just beginning to be tinged with gray. He flashed hazel eyes that could instantly turn dark when he was angered. His skin was tan, his stomach flat and tight. Physically, his only distinguishing feature was that he had no distinguishing feature. If he were so inclined, he could rob a convenience store and the clerk would be able to describe him only as a person of average height, average build, and average weight.

Where his appearance failed to set him apart his mind and his greed succeeded. He was brilliant in every nuance of the word. His mind made decisions quickly and almost always correctly.

"Just give me the facts," he would tell his key executives, "and I will give you the answers."

No one ever questioned him on that statement; and no one in his employ felt secure enough to second-guess him.

Returning to his desk, Quince put his feet up on his glass-and-chrome desk and leaned back in his jet-black leather chair. Behind him rain trailed down the window in sinuous rivulets. A small, knowing smile slid across his smooth face.

"How confident are you in this man's veracity?" Quince asked pointedly. "No chance that he's making this up?"

Quince listened to the response as he picked at his teeth with a fingernail. "Well, let me ask it this way: If it were your money about to be spent on this endeavor, would you invest in it?"

Again Quince listened quietly, offering only an occasional grunt in response. "That's a lot to believe and very little to go on. We need more information because, to be honest with you, it all sounds a little too mystical to me. I mean, who is this painter? Why is she painting these things?"

Another pause. "Well, I suggest we find out before we go much further. I'll make some calls. You keep an eye on your Dr. Bridger and see if he'll open up any more."

Quince lowered his feet to the floor. "Of course, you will be adequately rewarded, and if this turns out to be true—and that's a very big if—I'll fund another two years of your dig in Israel."

Releasing a small chuckle at his caller's words, Quince said, "No need to thank me, Dr. Newton. You have provided me with many wonderful pieces for my collection. I should be thanking you."

Quince hung up the phone and spoke to the empty office. "Interesting. Very, very interesting."

Twenty-Eight

"I'm trying to maintain a detached and clinical approach to all of this, Adam, but I must confess that I'm finding it difficult." Rachel took a sip of herbal tea from her cup and set it back on the dining room table. "Is he saying that Katrin's painting is the same as those done for the Keebler Nag-whatever?"

"Kebra Nagast," Adam corrected with a smile. "I think Keebler makes cookies."

"Cute. Now answer my question."

"Not exactly. What he said was that the painting is similar to those of the Kebra Nagast. He was quick to let me know that he was skeptical of the Queen of Sheba story."

"But it could be true?"

"Not likely."

"Is there any reason why it couldn't be true? Any compelling piece of evidence that makes it impossible?"

"Not that I can think of at the moment."

"In medicine," Rachel said, "we first try to diagnose what disease a patient has. If that fails, we work at demonstrating what he or she doesn't have through a process of elimination. So my question is, could this painting portray something else?"

"It could if we didn't have your vision lending credibility to the thesis that the ark was taken to Ethiopia. Whether it went in the manner described by Kebra Nagast or found its way by some other fashion is still debatable. The stone church in your vision and the ones in Ethiopia seem to be similar enough."

Rachel nodded. "The atlas you brought home from the seminary library shows several of the churches in Ethiopia and they sure look close to what I saw." The book Adam had borrowed was a pictorial atlas of Africa with articles on the people and the practice of each of Africa's countries.

"I feel that we've made some headway, but I still have more questions than answers."

"Me too. What about the second painting?" Rachel asked, sipping at her tea again. "Did Dr. Newton have any insights on that one?"

Adam lowered his head. "We didn't discuss it," he confessed. "I'm afraid that I lost perspective when he started talking about the ark and then mentioned those stone churches. It slipped my mind."

Laughing, Rachel said, "I'm surprised you found your way home without getting lost. Once that mind of yours takes hold of something it never lets go."

Adam just smiled and decided to save himself some embarrassment by not telling Rachel that he had indeed missed the freeway off-ramp he was supposed to take, a ramp he took every day.

"The second painting is different," Rachel commented. "I can see how the first one might deal with Africa. There are black men and women and vast open plains. But the second one looks like it has several ocean scenes in it."

Nodding, Adam agreed. "But what ocean? Assuming the water scenes do depict an ocean. Maybe they show a river like the Nile or the Amazon, or maybe a lake. It could be anywhere."

"No," Rachel disagreed. "I think it's clear enough to someone who has been to whatever place it depicts. It's just foreign to us."

"Probably, but I think we need to recruit some additional help to pull all this together. I can't help but feel that time is limited."

"I feel the same way, but I don't know why. Who were you thinking of asking for help?"

"The only person I can think of who might be able to solve all this quickly is Martin St. James."

"Good ol' Martin," Rachel said. "He was indispensable with the

Healer situation. You think he can do the same with this? I mean, this may be a little too surrealistic for Martin."

"Martin needs more exposure to the spiritual," Adam replied.

"He's a genius, I know that, but he's a genius with quirks."

"That's the definition of genius, dear," Adam said, raising his own cup of tea for the first time. "When you're that smart the world allows you to be eccentric."

"Are you going to go alone, or would you like some company?"

"I think we should all go," Adam answered. "It's important for the others to have a sense of ownership in the process. They need to be part of the solution. After all, they are the ones with the visions. Neither one of us can answer questions for them. Martin may pick up on things we would miss."

"OK," Rachel said, getting up from the table. "You call Martin and then I'll call the others. When should we meet?"

"The sooner the better. If Martin's available we can go tonight. Maybe Anna will invite us to dinner." Adam raised his eyebrows in anticipation.

"Oh, good. Then the rest of us can watch you stuff yourself until you are sick like last time."

"Hey," Adam protested, feigning shock and hurt. "That was more than four months ago. I've learned discipline and discretion since then."

"Discipline and discretion mastered in just four months? If she makes carne asada tacos again, I bet your discipline and discretion will go right out the window."

"I make no promises," Adam quipped. A smile crept across his face.

"What are you grinning at?" Rachel asked inquisitively.

"I was just wondering how the others are going to take to Martin—especially Lindsay."

"Well, I plan on taking the chair farthest away from them both. You had better sit near Martin."

"Why?"

"To hurl your body in front of him when Lindsay charges for his throat."

Twenty-Nine

Mozart's Salzburg Symphony No. 1 filtered through the room. Seated at a small card table two men were locked in a battle of wits, each attempting to distract, deceive, and outmanipulate the other.

A nearly imperceptible clack sounded as Adam moved the plastic chess piece forward one space.

Without moving his head, Martin St. James raised his eyes to stare at his opponent. Those eyes narrowed slightly as he said, "It's not going to work, Adam. You attempted that little charade last time we played. I'm not going to fall for it again."

"I don't know what you're talking about," Adam replied, raising his hands in a sign of innocence. "It's a perfectly innocuous move."

"There's no such thing in chess," Martin retorted. "There are only good moves and stupid moves. You tend to make the former and only occasionally make the latter."

"I'm honored by your admiration."

"Don't be. It wasn't meant to be a compliment."

"Well, I'm taking it as one anyway."

Martin grunted and pushed his queen into the fourth rank. "While you bask in your self-importance, I plan to decimate your defenses. This is the day you lose, my friend."

For dramatic effect, Adam slowly raised a hand to his mouth as if shocked by Martin's move. Then, without a word, Adam moved his queen's knight.

Martin blinked, shot Adam a wicked glance, and then said, "That's the same move you used three months ago. You didn't think I would forget, did you?"

"I won that game."

"No gloating allowed," Martin snapped. "Your problem is that you don't play the game correctly. You lack logic and the discipline of a well-formulated plan."

"I win every game we play," Adam said with a smile. "If I played the game by the book, I would lose all the time."

"Now you're catching on," Martin replied, then moved his queen again. "You're the only one who has ever beat me and it's all because you play by instinct rather than logic."

"I should feel bad about that?"

"I don't care how you feel, as long as you understand that I'm going to beat you at this game. You are my last challenge in life."

Adam slid his bishop across the board. "Check."

"What?"

"We can't have you going through life without challenges, you know. It just wouldn't be right."

"Don't get cocky," Martin retorted quickly. "It's just check, not checkmate."

"Yet."

The doorbell rang, chiming out a measure of Beethoven's Fifth Symphony, which clashed horribly with the Mozart that was wafting through the mansion's customized sound system.

"It sounds like your reinforcements are here," Martin quipped. "No kibitzing allowed."

"Don't need it. We'll be done in about three moves."

"In your dreams, preacher man, in your dreams."

"I'll get it," Anna shouted as she quickly walked from the kitchen to the door. "It's so good to have guests."

Martin mumbled something unintelligible. Adam couldn't help but think of the differences between Martin and his sister Anna. Martin was painfully thin with a drawn face and an anemic look about him. The only thing positively striking about him was his clear blue eyes that exuded the rare intelligence that Martin possessed. Anna, on the other hand, was a large woman with ample gray in her hair. She was gregarious, gracious, and loved people. Martin was the complete opposite.

"Unbelievable!"

Adam heard the word and turned to see Nick standing at the threshold of the foyer and the gigantic living room. Behind him stood Pruit, Katrin, and Lindsay, all bordered by Anna and Rachel.

"Please come in and have a seat," Anna said sweetly. "May I get anyone some coffee or tea?"

"Look at the view," Katrin exclaimed. "The whole wall is glass from floor to . . ." she paused midsentence as she looked up at the ornate ceiling that hovered twenty feet over her head. She then let her eyes drop to the ocean view outside the window. The sun was setting over the hazy horizon, and a man, suspended from a multicolored hang glider, leisurely sailed by. "Wow!"

Martin leaned back in his seat to view his visitors. He watched them for a moment then without comment turned his attention back to the game.

"I could learn to hate you, Adam," Martin said firmly. "You have me in checkmate in three moves and there's nothing I can do about it."

A laugh erupted from Adam. "You couldn't hate me, Martin. I'm just too lovable."

"Don't bet on it!" Martin reached across the chessboard and knocked his king over, indicating in centuries-old tradition that he was resigning himself to defeat. "Do you know what your problem is? You're too erratic. Your moves make no sense. You were supposed to push your queen's pawn and not retreat your knight—everyone knows that!"

"I guess there's something to be gained by being ignorant."

Martin pressed his lips together in frustration. "I will beat you someday, Adam."

"No doubt, but not today." Adam stood. "Let me introduce my guests."

"No need," Martin said with a wave of his hand. "I've done my research. You, sir," Martin pointed at Nick, "are Nick Stern. You, young lady, are Katrin Couer, the painter. You, sir, are Pruit Bain, advertising magnate, and you are . . . a mystery, Ms. Blair. I see you appreciate art." Lindsay stood silently before a large painting that hung on the foyer wall.

The group entered the spacious room and sat down, all except Lindsay.

"I have a fondness for art, Mr. St. James, especially the Monet you have hanging on the wall. It's rare that I meet anyone who actually owns an original Monet."

Martin surrendered a knowing smile. "Anna decorates the house; I don't have a head for such things."

"What did you mean when you said I was a mystery?" Lindsay asked firmly, turning to join the rest.

"Your past is . . . spotty at best, Ms. Blair," Martin replied calmly. "Outside of a few old school records you don't exist."

"You had somebody run a check on me?" Lindsay's tone darkened and her words carried a razor's edge of anger.

"Of course not," Martin replied with a dismissive wave. "I did the check myself."

Adam saw Lindsay's jaw tighten. This was not a good beginning.

"You see," Adam began, "Martin specializes in . . ."

"Who gave you authorization to do a background check on me?" Lindsay nearly growled.

"I did." Martin said nonchalantly. "And why shouldn't I? Should I allow people I don't know into my house? Adam asked for my help and because he is my friend—my only friend—I have agreed. To do my job, I must have all the information possible. That includes information on all of you."

"Why, you little . . ." Lindsay took a step forward.

Martin raised his hands. "No need for hysterics, Ms. Blair. I can assure you that I am completely trustworthy in all matters. The Pentagon trusts me as do more than 100 of the Fortune 500 companies."

"Lindsay," Rachel said soothingly. "I know how you feel. When I first met Martin he had already peered into my bank account as well as that of nearly every employee at Kingston Memorial Hospital. I reacted the same way as you. But I have found Martin to be a man of his word."

"Where I come from," Lindsay blurted, "such acts are illegal."

"So it is here," Martin stated matter-of-factly. "Do illegal things bother you, Ms. Blair?"

"What's that supposed to mean?"

Martin sighed heavily. "Sit down and I'll tell you."

Reluctantly Lindsay sat in an overstuffed chair. "Yes, I did a background check on each of you. No, neither Adam nor Rachel asked me to. In fact, I imagine that Adam is rather upset with me."

"We've had this discussion before, Martin," Adam said evenly, not attempting to mask the tension in his voice. "I cannot condone such actions."

"As I've said," Martin responded calmly, "Adam is my only friend. I owe him everything. However, I am my own man. I do a very special kind of work that few others can do. I do such work for major corporations and secret government agencies that even Congress doesn't know exist. Therefore, I am allowed a certain latitude.

"Look at it from my perspective," Martin continued. "Adam calls me with a mysterious story of visions and dreams and cryptic paintings. He feels a certain urgency about the matter. He asks if I will help and if I will meet with all of you. I am not a social butterfly. I do not normally entertain guests. Nonetheless, here you all are."

"Adam asked for your help," Lindsay interjected. "We didn't."

"I understand," Martin said. "If you don't want answers, please feel free to leave at any time."

The atmosphere in the room became heavy, but no one moved.

"Wasn't there a better way?" Rachel asked. "Couldn't you just have asked them about their backgrounds?"

"While I am quite good at recognizing lies when they're being fed to me, I am not infallible. I prefer some facts to start with and then begin my investigation."

Pruit spoke for the first time. "All right, we're here; let's push on and see what young Sherlock Holmes can or has discovered."

"I am no detective, Mr. Bain," Martin said. "I am an information broker. I uncover information and apply techniques of logic and creativity to arrive at a solution to any problem presented me. It has made me a fortune."

"Great," Lindsay uttered harshly, "so let's hear what you've discovered."

"Not so fast," Martin said. "First I will hear from each of you. Then I will ask questions. By that time, Anna will have dinner on the table for us. After dinner I will look at the two paintings . . . You did bring the paintings with you?"

Katrin nodded.

172

"Good," Martin said. "After dinner I will examine the paintings. If they're decipherable, then I will do so. If not, I'll send you on your way, for your task will be hopeless."

"You're an arrogant little toad, aren't you?" Lindsay said.

"Just very confident." Martin turned and looked at Nick. "Let's begin with you, Mr. Stern. Start from the beginning and tell me everything. Leave nothing out."

"Look," Nick said, "I'm a pretty casual guy. Can we switch to first names?"

"If you wish," Martin answered.

Nick Stern told his story from beginning to end. From Adam's perspective there was nothing new in the account. Martin watched Nick closely, allowing his eyes to dart about the man on the couch. Adam knew that Martin was looking for any physical signs that Nick was lying: excessive blinking, changes in skin tone, or frequently raising the hand to the face.

"When you were in this picture," Martin inquired directly, "was the restaurant in color or black-and-white?"

"Color. Why do you ask?"

"Please humor me, Mr. . . . Nick." Martin shifted his weight. "What did the chair feel like?"

"Like any chair. It was wood, and a little uncomfortable."

"Thank you," Martin said. "Let's move on. Katrin, if you don't mind, please."

Taking a deep breath, Katrin retold the story, fidgeting as she did. Her story took less time than Nick's, but she held back no details.

Martin had no questions.

Rachel was next to recount what she saw. And strangely, Martin had no questions for her either.

Things changed when Pruit shared his experience. Martin allowed him to tell the story uninterrupted. When Pruit was done, Martin leaned back in his chair and tightly closed his eyes. The room was silent as Martin sat motionless with only the occasional movement of his right index finger, which jerked about as if Martin were writing on a blackboard.

Five minutes later, Martin opened his eyes and leaned forward. "Mr. Bain, you are a highly successful advertising man. Judging by the articles on you that I downloaded from the Internet, you are also highly respected. You are also a liar."

"I beg your pardon!" Pruit was instantly on his feet. "How dare you. Of all the gall, to sit there and call me a liar! I don't care how smart you are, or how rich you are . . ."

"Mr. Bain, sit down." Martin commanded. "Do not raise your voice in my house. I say you are a liar and I shall prove it. But don't take that tone with me. I'm not a moralist. Whether you are a liar or not is of no concern to me. Such things may bother Adam and Rachel here, but I am not one of their flock. I am not a spiritual man with a spiritual code of conduct."

"Yet," Adam interjected.

Martin cut him a quick look and then continued on. "Your words and actions give you away, sir. The basics of your story ring true, but some elements are false. I can't know for sure, but I don't think you were driving when the first evidence of stigmata appeared. Nor do I believe you were on a business trip. I think you were about some other kind of business—secret business. I am right, aren't I?"

Pruit said nothing but sat down.

"What is it that you are hiding, Mr. Bain? What secret have you withheld from the group?"

Pruit remained stone silent.

"Mr. Bain," Martin said in the measured tones of a counselor speaking to a troubled client. "I believe that I already have a good feel for what's going on with all of you. I can't tell you the why, but before the night is over, I will tell you the what. If I am right, and there's a very good chance of that, then the people in this room may end up saving your life. At some point you have to learn to trust them. When you entered my house, I immediately told you of the background searches I've done. Ms. Blair was absolutely right in judging those searches to be illegal. I have confessed as much before each of you. In so doing, I have exposed myself to strangers. I'm asking you to do the same."

Pruit uttered no words, but some of the tension in his body melted away.

"OK," Martin said. "Let's do it this way. You're having an affair."

"I most certainly am not!" Pruit exploded.

"Your wife is having an affair."

"Don't be ridiculous."

"You're extorting money or skimming funds from your organization."

"That's absurd as well as impossible, and if you think I'm going to sit here and let you . . ."

"You're using drugs."

Pruit stopped abruptly.

"Well, that numbers you with about 10 percent of the population. My suspicion is that no one knows of your addiction. The question is, what drug." Martin studied Pruit for a moment. "You're thin but not so thin as to make me think that you have a problem with heroin. Crack and the like would be beneath a man of your stature, and wild mood swings would soon make the addiction noticeable. No, most likely it's amphetamines or cocaine. Performance enhancers like speed might have been useful when you started your company, all those late nights and so on. But that would be too noticeable, too difficult to conceal for years. It's cocaine, isn't it, Mr. Bain?"

Pruit was stunned beyond words. Unknown to him, his mouth had dropped open.

Adam had watched the exchange, too dazed to speak. In a matter of moments, Martin had plucked a deeply held secret right from Pruit's mind.

"Mr. Bain," Martin spoke softly, "please understand that I have no wish to embarrass you. But if my first hypothesis is remotely correct, then you and the others are involved in something truly earthshaking. Something that will change history. With so much at stake, there can be no secrets between you. Now, what were you really doing when the stigmata appeared in your palms?"

"I was . . . I was . . ." Pruit, stunned and shattered, struggled for just the right words. "I was preparing to drive my car off a cliff into Long Island Sound."

Bewildered silence.

"You were on the verge of committing suicide?"

"That was the idea," Pruit divulged. "I can't live without the stuff. I never meant to become an addict, but I have. I'm going to lose my family and my business."

Lindsay could contain herself no more. "Listen, you little weasel. What right do you have to go mucking about in someone's private life? Who do you think you are? God?"

"I'm an agnostic, Ms. Blair. Much to my friend Adam Bridger's dismay. Despite years of efforts on his part and my sister's, I still hold no belief in or about God or gods. And as to what right I have to

... how did you put it? ... muck around in someone's life, well, the answer is simple. The truth you just learned may save your life, or his life, or Adam's life."

Anna, who had strategically placed herself at the table in the dining room—a space that was less a room than it was a raised extension of the living area with nothing but a rail separating the two spaces, spoke up. "Maybe now would be a good time for dinner."

"Not now, Anna," Martin said quickly. "We still have to hear from our mystery woman, Lindsay."

"I'm not sure I want to cooperate," Lindsay said coolly. "I'm not in the mood for an interrogation."

"Just tell us everything you saw and heard and there will be no need for an interrogation." Martin's words were quick and firm.

"Didn't the Right Reverend Bridger fill you in?" Lindsay retorted bitterly.

"As a matter of fact, he did. He told me that you had a very unpleasant vision of hell. He spoke of the creature that touched you, spoke to you, and tormented you. He also said that the creature broke off a branch—the only visibly living branch in sight—and gave it to you."

"Well then, you know everything I know," Lindsay said.

"Not so," Martin responded. "I think there's more."

"On what grounds do you make that accusation?"

"Frankly, Ms. Blair," Martin said coolly, "you are a woman of mystery. As I have already revealed, I have done some research on all of you. You, Ms. Blair, are a woman with a well-concealed past. I was able to find a few references to your education and the like, but for the most part, you simply do not exist.

"To conceal one's past so assiduously," Martin continued, "requires diligence, special knowledge, and a high level of sophistication. That means that you are one of three things, Ms. Blair. You are either part of a witness protection program, a spy involved in covert operations, or you are a thief. Which is it?"

"You are awfully sure of yourself, Mr. St. James," Lindsay said. "Does the rest of your family have any ego or did you get it all?"

"I am not the subject here, Ms. Blair, you are. Shall I give you my best guess about your need for secrecy?"

"You're going to tell us whether I give my consent or not."

"True," Martin closed his eyes for a few moments, then spoke again.

"I doubt the witness protection scenario since the name you use today is the same as that which is on your childhood school records. If those records were planted, then there should be an unbroken stream of information—meager perhaps, but still steady. As it is, there is just the childhood records then nothing. If a new identity were created for you, that identity would be complete, not fragmentary. So I dismiss that idea out of hand.

"The spy scenario is equally weak," Martin continued. "While I doubt that skullduggery is beneath you, you don't seem the type to be a team player. Besides that, covert operatives thrive on anonymity. Your very physical presence draws attention to you. Even your choice of clothing, which is clearly expensive, demonstrates that you prefer to be noticed even if you prefer to remain undisturbed. A spy chooses to blend in; you've chosen to stand out. It is clear that you have taken steps to magnify your beauty, not hide it."

"Is that flattery?" Lindsay asked with a smirk. "It's a poor effort if it is."

"It was not meant to be such," Martin replied, unscathed by Lindsay's verbal dig. "I am simply stating the obvious."

"So where does that leave us?" Nick chimed in.

"Ms. Lindsay Blair is a thief," Martin uttered casually. "My guess, taking into account her obvious intelligence and quick wit, is that she is a very good thief. Probably works alone, as demonstrated by discomfort in intimate group settings such as this."

Martin paused and Adam watched as he studied each person's reaction.

"So what is it, Ms. Blair?" Martin inquired casually. "Nothing so mundane as the theft of money, probably something far more valuable and even esoteric. Industrial secrets? Computer piracy? Jewelry?"

A thin smile was etched across Lindsay's face. Still, she said nothing.

"Come on, Ms. Blair," Martin prompted forcefully. "You know as well as I that your position is safe here. Even if one of us wanted to turn you in we would lack evidence. We can show no motive, means, or opportunity. It would be our word against yours. In both our countries the accused is innocent until demonstrated otherwise. You are safe here."

"Art," Lindsay blurted out. "Art and antiquities."

"You steal art?" Katrin was nonplussed.

"Mostly antiquities for collectors. Occasionally, if the price is right, I'll steal paintings and sculptures. And yes, I have even stolen a painting or two of yours, Katrin. Actually that was done as a favor for someone. As you know, an artist's works improve in value when the artist dies."

"I don't believe this," Nick said. "An honest-to-goodness cat burglar."

Adam looked at Rachel and could see her perplexity at this revelation.

"We're quite a team, aren't we?" Lindsay said with a laugh. "An art thief, an injured fireman, a cocaine-addicted businessman, a timid artist, and a surgeon. Nobody would believe this story."

"This story is far from complete," Martin interjected. "I appreciate your forthrightness, but there's more, isn't there? Not about your . . . occupation . . . but about what you saw in your vision. You haven't told the whole story yet."

"The rest doesn't matter," Lindsay snapped. "I've told you more than you need to know."

"Have you?" Martin leaned forward. "Ms. Blair, the people around are all caught up in the same mystery. Now I think I already have a good grasp of what's going on, and unless I am way off track, you and the others are at just the beginning. This thing is far from over. It is even possible that your life may rest in their hands. Honesty is not only prudent at this point, it's essential. Tell us what else you saw, and tell us now!"

"I saw my father in hell!" Lindsay shouted, her jaw clenched tight. "I saw the only person I have ever loved writhing in anguish. His skin was boiling. Not burning, but boiling like water in a pot. He kept calling my name, pleading for help, but I could do nothing . . . nothing at all. I could only stand there and watch him begging for relief, relief that I couldn't give."

"Oh, my God." Adam uttered the words, not as a cliché but as a genuine prayer from the heart.

"I have always had good memories of my father. He was wonderful to me. Now those memories have been replaced by what I saw. I see them at night and during the day. His voice keeps echoing in my ears. I can't stop it. I can't stop it."

One lone tear trailed from Lindsay's eye. Adam knew that it was one tear more than she wanted to shed. Suddenly Lindsay was on her feet and looming over Adam, pointing her finger in his face.

"It was your God who put him there, preacher. Your God! My father burns in hell because of your God! What are you going to do about it?"

Thirty

Morose was the only word Adam could think of to describe dinner. The food itself was sumptuous in every respect. Adam felt sorry for Anna because he knew she had spent hours preparing the Mexican dinner and no one was eating much.

Martin, after having eaten one carne asada taco and a tiny helping of rice, quaffed a glass of water and bolted from the table. "I want to study the paintings while you eat," he had said.

Katrin offered to retrieve them, but Martin insisted that she remain at the table. "When you are done, we will all talk again."

Conversation was minimal. Two of the party had just laid bare tender and wounded souls, casting a dark pall over the gathering. No one knew what to say. No conversation seemed important.

It was Adam who suffered the most. He had seen the terror and anger in Lindsay's eyes. "It was your God who put my father in hell," she had said, spewing forth her sorrow in massive waves of ire. Adam, a man seldom lacking for words, came up short. What could he say? "Your father must have been a really rotten person? I'm sure he got what he deserved? Hey, blame God, not me?"

The truth of the matter was that Adam had no words to say. He had preached on hell a few times in his ministry. He had taught several adult Sunday School classes, and in training his new deacons

180

he had elaborated on the doctrine. That was fine when hell was discussed as a future, abstract principle. It was quite another when facing someone who had been there and who had witnessed the one love in her life in pure and abject torment.

Years ago, Adam had been reading a book written by the great British preacher Charles Haddon Spurgeon. The book was Spurgeon's advice to young ministers. In it, Spurgeon admonished his charges that they should always preach about hell with tears in their eyes. Adam understood the sentiment. While many through the ages had used hell as a club to beat fear into wayward people, he found no joy in the subject.

The challenge Lindsay issued rang in his ears: "What are you going to do about it?" What could he do about it? Nothing. What words of comfort could he offer? None. What advice could he give? None. What suggestions could he make? None. Nothing. None.

Adam had never felt more useless in his life.

A distant voice: "Adam, are you all right? Adam?"

Looking up, Adam saw Rachel gazing at him from across the table. "Uh, yes, I'm fine. I'm just distracted." Then to Anna he said, "Anna, as usual, this is wonderful. I only wish my appetite had been up to the task."

"Thank you, pastor," Anna replied softly.

"But if you'll excuse me, I think I'll go see how Martin is doing on those canvases."

"I'll join you," Katrin said.

The guests around the table said a word of thanks to Anna and then left the table, their meals hardly touched, and walked back into the large living room, where they found a contemplative, almost meditative Martin St. James.

Seated on the floor with his thin legs crossed, Martin studied the two paintings, which he had propped against a pair of folding chairs. He said nothing when the group arrived. It was clear to all present that Martin had immersed himself in the images before him. From Adam's place on the davenport he could see Martin's eyes dart about as he took in each frame of the picture.

No one said a word; no one interrupted. Not even Pruit or Lindsay, who had reasons to be angry with Martin. Despite his caustic, straightforward approach, they must have recognized his brilliance.

"This is too easy," Martin said standing up. "Once you understand the basic flow and have a little information, the puzzle unravels itself right before your very eyes."

"You think you know what it means?" asked Katrin.

"I'm certain of my interpretation," Martin answered confidently. "It's not especially difficult or obtuse. Actually it is quite straightforward. But that's to be expected, isn't it?"

"What do you mean?" Adam asked.

"Adam," Martin said with astonishment, "you of all people should know the answer to that. These weren't created to keep a truth secret; these were created to make a secret known. And if I buy into your spiritual theory—and that seems to be the only thing that makes sense at this point—then we have God or one of His agents laying out a plan for you."

"A plan?" Nick asked. "What kind of plan?"

"It seems, boys and girls," Martin replied playfully, "that you need to start packing your bags. You all are going on a trip. Two trips to be precise, and you don't seem to have a choice in the matter."

Six people simultaneously shifted uncomfortably in their seats.

Martin turned to Adam. "Did you do the research I asked you to?"

"Yes," Adam answered. "The best I could in the time I had. Do you want me to share it with you now?"

"No," Martin said as he got up from the floor and crossed to his chair by the chess game. "I'll ask questions. It will make things move faster."

"What research?" Nick asked.

"Martin requested that I check my commentaries and biblical reference books for information on the ark of the covenant."

"That's what we were talking about at your house," Katrin voiced.

"True, but I needed to review the topic for more detail."

"First question, Adam," Martin began. "What is the ark of the covenant?"

"It's a box made of acacia wood and gold," Adam replied. "It was covered in gold both on the inside and the outside. It was carried on acacia-wood poles that were also covered in gold. The poles went through four rings, two for each pole. The rings were made with gold."

"How thick was the gold?" Martin inquired.

"No one knows. It could have been a wooden box with a gold box inside and a gold box on the outside, or it could have been just gold-plated."

"What would something like that be worth?" Nick asked.

"Please." Martin held up his hand. "This will move more easily if I ask the questions. Its worth is immaterial at the moment." Turning to Adam he said, "You say that the ark was carried? By how many men?"

"It was to be carried only by a special group of people." Adam reached into his back pocket and pulled out several pieces of paper that he consulted. "The Kohathites—that is, the sons of Kohath—were responsible for the care of the ark. That's found in the Book of Numbers, chapter 3."

Martin paused for a moment. "Gold is heavy. If there were too much gold, it would be difficult to carry. Still, four men could carry a fairly heavy object. How big was this box?"

"It's hard to be specific, because its dimensions are given in cubits. A cubit was the distance from the tips of a man's fingers to his elbow. As you can imagine, such a measurement can vary substantially. A cubit is somewhere between sixteen and twenty-two inches. Most scholars use the length of eighteen inches as a basis of measurement. The Bible lists the size of the ark as two-and-a-half cubits by one-and-a-half cubits by one-and-a-half cubits. That would make it about . . ."

"Three point seven-five feet by two point two-five by two point two-five feet," Martin said. "What was it used for?"

"Several things," Adam answered. "First, to be a visible sign of God's presence. Second, God spoke to Moses from between the two cherubim on the mercy seat."

"The what?"

"The mercy seat. It was the ark's lid, and the craftsmen who made it," Adam consulted his notes again, "Bezalel and Aholiab, constructed the gold lid with two kneeling angels whose faces were turned down toward the ark itself. It is said that God spoke to Moses from between the cherubim, that is the angels."

"I understand. Go on."

"The ark was also used to carry a special cargo: the Ten Commandments written on two stone tablets, a golden jar of manna, and Aaron's rod that miraculously budded."

"I want to come back to those in a minute," Martin said, "but let me first ask this: What happened to it?"

"No one knows," Adam confessed. "The Bible just ceases mentioning it. Some think an Egyptian pharaoh took it, some think the Babylonians captured it when they conquered Jerusalem. And as I told you, there is an Ethiopian legend too. Some have even taught that Jeremiah carried it to Ireland, but no serious scholar promotes that idea."

"So the ark traveled with the Hebrews until they settled in what is now Israel?"

"Yes. It spent most of its time in Shiloh, which is about twenty miles north of Jerusalem."

"How long was it there?"

"About 400 years."

"Where did it ultimately end up?"

"In Solomon's temple, which was complete around 960 B.C."

"Was it intact then?"

Adam shook his head. "No. In 1 Kings 8, we are told that only the two tablets of stone were still in place. No one knows what happened to the other items."

"It's not likely the Jews would have removed the items," Martin said. "Did anyone else have possession of the ark?"

"Actually, yes," Adam replied. "The Philistines captured the ark after the battle of Aphek. They first put it in the temple of their god Dagon to prove his predominance over Jehovah. But the next day they found the statue of Dagon had been toppled over. They re-erected the statue only to find the next day that Dagon had been toppled again and this time Dagon's head and hands had been cut off."

"So the ark was making a point?"

"Well, God was making a point. But the Philistines didn't catch on. Soon they were afflicted with tumors—some scholars translate the Hebrew word as hemorrhoids—and plagued with mice. As each plague broke out, the Philistines would send the ark to the next town. A plague would soon break out there too. After the ark had been sent through the five major cities of Philistia it was returned to the Hebrews."

"But the ark was out of the hands of the Hebrews, true?"

"Yes."

"Well it all makes sense," Martin said, surrendering a small smile.

"How so?" Rachel asked.

"Not yet," Martin said raising a hand. "In one of our long discussions in which you've tried to convince me that the Bible is a unique book and that it is the very Word of God, you told me that many things in the Old Testament are symbols for things that occur in the New Testament. Did I get that right?"

"Yes."

"Is the ark an Old Testament picture of a New Testament event?"

Adam nodded. "Yes. Biblical scholars see the ark as a type of Christ. The word 'type' means a foreshadowing picture. The ark was composed of wood and gold; Christ is both fully human, represented by the wood, and fully God, represented by the gold. The ark contained the Law of Moses, that is, the Ten Commandments; Christ is called the Word in the Gospel of John; the ark held the golden jar of manna, which was the food that sustained the Israelites during their forty years of wandering; Christ referred to Himself as the Bread of Life; the ark held Aaron's rod that budded—which was probably a dead almond branch that miraculously began to produce almonds even though it was not part of a living tree—which signified that Aaron was God's choice for priestly leadership; in the New Testament, Christ is called the High Priest."

"Well," Martin said matter-of-factly, "there it is."

"There's what?" Rachel asked.

"Don't you see?" Martin asked in amazement. "It's simple, really. You all are to find the ark and return its contents."

"I don't follow," Pruit said.

"Look," Martin began. "Rachel, in her very elaborate vision, sees the ark of the covenant in a stone church. It matches the description of the biblical ark. Nick here is caught up in a dream or vision in which he is seated in a restaurant where he is served a sweet-tasting food from a golden jar. That's the manna. Lindsay is dragged to hell but is sent back with the image of a branch with leaves on it—a branch taken from a dead bush. There's Aaron's rod. What else could it be?"

"And we're supposed to go looking for the ark of the covenant?" Pruit said in disbelief. "But it's been missing for millennia. It's probably turned to dust by now."

"Not so," Martin quickly responded. "We have gold objects of much greater age in museums. The ark could very well exist."

"But wouldn't someone have found it by now?" Katrin asked. "It must be priceless with all that gold."

Adam spoke up. "Almost every year someone claims to have found the ark, but no one can produce it. I have always assumed that God hid it for a purpose and that it would never be found until He was ready."

"It sounds like He's ready," Rachel said. "And it seems that we're part of His purpose."

"But where do we begin?" Katrin asked. "We still don't know where the ark is."

"We have some idea," Martin said. "But everyone needs to understand that the ark has been separated from part of its contents. Isn't that right, Adam?"

"It is true that when the ark was finally placed in the temple built by Solomon that only the stone tablets remained, the other two items were gone. No one knows where or why."

"I do," Martin said, not caring if he sounded arrogant. "The where I can only describe in general terms now, but I think the details will become clearer the more I study the paintings."

Walking to the paintings Martin continued: "The paintings are laid out in an orderly fashion if you know what to look for. I started with the assumption that they were a means of communication, just like the visions. So I applied Occam's razor."

"Occam's what?" Nick asked.

"Occam's razor," Martin answered. "It's a principle applied by scientists. William of Occam was a fourteenth-century philosopher who said—and I'm paraphrasing a much more complex idea, 'When faced with a difficult question, start with the simplest explanation. It is usually right.' So instead of searching for hidden secrets, I looked for the simplest answer, and that was that the paintings should be easy to read. And sure enough they are—for the most part."

"Then you've made more headway than I have," Adam said.

"It's simple, really," Martin pointed at the first painting. "This first row of images is easy to understand. The first one is of someone painting; the second is the San Diego skyline; the third image is of Kingston Memorial Hospital."

"That's how I found Rachel and Adam," Katrin offered.

"As you have said," Martin interjected. "The next image is of our own Rachel. The following few images are of Pruit, Katrin, Nick, and Lindsay. It's very much like the opening credits of a movie.

"It's the next set of images that becomes confusing," Martin went on, "but only if taken individually. If we combine what we know of Rachel's vision with the information about the Ethiopian ark legend that Adam received from Dr. Newton, then we begin to see the communication come through. As you can see, there are a number of dark-skinned people, vast plains, and what looks like a rudimentary map. At the end of the painting is the blurred image of the ark. The meaning of the frames in between are still unclear, but they won't hold their secrets for very long."

"How do you know that one frame is a map?" Pruit asked. "It looks like a dark square with a white, squiggly line through it."

"I just know," Martin said, "but I'll prove it to you in a moment. First let's look at the second painting. As you can see, it starts with the same characters, but then it moves in a different direction. You can see a great deal of blue water. On the water is an ancient sailing ship. Does everyone see that?"

The group had gathered close as Martin had begun his explanation. A chorus of yesses was voiced.

"I need to confirm this," Martin continued, "but based on what Adam has told us about the ark, I'm willing to go out on a limb and say that sailing ship is a representation of a Philistine vessel. Now look at these dark irregular shapes on the blue background of this frame. Those are islands. Which islands? you might ask. Well, to where could the Philistines sail?"

"A great many places," Adam answered.

"I agree, but I have a place in mind. Let's see if I can't prove it. Everyone, please follow me."

Moving quickly from the living room, Martin led his band of students to the foyer, through a door, and down a narrow stairway. Only Adam and Rachel knew that Martin's private office was secreted on an underground floor. At the end of the stairs, Martin passed through another narrow door into a small, drab, windowless cubicle. A few books were scattered about, and one lone computer was situated on a cluttered desk. Martin sat at the desk and booted up the computer.

Adam was the last to enter the room. His progress was slowed by Nick's difficulty in negotiating the stairs. Once inside Martin's tiny office, Adam watched as Nick leaned against the wall, exhausted.

"Are you all right?" Adam asked, concerned. "Those stairs couldn't have been easy on you."

"I'll be fine in just a minute," Nick said. "Getting back up them is going to be the problem."

"Let me know if I can help."

"I'll make it, but thanks anyway."

"Adam!" Martin called. "Did you bring those photos you told me about—the ones of the paintings?"

"Yes." Adam was glad he had grabbed them before coming downstairs. When he had first arrived at Martin's, he had showed him the photos, but Martin took little interest in them at the time, preferring to play chess.

Martin took the small stack of Polaroids and began shuffling through them. When he came upon the one he was looking for, he pulled it from the stack and placed it in a scanner next to his computer.

He explained as he worked. "This is a digital scanner. It will convert the photo into pixels—small, shaded squares—so the computer can read it. I will then be able to see the photo's image on the computer monitor." The group watched as line by line the photo appeared on the screen. "Now I'll run an atlas program. This is a good one. It's used by the CIA to generate images of the world for reports. It's the best one available."

A blue-and-green orb appeared on the screen and began to rotate slowly.

"It's a globe," Katrin said.

"That's right," Martin responded. "And by clicking on a section of the world with my mouse . . ." Martin selected Africa and clicked the left button on his mouse. Instantly, a map of Africa appeared with the names of each country emblazoned in yellow. "Now let's select Ethiopia in East Africa." An image of Ethiopia filled the computer monitor. "One more click ought to do it." Pointing at a river that was represented by a twisted, convoluted blue line, he watched a portion of west Ethiopia zoom to fill the screen.

"Impressive," Pruit said.

"Now all I need to do is superimpose our photo over the map, size it to scale, and . . . voilà. A pretty good match."

Everyone in the group was silent.

"Katrin," Martin said. "You are a fine artist. Every major turn in the river corresponds. This, my friends, is the Blue Nile. It begins in the highlands of Ethiopia and flows into the Nile. In fact, eighty percent of the Nile's water comes from the Blue Nile."

"Incredible," Adam said. "It's a perfect fit."

"It is also proof that some of you will soon be on your way to Ethiopia."

"What about the islands on the other painting?" Nick asked.

Martin sifted through the stack of Polaroids again until he found the one that had captured the image of the islands on the blue background. "I think I know where this is," Martin said, "but let's verify it."

"Greece," Lindsay blurted.

"Very good, Ms. Blair. My thoughts exactly." Martin repeated his previous actions of scanning the photo, sizing it to scale, and superimposing it over the Cyclades and Dodecanese islands southeast of Greece and west of Turkey. They too matched perfectly.

Everyone began to talk among themselves, causing a deafening clamor in the tiny room.

"Silence!" Martin shouted. "Let's move back upstairs. Anna will fix us some coffee and we can complete our discussion."

"But what does it all mean?" Katrin asked seriously.

"It means the five of us are going to be doing some traveling," Nick said with an excitement not shared by the others. "We're going to make a difference."

"Correction, Nick," Martin said. "The six of you."

"Wait a minute," Lindsay objected. "I didn't see his face in the paintings." She pointed a well-manicured finger at Adam. "He hasn't had a vision, either."

"You didn't look closely enough," Martin corrected. "Adam's face doesn't appear in the . . . shall we call them the opening credits? His image doesn't need to appear, nor does he need a vision."

"Why?" Pruit inquired.

"Because he doesn't need to be convinced of God's ability to work in the lives of individuals. None of you are believers—except Rachel and Adam. And before you ask, let me give the answer: Rachel received a vision to give credibility to your stories. She is the cord that binds all of you together."

"I'm still not convinced," Lindsay said bitterly.

"Well," Martin said glibly, "how then do you explain the appearance of six players in the paintings and not five? And if you'll look closely, you'll see the sixth player is Adam."

"Odd," Adam said, puzzled. "I don't recall seeing that before. I must have overlooked it."

"Now what," Katrin asked confused.

Martin answered with a small smile. "Now your lives change forever."

Thirty-One

A slight drizzle spotted the windshield as Adam steered his way off the freeway and onto the surface streets. The clouds overhead shrouded the stars and moon from view. A darkness, fed by weariness and apprehension, filled the car.

"Are you OK?" Adam asked.

Rachel turned her view from the moist streets outside her window to her husband. "Yes, I'm fine," she replied. "Just a little depressed."

"Depressed?"

"Slightly," she acknowledged. "Nothing to worry about. It's probably just Lazarus syndrome."

"What's that?" Adam glanced from the road ahead to glimpse his wife. She was clearly weary. Not from physical exertion or even the coma, but from the mental strain of trying to sort out all she had seen and heard.

"Surgical patients who have faced life-threatening illness suffer from it occasionally. They've been close to death, the surgery saves their lives, they're happy, but soon become depressed. It's part of the trauma. The emotions rise and fall like an elevator."

"I thought you were excited about all of this."

"I am most of the time, but I think it's all caught up to me. My emotions are wearing thin. There's so much to do and we still know so little."

"And things are moving fast—real fast," Adam agreed.

"Is this really happening, Adam? Are we really about to go hunting for the ark of the covenant?"

Nodding in the dark, Adam said, "It sure looks like it."

"Aren't you afraid at all?"

Adam shrugged. "I don't know. I've been so caught up in this that I haven't had time to really think about it. It's simultaneously thrilling and frightening."

"I remember when I was in medical school," Rachel said, repositioning herself in the seat to better look at her husband. "I was on my first surgery rotation. Mostly I observed and aided the surgeon, but this one day the surgeon hands me a scalpel, points at the patient's abdomen, and says, "It's your turn to make the first cut."

Rachel chuckled. "I remember taking the scalpel, looking at the patient, then at the surgeon, then at the nurses. Except for the patient who was under anesthesia, everyone was looking at me. I was scared beyond belief. But I knew what he was doing. There comes a time when you have to pick up your first scalpel and make your first incision. First things are always hard.

"That's how I feel now," she continued. "I am—we are—about to do something that we have never done before. There's no precedent for it. It has to be done, but the doing of it is scary. Do you know what I mean?"

"I understand," Adam replied. "Yet, I also know that God has chosen us for something of historical importance. And I know that He didn't call us to failure. If He has gone through this much trouble to get us started, then He won't abandon us."

"But there are so many questions and unknowns," Rachel exclaimed. "Where do we look in Ethiopia? What is to be done in the Greek islands? And why did God choose four people who aren't even believers?"

"My answer to all three questions is I don't know. But I think we will know soon enough."

Slowing the car, Adam made a right-hand turn onto their street. "We'll be home in a few minutes. We can catch some sleep, and things will look better in the morning."

"I hope so."

The drizzle had turned into a light rain. Black pools of water set-tled in the depressed areas of pavement. A tiny river ran along the curb. The street lamps cast an eerie blue light on the moist yards, sidewalks, and driveways.

As Adam turned the car into the driveway the headlights cast a passing beacon across the front of their yard. A dark shadowy shape moved quickly beside the side of the house, catching Rachel's eye.

"What was that?" she asked, pointing toward the fence that ran between their yard and the neighbor's.

"What's what?"

"I thought I saw something by the house. It was too dark to make out."

"Probably the neighbor's dog," Adam said evenly. "That thing gets out almost every night."

"I suppose it could be a dog," Rachel admitted. "I guess I'm just getting jumpy."

"You need some sleep, kiddo."

"You're right. The thought of closing my eyes for the night sounds wonderful."

Moments later, Adam Bridger and his wife, Rachel, stepped out of the rain and into the warmth of their home. Fifteen minutes later they were in bed asleep.

Twenty minutes later, a stocky man dressed in black stepped from the side yard, crossed the lawn, and hurriedly walked to a nearby van, which he entered. A minute later, the van drove away.

Thirty-Two

Seattle, Washington

The sun was quickly slipping below the western horizon, casting its last golden rays through the moist atmosphere and illuminating the patchwork clouds, causing them to glow as if they were the source of their own light instead of mere mirrors of something greater.

Gerald T. Quince watched the encroaching night push back the failing sunlight. It was close to 8:15 and it seemed unnatural to have night just now approaching, but Quince knew what every resident of Seattle knew: the farther north one traveled the later the sun set.

On the street below him, the last diehard employees of Datadyne were pulling out of the parking garage and making their way to home and family. Quince had no family, but he did have a home—a large, ornate home in which he entertained guests frequently.

"I think they're getting ready to move," a striking man with a clear, smooth voice intoned. "We've had them under surveillance for two weeks, twenty-four hours a day. Over that time we've collected a great deal of data, but we still don't have the crucial stuff. My guess is, they don't know where to look either—apart from the general areas of Greece and Ethiopia."

Quince turned to look at the man speaking. Jason Beck could have made a better than adequate living in the movies. At six foot two, with thick wavy brown hair, he looked like a tall Kennedy. An image enhanced by his judicious use of a captivating Massachusetts accent.

Beck was a private investigator—a very expensive private investigator who was more than willing to sully his hands in industrial espionage. Quince had used him on many occasions to investigate—spy on—other software companies. Trained by the military, Beck was as intelligent as he was shrewd. In less than ten years he had turned a one-man office into a firm of more than 100 operatives, each with special skills, and some with skills considered illegal in all states.

Sitting next to Beck was Dr. Julian Newton, who frequently revealed his discomfort by incessantly clearing his throat.

"All the wiretaps are working?" Quince asked.

"On all subjects except this St. James character," Beck answered. "I don't know who this guy is, but his phone and ISDN computer connections are virtually tap-proof. The only thing I've ever seen like it are those systems used by the FBI, Pentagon, and others."

"It's uncrackable?" Quince asked.

"So far, and I'm out of ideas."

Quince frowned deeply and walked to the conference table in his office.

"I finally got a picture of all of them together at St. James' mansion." Beck pulled an eight by ten photo from a file and slid it across the table toward Quince. "It wasn't easy. The front of the house has no windows. All the windows face the ocean, and since the house is on the edge of a cliff . . . well, you see the problem. I got that picture by having one of my operatives sail by on a hang glider. We had a small video camera attached to the frame. We then downloaded one frame. That's what you have there."

Quince studied the photo intensely. The image was hard to make out, but he could see a group of people sitting around a table.

"Go on," Quince ordered.

"We've monitored all their movements and phone conversations—except St. James', of course—and they have been dividing up the work. The Blair woman has been making travel arrangements. Pruit

Bain has been making calls to free up his schedule. Couer has spoken to her mother several times but hasn't told her anything, and ..."

Raising a hand Quince cut Beck off. "I get the idea. What's their plan?"

"Two teams, three people each. One will travel to an island in Greece, but they haven't said which one. That team will be composed of Nick Stern, Lindsay Blair, and Katrin Couer. The second team will fly to Addis Ababa in Ethiopia. That team consists of Adam Bridger; his wife, Rachel; and Pruit Bain."

"Why don't we know which Greek island?"

"Because they don't know," Beck answered quickly. "We picked up one conversation in which Adam asked St. James about the picture faxed to the tourism board in Greece. Apparently they have some photo or drawing with a building on it. They're attempting to identify the island by the building."

"Clever," Quince admitted. "When do you think they will leave?"

"Any time."

"Do they have a contact in Ethiopia?" Newton asked, speaking for the first time since the meeting began.

"Yes," Beck responded. "A missionary and his wife."

"You have their names?" Quince inquired.

"Absolutely, and I have operatives running down their location and gathering other information."

"Good," Quince said smiling. "Very good."

Beck acknowledged the compliment with a simple nod.

"All right," Quince said as he began to pace the room. "I want us to be ready to go at any moment. Beck, make sure that you have at least one operative tailing each team. I want reports at least twice a day. Don't worry about expenses. Make sure they are equipped with the best communication devices. I don't want them depending on local phones."

"It's already been taken care of, sir."

"Great. I'll have the company plane ready to fly at a moment's notice. I want both of you to be ready to depart when I call."

"Both of us?" Newton said with surprise. "What do you need me for?"

"You're an archeologist, Newton, and a good one. When they

find what they're looking for, I want you there to authenticate things. I don't want to leave anything of importance behind. Besides . . ." Quince trailed off.

"Besides what?"

Quince exchanged a knowing glance with Beck. "Besides, some of what we may be called upon to do is illegal. Actually, the wire-taps and listening devices are already an invasion of privacy. The point is this: You're involved, lock, stock, and barrel. I want to keep you involved in case you get cold feet and decide to talk. I need you as guilty as the rest of us."

"That's not really necessary," Newton said. "I can assure you . . ."

"I don't want your assurance, I want your compelled loyalty." Quince approached the table, placed his palms on the shiny finish, and leaned forward, close to Newton's face. "You've made a deal with the devil here, Newton, and there's no backing out. We are about to find the most prized possession on the planet. Its value is unimaginable, and it's going to be mine."

Standing up, Quince took a more relaxed posture. "Everyone gets what he wants here, indeed, more than he ever dreamed. That should buy some loyalty. Understood?"

"Yes, sir," Beck said quickly.

"I . . . I guess so," Newton stammered.

"This," Quince said raising his arms high, "is going to be our finest hour. The ark of the covenant, the most valuable object in the world, and it's going to be mine. All mine!"

Thirty-Three

San Diego, California

The silence was palpable; the tension tangible. Eight people sat around Martin St. James' dining room table in a stunned hush.

"Your kidding! Right?" Nick Stern said, finally cutting the heavy shroud of silence. "This is a joke."

"It's no joke," Lindsay replied crisply, her heavy British accent made all the more noticeable by the force of heated emotion. "I don't plan on making long explanations. All you need to know is that I'm out. I don't know why I've wasted more than two weeks of my life with you people, planning and going over the details of what is clearly madness."

"But it's not madness," Rachel cried. "How can you say that after all that we've been through? Your own experience alone ought to prove . . ."

"Prove that I've had some psychotic episode," Lindsay interrupted sharply. "For all I know, I have a brain tumor that caused that . . . that . . . fantasy. I don't know what it was, but I do know that flying off to Greece to look for some mythical object is insane. Especially if I'm in league with a group of insane people."

Adam spoke up. "The objects are not mythical but historical, and neither you nor any one of us is insane. You're just a little nervous, that's all."

Lindsay guffawed loudly. "Preacher, I have never been nervous in my life. You know my line of work. I do things that even Hollywood screenwriters can't conceive. I assure you, nervousness has nothing to do with my decision."

"Then what?" Adam raised his voice louder than he intended, but weariness and frustration had worked him to his last and very frayed nerve. "Why this sudden change?"

"Because I've come to my senses," Lindsay snapped. "Look at yourselves. You're not some trained group of explorers about to go on expedition. You're a group of dysfunctional people with a Don Quixote complex."

"Now just a minute," Pruit said. "I don't like this any better than you . . ."

"What a group," Lindsay ranted. "A preacher man leading a brain-damaged surgeon, a drug addict, a bitter fireman, and woman artist who can't climb out of her adolescent bashfulness. And you expect me to go globe-trotting with you. Not a chance. I've wasted all the time I'm going to. I leave for London tonight."

Sharply, Lindsay turned to leave. Adam leaped from his chair and followed her. Within four steps he was close enough to reach forward with his left hand and seize her right elbow.

"Now listen for a minute . . ." Adam began, but his words were cut brutally short. In a swift, fluid motion Lindsay raised her arm in an arc that allowed her to pin Adam's outstretched arm under hers. Then, before Adam could think or respond, she took one step back and viciously kicked his left foot forward. Adam was instantly airborne and falling hard. Lindsay released his arm. He crashed shoulder first on the carpeted floo;, the impact forced the wind from his lungs.

Those around the table were instantly on their feet, but only Rachel moved forward, racing to Adam's side.

"Don't even think it!" Lindsay bellowed. "I have taken care of men three times the size of any of you. I can handle one of you or all of you together. And right now, I'm angry enough to welcome the challenge."

The silence returned.

Lindsay turned and stormed from the house.

Adam gasped for air. The front door slammed with a resounding crash. A car's engine started. Tires squealed on the pavement.

"Are you all right, Adam?" Rachel asked. "Maybe I should look at that shoulder."

Shaking his head, Adam sighed, and then took a deep breath. The shock of the fall was wearing off and his breathing was returning to normal.

"Can I . . ." Rachel began, but Adam cut her off with up-raised hands.

"No! I need a minute to get hold of myself." Adam was struggling with an invasion of emotions. He was angry at Lindsay's words and actions; he was embarrassed at having been so easily thrown to the ground; and he was dispirited by her cavalier dismissal of them all.

Struggling for words, Adam realized that what he really wanted to do was to scream. But he wouldn't allow it. Composure. Reason. Measured response. That's what was needed.

Slowly he rose to his feet, rubbing his shoulder and moving his arm in a small circle. "Well," he said, "I didn't expect that."

"Highly unreasonable," Martin said, his eyes still wide at the act of violence he had seen in his own home. "That's why I don't like people in my house. They're so unpredictable."

"Would you rather we left?" Pruit asked hotly.

"Enough!" Adam uttered loudly. "Let's not turn on each other. Let's give ourselves a moment to let the adrenaline settle down." Turning to Anna, Adam said, "May I have some aspirin and some water?"

"Certainly," Anna replied and quickly moved into the kitchen. A moment later she returned with a bottle of white tablets and a tumbler filled with water.

Taking the items from Anna, Adam said, "Let's all be seated. It looks like we have some decisions to make."

"What do we do now?" Katrin asked quietly, clearly frightened. "There were supposed to be six of us and now there are only five."

"Yeah," Nick agreed. "And Lindsay was on my team. Personally, I'm glad she left now and not somewhere in Greece."

"I don't think Nick and I can do the job alone," Katrin said. "And I don't mean that as an insult to you, Nick."

"You're right," Nick said morosely, "I'm not much good, especially at the physical stuff."

"Maybe one of us should join your team," Pruit offered. "I'd probably be more comfortable in Greece than Ethiopia anyway."

"No," Adam said rubbing his eyes. "I think we need to stay close to the plan laid out on the paintings."

"But . . ." Katrin interjected.

Adam raised a hand. "I agree that you two should not go to Greece alone. Three people were supposed to go, and three people should go."

"Maybe we could all go to Greece first, then all go to Ethiopia together," Rachel said.

"The paintings show two distinct teams," Martin said. "I agree with Adam in that much. I'm not sure what all this vision stuff is yet, and I'm not willing to attribute it to spiritual communication from God, but sticking with the plan is still the best idea. At least the best I can see at this time."

"What about you?" Pruit asked of Martin. "Would you be willing to go?"

"No." Martin's answer was quick and to the point. "I seldom leave my house. Besides, someone needs to coordinate the communications. And there's still some interpretation of the paintings to be done."

"Well," Nick said. "I don't know anyone who can just pick up and go off to Greece, not to mention someone who would believe the whole story in the first place."

"I do," Adam intoned firmly. "I know someone."

"Who?" was the unanimous question.

"May I borrow your phone, Martin?"

"Sure, Adam, but who are you going to call?"

"The one person who will believe us—Dick Slay."

At ten minutes past eight that evening, Dick Slay arrived. He sat comfortably in a Barchalounger listening to the story being told him. He listened in silence, moving only to sip Anna's special coffee and to occasionally scratch his stubble-laced chin.

They each took turns, telling their personal tale in great detail. After the last had finished, Adam brought Dick up-to-date on the plans and research. All totaled, it took nearly ninety minutes to lay open all they knew and had experienced.

When Adam had finished, he leaned back in his chair, crossed his arms, and said, "Well?"

At first Dick said nothing. He slowly looked around the room as if judging the character and sanity of each person. Finally his eyes fell on Anna. "The coffee is wonderful, Anna, could I have another cup?"

"Coffee?" Adam was aghast. "We pour out our souls to you and all you can do is ask for more coffee?"

Dick smiled and then turned back to Anna, "You wouldn't happen to have some cake, would you? You know, the kind you bring to the church potluck?"

"I sure do," Anna said with a brilliant smile, happy to be involved in some way. "Would anyone else like some?" Only Nick took her up on the offer.

"Cake? Coffee?" Adam was distraught. "Come on, Dick. I'm dying here."

"What do you want to know?"

"Do you believe us and will you help? That's a good place to start." Adam replied.

"Of course I believe you," Dick said casually. "Why wouldn't I?"

"Well," Adam said. "It is pretty wild."

"Haven't you been teaching the church that God is still a God of power and miracles? Haven't you taught us that He is still active in our everyday lives?"

"Yes, that is what I've always taught."

"Then why are you so shocked when God acts?" Dick asked without a hint of sarcasm. "So God has stepped up the level a notch or two, but that doesn't change my belief or yours. It's just our turn to act."

"Then you'll help us?" Rachel asked.

"Of course," Dick said with a laugh. "I wouldn't miss this for anything." Anna returned with the cake and coffee and served Dick, whose smile broadened measurably. Holding up the small plate with the large slice of chocolate cake, he said, "See, I'm already benefiting from being part of the team."

Laughter and sighs filled the room. Dick continued, "I suppose you want me to replace this Lindsay woman."

"Yes," Adam said quickly. "She was supposed to go to Greece with Katrin and Nick."

"Good," Dick said with his mouthful. "Nick is clearly intelligent."

"What makes you say that?" Nick asked, puzzled.

"You were the only other one smart enough to take up Anna's offer of cake. That's the sign of a solid character."

Nick laughed. "I think I'm going to like you, Dick."

Adam looked at Rachel and smiled, then he released a long sigh and began to rub his aching shoulder.

"I still think we should have followed her," the thick man with a bald head said. "She took outta here pretty fast. She may be up to somethin'."

The thin man with gray eyes shook his head. "We're assigned to maintain surveillance here. Another team will pick her up when she reaches the hotel. That's why I called them on the cellular phone, so they would be waiting for her."

"Well, it's not like we're doing any good here. We can't hear or see a thing."

"We get paid good money to do what we're told. I'm not jeopardizing that. Now sit back and relax. You're making me nervous."

"The people in that house should be the nervous ones. Beck is spending a boatload of money keeping track of them."

"I don't care, as long as I get my share."

"Amen to that, partner. Amen to that."

Part 3
Between the Cherubim

And there I will meet with you, and from above the mercy seat, from between the cherubim which are upon the ark of the testimony, I will speak to you about all that I will give you in commandment for the sons of Israel.
— Exodus 25:22

And the temple of God which is in heaven was opened; and the ark of His covenant appeared in His temple, and there were flashes of lightning and sounds and peals of thunder and an earthquake and a great hailstorm.
— Revelation 11:19

Thirty-Four

Disorientation swept over Adam. Walking from the old Boeing 727 that had touched down fifteen minutes before and was now disgorging it contents of passengers on the tarmac, Adam saw the green-yellow-red flag of Ethiopia flapping gently in the cool African breeze. Adam had never traveled much, not even to cross the border into Mexico which was less than an hour's drive from his home. Seeing a foreign flag flying high against a sharp blue sky made him feel uncomfortable and out of place.

"Is that them?" Rachel asked, nodding in the direction of a white man and woman dressed in casual clothes. The man stood less than six feet tall, had brown hair cut close to the scalp, and wore tan pants and a chocolate-colored golf shirt. The woman was a good six inches shorter, with blond hair parted through the center that hung limply down to the middle of her neck. Both were smiling broadly and waving.

"Yes," Adam responded, "that's them. I haven't seen Ted and Lisa for more than ten years. They both look good."

"You said you went to seminary with him?" Pruit stated.

"That's right. We weren't close, but we belonged to the same study group. We were both working on our master of divinity degrees."

"I didn't know divinity could be mastered," Pruit said with a wry smile.

"That's just the degree's title," Adam responded. "You know, master of arts degree, master of science degree, and master of divinity."

"It was a joke," Pruit said lightly. "I knew that."

"Of course," Adam replied.

Rachel shot Pruit a glance and winked. Pruit returned the wink instantly. It was good to see him loosening up. The three continued across the tarmac until they reached a chain-link fence that delineated the outside waiting area.

"Adam," Ted Hawthorne uttered warmly as he extended his hand. "It's good to see you again. It's been a long time, but you haven't changed a bit."

"You're lying, of course," Adam responded with a smile. "I've gotten older and even put on a couple of pounds, but thanks for the compliment. I would like you to meet my wife, Rachel, and our friend Pruit Bain."

"I'm pleased to meet both of you." Ted spoke quickly, firing his words out as if he were on a time limit. "This is my wife Lisa. Let's get your baggage. I have a car waiting."

It took more than forty-five minutes to retrieve their luggage, which they had purposely kept as small as possible to make travel easier. Fifteen minutes after that, they were seated in the back of an old blue Volvo station wagon as it motored down the paved streets of Addis Ababa, Ethiopia's capital.

"We don't get many guests out this way." Ted was driving, but as he spoke he turned his head to direct his words to the passengers in the back seat, a habit that Adam found disconcerting. "Ethiopia isn't one of the hottest tourist attractions, you know. Too much trouble, too much insecurity."

"How long have you been here?" Pruit asked.

"About eight years," Ted answered, snapping his head around again. "When I left seminary, I pastored for the better part of a decade, but I never felt completely comfortable in it. You know what I mean? I always felt that I was supposed to be doing something else. Well, Ethiopia was in the news a lot back then: famine, civil war, disputes of borders, and Eritrea's succession and all. I kept seeing pictures of Ethiopians, especially the children, and then finally realized that I needed to be here."

"So you came as a missionary?" Pruit asked. "What kind of work do you do here? Do you have a church?"

"Actually, no. We operate a literacy mission. Only about 25 percent of the people can read. So we've set up a mission school for adults. Ethiopia has compulsory education for children ages seven to thirteen, but that's not much.

"Lisa is a nurse," Ted continued, "so she provides some medical care, but it's limited. Still, she does a good work. There is only one doctor for every 100,000 people. The infant mortality rate is more than 12 percent. That's pretty high. A child born today, if lucky, can expect to live about fifty years and that's it. And depending where he is born, he will spend a lot of those fifty years hungry and fearful of civil war."

"Or she," Lisa added.

"Or she," Ted agreed.

Rachel leaned forward and asked, "Do you like it here? Does the government give you much trouble?"

"I love it here," Ted said enthusiastically. "And I love the work. I feel fulfilled. As for the government, they've been pretty good. It's still a transitional government, you know, and they have a lot to deal with. There are still rebels in the hills, and there is always the problem of famine, especially in the lowlands."

"Lowlands?" Adam inquired.

"Yes, we're in the highlands now. That's why the weather is so nice and cool. The rainy season begins in June. Which reminds me: What kind of visas did you get?"

"Tourist," Adam replied.

"Good, that gives you up to thirty days in the country."

Seizing a break in Ted's constant dialogue, Lisa spoke up: "How is everyone feeling? Anyone feeling lightheaded?"

"A little," Rachel said. Adam and Pruit agreed.

"I'm pretty tired," Pruit added.

"That's to be expected," Lisa said. "Some people suffer from altitude sickness. We're pretty high up here. Addis Ababa is 8,000 feet above sea level. Coming from San Diego, which is as close to sea level as you can get, you'll probably experience fatigue and maybe headaches. It will take a few days for you to get acclimated."

"I thought it was just jet lag," Rachel offered.

"Well, there's that too," Lisa replied. "There's eleven hours difference between here and the West Coast."

"Almost half a day," Pruit said.

"That's right," Ted jumped in. "It's about four in the morning back at your home."

"Pruit's from New York," Rachel interjected.

"Never been there," Ted said, "except to change planes on our way over here. By the way, did you guys come through Rome?"

"No," Adam answered, "we flew from San Diego to New York to Cairo, then to Addis Ababa. I wish we had time to spend in Egypt. There are many things I'd like to see."

"You do seem in a hurry," Ted said as he steered the car down Churchill Avenue. "Not to mention secretive. You on some kind of mission or something?"

"Sort of," Adam said. "I'll explain when we get to your place. Just where is your place anyway?"

"We're about an hour and a half outside the city limits. That's where the need was the greatest. So sit back and enjoy; we'll be there in just under two hours. Sleep if you want to. I'm sure you're tired."

"We are that," Adam said wearily. "We are indeed that."

The stars overhead shone more brilliantly than Adam had ever seen. The Milky Way spread its gigantic wings of galaxies across the sky. The stars glimmered against the pitch-black sky like glitter cast into the air.

"Beautiful, isn't it?" Ted said, zipping up his coat. "I bet you don't see a sky like this back in San Diego."

"Not where we live," Adam admitted. "We have clouds almost every morning and night. It comes with living close to the coast."

"I see these stars every night," Ted said softly. "They're like diamonds that can't be touched. Every time I step into the night I pause to take in the beauty of it all. It would seem criminal not to do so."

"You don't get used to it?" Pruit asked, rubbing his hands together to warm them from the night chill.

"Not yet," Ted replied, "and I pray that I never will." Seating himself at the old picnic table that was situated at the rear of the building where Ted and Lisa lived and taught, he quickly glanced at his guests. "You look a little more rested. How's the headache, Rachel?"

"Better. The ibuprofen has helped. Not to mention the few hours of sleep."

"You'll adjust quickly enough," Ted said. "Just don't overexert yourself for a few days. The air is pretty thin. And to help everyone feel better, Lisa is bringing some coffee—African coffee. I think you'll like it."

"African coffee," Rachel said, surprised. "I didn't know Africa grew coffee."

"Oh, yes," Ted answered with a broad smile. "Africa grows some of the world's best. It's one of the few things that Ethiopia has to export. Trust me, you'll like it."

As if on cue, Lisa appeared with a tray of mugs and a steaming glass carafe of coffee. To Adam it smelled wonderful, and the thought of consuming a warm fluid to fight the night chill was compelling.

After the coffee was served and praised by all, Ted spoke: "It will be getting cool soon so we'll need to move inside. But maybe you can tell me what all this is about. Don't get me wrong. I'm tickled that you're here, and I hope you stay for a while, but the mystery is killing me."

Adam looked at the others. Before leaving the States they had spent some time discussing how much to reveal to Ted and Lisa. They debated the issue for several hours before finally settling on an honesty-is-the-best-policy approach.

"Let me begin with a few questions," Adam answered. "I understand that Ethiopia has a long Jewish and Christian tradition. What can you tell me about the Black Jews? I think they're called the Falasha."

"That's right: Falasha is an Amharic term. It means 'exiles' or 'landless ones.' They called themselves Beta Esrael, which means 'house of Israel.' Interesting group," Ted said, sipping his coffee. Steam rose from his cup. "The Falashim have a very ancient tradition in Ethiopia. They believe they are the descendants of a union between Solomon and the Queen of Sheba. That story is doubtful, but they are a very old Jewish group. So old in fact, that they continued animal sacrifices long after the other Jews in the world stopped. They knew nothing of the Babylonian or Palestinian Talmud. Apparently they had been isolated for millennia. They're all gone now."

"You mean there aren't anymore?" Pruit asked.

"Very few in Ethiopia," Ted answered. "Nearly all of them were airlifted to Israel between 1984 and 1991."

"You don't believe the story told in the Kebra Nagast?" Adam asked.

"Oh, you know about that, huh?" Ted took another sip of coffee. "I'm doubtful, but then again, such legends are not my forte. The Falashim have a very ancient lineage, but I don't know that it goes back to Solomon. I suppose it could, but I'd be surprised."

"Do you think they ever possessed the ark of the covenant?" Rachel inquired, leaning forward over the table.

"Don't tell me you guys are trying to be the next Indiana Jones," Ted said.

"Humor us for a little while," Adam encouraged.

"The Ethiopian Christian church believes it possesses the ark of the covenant, but no one has been able to verify that. Every church has a *tabot*, which is a representation of the ark. Sometimes it's nothing more than a small box or even a slab of wood. The church of Saint Mary's in Axum, however, is the one with the real ark— according to tradition. The ark is brought out only once a year to celebrate Timkat."

"Timkat?" Pruit said.

"The celebration of Epiphany," Ted explained. "It's a holy day they observe every January."

"They actually show the ark every January?" Rachel said. "You mean people actually see it?"

"Not really," Ted said shaking his head. "While every church is said to have a *tabot*, only the Axum church is said to have the real ark. But I don't think they have it, and if they did I don't think they would bring it out, even during Timkat. As far as seeing the *tabot* goes, well, no one sees any church's *tabot*. It is always covered with an ornate and heavy covering. The best you could see is the high priest leading an entourage of priests with a concealed *tabot* carried above their heads. The ceremony is worth seeing, though. The crowd goes absolutely wild with excitement and they dance and gyrate before the *tabot*. It's quite a sight. Lisa and I have seen several Timkat celebrations."

"But you don't think the ark is in Axum?" Adam asked.

"Doubtful," Ted answered. "Think about it. Would you keep the ark in a church? Even in the new one they built some years back? I wouldn't. True, whatever is there is closely guarded by a priest and by others, but not nearly enough to protect it from someone or perhaps a group that wanted it. No sir, something that valuable is going to need a great deal more than a priest to protect it."

"A priest guards it!" Pruit asked. "That's it?"

"One priest is assigned to protect and serve the ark and that assignment is for life. When he dies, another is selected and that priest will spend the rest of his days in the presence of the *tabot*. But don't be mislead. It's more than one priest who guards the *tabot*; the people guard it, too. I wouldn't want to be the one to sneak in there to catch a glimpse of the ark. If the people found out, you'd probably be dead before you knew it."

"All right," Rachel said. "If you wouldn't keep it in a church then where would you keep it?"

"I have no idea," Ted replied. "Now it's getting cold out here. Let's go inside and finish our coffee. Perhaps you can tell me what all this is about."

Adam, Rachel, and Pruit exchanged knowing glances.

In Addis Ababa another aged Boeing 727 bounced down the runway toward the white terminal building. Inside, a thin man with gray eyes and a thick man with a bald head unfastened their seat belts and prepared to deplane.

"So, Hector, do you think we'll see any elephants or lions while we're here?" the thick man asked.

"The only lions and elephants I want to see, Carl, are those locked behind the bars of a zoo." The thin man shifted in his seat. "Besides, we're here to work, not sightsee."

"I know, I know, but I can hope, can't I?"

"Let's just do our jobs, and then we can go home."

Thirty-Five

San Diego, California

The early morning marine layer cloaked the sky with a soft but thick cushion of clouds. Light, softened by the filtering effect of the overcast, oozed through the large living room windows of Martin St. James' mansion filling the space with a pale, almost dreamy radiance.

Seated on the floor and wearing nothing but a pair of white shorts was Martin. Next to him a cup of coffee sat on the floor untouched. Three feet in front of him, still propped against a folding chair, were Katrin's two paintings. Martin had arisen early to study the illustrations and had not moved from his place on the floor for more than two hours.

"You're worrying me, Martin," his sister Anna said. "You've refused breakfast and now you've let your coffee get cold."

"I'm working."

"Breakfast would ruin your work?" Anna sighed heavily. "No wonder you're skin and bones. Just look at you."

"Mom died years ago, Anna, and I don't need you to replace her. You're my sister, remember?"

"I just worry about you. I've seen you go days without eating. Once

212

you get your head into something you forget about everything, including life's basics."

"All right," Martin acquiesced. "I'll have breakfast, but nothing too filling. A roll maybe."

Smiling at the slight victory, Anna went into the kitchen to prepare a roll, a hard-boiled egg, and a glass of orange juice. Martin would protest that the meager meal was too much, but she would threaten to nag him, preventing him from concentrating, unless he swallowed every bite. He would do it. He wouldn't like it, but he would do it.

Fifteen minutes later, Anna left the kitchen with a small platter of food. Martin was still seated on the floor like a stone statue, his head resting motionless in his hands, his elbows planted squarely on his knees. The only movement she could see was the occasional blinking of Martin's eyes. But she knew that inside his head there was a great deal of activity: thoughts, questions, suppositions, trial answers, and more. Martin's body might be sedentary, but his brain was one of the most active on the planet.

"Here's your breakfast," she said, "and you need to eat every bite of it. Unless you want me to nag you all day."

"This is stupid," Martin spat.

"No, it's not. It's important that you eat . . ."

"I'm not talking about that, Anna. I'm talking about these paintings. They're driving me crazy. The overall message was easy to ascertain, but the details . . . the details are just out of my grasp."

"Well, if anyone can figure it out, it's you."

"I don't share your optimism, Anna," Martin said bitterly. "Adam and his team are already in Ethiopia, but they have no idea what to do next. Dick, Katrin, and Nick will be landing in Crete in a few hours. Once there, they'll make their way to Karpathos and then sit in a hotel room waiting to hear from me—and I don't have anything to offer them."

"Maybe you're trying too hard. Maybe you should relax more and then answers might come to you."

"I wish it were that simple, but it's not." Martin was exasperated. "Some of these images are blurred—indistinct. They lack sufficient detail for me to trace them. These islands, for example," he said, pointing at the second painting. "Identifying them as the Greek islands in the Aegean was easy. But there are dozens of islands, and probably some that don't appear on any map." Martin threw his arms in the air. "It doesn't make sense."

"But it will, Martin. I know it will."

Martin got up from the floor and began pacing. "It's not just the details that don't make sense, Anna, it's the whole concept. Adam believes that these visions are from God. And that these paintings are His way of communicating."

"I think he's right."

"But how can he be?" Martin exclaimed. "The simple logic of the matter dictates otherwise."

"What do you mean?"

"I'll tell you what I mean," Martin said as he approached the paintings. "If I were God and I wanted to send a message I sure wouldn't use a means like this. And if I did . . . and this is the important point . . . I would make sure that the paintings were clear enough to be understood." He turned to face Anna. "They wouldn't be cryptic. Too much is at stake. No sir, if these were truly from God, then you'd think that He would have made them more understandable!"

Martin stopped his tirade and looked closely at Anna. "Anna? Anna, what's the matter with you? Are you sick or something?"

Anna didn't answer directly. Instead she slowly raised one hand to her mouth and with her hand pointed a shaky finger at the paintings. She was ashen.

"What?" Martin asked. "What?" He turned and looked at the illustrations, gasped, and took a step back.

"Umm . . ." was all that Anna could say.

"No. No." Martin stuttered. "No, this isn't happening. I don't believe this." Quickly Martin slammed his eyes shut, pressing his lids together hard. Then he opened them again.

"Unbelievable," Martin said softly then approached the paintings. Stooping down, he put his face close to the canvas. "Unbelievable."

The paintings were changing. Certain of the frames began to move; colors mutated; brush strokes altered. Images that were blurry sharpened to crisp clarity. Hazy lines became distinct, and vague images became certain.

Anna and Martin watched, dumbstuck.

"This is not possible," Martin repeated. "The paint was dry. It was set. It can't change like this."

"But it is," Anna said in awe. "God is answering your prayer."

"My prayer? I wasn't praying!"

"Maybe not in a traditional way, but you were calling out for help."

Stunned, Martin turned back to the paintings and watched as his world of skepticism, logic, and cynicism melted away.

"I . . . I don't know what to say," Martin stammered. "I never thought that such a thing was possible. It's a . . . it's a . . ."

"Go on, Martin," Anna prompted quietly. "Call it for what it is."

"It's a miracle." Martin exclaimed, shocked by his own admission, but unable to deny his own eyes.

Anna began to weep softly for joy.

Thirty-Six

Iraklion, Crete

The pungent smell of saltwater hung heavy in the clear open air. A gentle breeze caressed the surface of the azure ocean and brought its unique perfume to the ferry that pushed its way through the water. Above, gulls dressed in brilliant white plumage highlighted with dark gray serenaded the passengers with sharp calls and struggled to stay airborne over the slow-moving boat.

"This is glorious," Katrin said, hugging herself. "Look at that sky. It's so blue, so rich in color. And the ocean is majestic. I could spend a lifetime trying to catch this image on canvas and I don't think I would do it justice."

"It is magnificent," Dick agreed. "If my wife knew how picture-perfect this place is, I'd be in big trouble for not bringing her along."

Nick sat leisurely in a deck chair, his face turned skyward and his eyes closed as the sun poured its light over him, and serenely smiled.

"How are you doing, Nick?" Dick asked. "You've been awful quiet since we left Iraklion."

"When you're in heaven, words are only distractions." Nick lowered his head and opened his eyes, drinking in the beauty of the Aegean Sea. "I have spent the last few years of my life holed up in a tiny, dingy little apartment in downtown Fort Worth. The view out my windows is of an overcrowded street and an office building. Which was OK at the time since the view out my window matched my mood. Things have changed now." Nick closed his eyes again and turned his face skyward.

"Do you mind if I ask you something?" Dick inquired, turning to face Nick.

"Shoot."

Dick leaned back against the guardrail. Less than six feet below him, the ocean gently swept by, releasing a symphony of soothing splashes, gurgles, bubbles, and babbles. The sound was as serene as the day was beautiful. "You're not like the others," Dick began. "The rest of the team has concerns and fears about the . . ." Dick looked for the right word ". . . mission. You, however, are like a kid in a candy store. You seem to be having fun."

"Not fun," Nick corrected. "I'm livin' again. I was dead before and my apartment was my tomb, my one-bedroom coffin. I had stopped livin' the day I fell through that floor and burned my legs. But now my perspective has changed."

"Because of the vision?" Katrin asked.

"Exactly," Nick replied leisurely. "Now I have a purpose. A man needs a purpose, don't you agree, Dick?"

"Absolutely."

"I thought the fire burned away my abilities and my direction. Now I know better. This mission has been my salvation." He paused and let go a long, wonderful sigh that had its origin not in weariness, but in long-missing bliss. "Do you know who Stephen Hawking is?" Nick asked, opening his eyes and looking at Dick and Katrin.

"I've heard the name," Dick answered. "But I couldn't tell you who he is."

"Me either," Katrin agreed.

"Stephen Hawking is a man who is bound to a wheelchair by a muscle disease," explained Nick. "He can't feed himself or dress himself. He can't even talk in a way that we could understand. But that doesn't stop him. He's a world-famous physicist. Now I only know about him because there was an article on him in the *Time* magazine I was readin' when all this started. He does all his work in his head. Huge calculations and he writes them in his head. They say he's the smartest man since Einstein. He thinks things the rest of us can't even understand."

Dick nodded. "I think I saw him on television once."

"I was thinkin' about him on the flight to Crete," Nick continued. "I wonder if he would be as smart if he were healthy? I mean, if he were like everyone else, would he bother with how the universe started and things like that? I don't know if he would agree with me, but he may be a better scientist because he's not like the rest of us."

"That's possible, I suppose," Dick answered.

"Well, I got to thinkin'. I wonder if my injuries might not make me a better person. I'm not confined to a wheelchair like Hawking. I can still walk, just not as fast, and not as far. I can still sit in a chair and get up on my own, with no help from nobody, so I've got that workin' for me. So maybe, just maybe, I'm not so bad off after all. Maybe there's still hope for me."

Dick laughed out loud. "Man, if you can think thoughts like that, then there's a whole world of hope for you."

"I have a question," Katrin said. "It's been bothering me for a long time; well, since the beginning anyway."

"Ask away, young lady," Dick replied. "We're going to be on this tub for a couple more hours at least."

"OK," Katrin offered. "Why us? We're not church people. Why did God choose us and not some others?"

Shaking his head, Dick responded, "I can't know for sure. After all, I'm the new kid on the block. Maybe we ought to ask it the other way. Why not you? God has used a variety of people to do His will. Adam knows more about this than I do, but I know that the Bible was written by more than forty different men over 1,500 years. Some of the books were written by kings and priests, others by common laborers. Some were educated, some were not. According to the Bible, God even used nations like Babylon and others to carry out His will. So God can use any person He wants."

"But why me? I'm just a painter."

"You're more than just a painter," Dick said. "You are more than what you do. God picked you for a reason. I can't tell you what that reason is, but I know He did."

"Maybe we'll find out when we get where we're goin'," Nick interjected.

"Perhaps," Katrin said, frustrated that she possessed no concrete answer.

"You gotta admit," Dick said, "if you're gonna get sent on a mission, then the Greek isles are a pretty good place to get sent."

"Hear, hear," Nick agreed. "I wonder how the others are doing in Ethiopia?"

"Especially Pruit," Katrin voiced.

Dick couldn't help notice a pained expression quickly dart across Nick's face.

"Why Pruit?" Dick asked.

"Because of his problem." She lowered her voice to a conspiratorial tone. "The drugs, I mean."

"I hope he was smart enough to leave all that stuff home," Nick said firmly. "Transportin' cocaine across international borders can be dangerous. Some countries lock you up and don't let you out until your trial—a decade or so down the road."

"I overhead Martin talking to him," Dick said. "He was telling him the same thing, and doing so in no uncertain terms."

"Good," Nick said. "If he's not careful, Pruit could ruin everything."

"He's a smart man," Katrin replied defensively. "I don't think he'd do anything stupid."

The pained look returned to Nick's face.

Turning his gaze back over the railing, Dick pondered their situation for a moment. "I wish we knew more," he said. "There are a lot of Greek islands around here, including some that are too small to appear on most maps. If we have to investigate each one individually, then we may spend the rest of our lives here."

"I can think of worse things," Nick said. "I can think of a lot of worse things."

Dick and Katrin chortled.

Twenty-five feet across the ferry's deck a young and studious looking woman with short fawn hair slipped her arm in the crook of the elbow of an equally studious looking man. She smiled lovingly, but her eyes were questioning.

The man, slim with sharp features and wire-rimmed glasses, removed the headset that he had been wearing, reached down to the small radiolike device attached to his belt, and turned down the volume.

A middle-aged couple strolled by the man and woman. "It's about time you turned off that music and paid attention to me," the woman said. "This is our honeymoon, you know."

The couple walked on, casting each other a small, knowing smile after having overheard the two lovebirds.

A few moments later the tourist couple was out of earshot.

"You getting anything?" the studious woman asked.

Raising his hand slightly, the man with the glasses nodded in the direction of the device he held. It was a small, palm-sized parabolic dish. Quickly he redirected the dish at Dick, Katrin, and Nick.

"Yeah," the man said. "It's working fine. I'm getting everything on tape."

"Good," the woman said. "Beck is going to meet us tomorrow on Karpathos. He's going to lead this side of the investigation. He'll want that tape."

"Not much on it, I'm afraid. They appear to be lost."

"They got this far. They know something. Perhaps they're being coy."

"Maybe, but I don't think so. I think they've come to the end of the trail."

"I hope not. For their sakes and ours, I hope not." The woman's tone was serious. "Do you know who the new guy is yet?"

"No more than we had when we flew out of the States. Dick Slay is his name. Seems like the leader type. The other two are deferring to him."

"Are they still talking visions and that nonsense?"

"Don't be such a skeptic," the man admonished. "This line of work calls for an open mind. To answer your question, yes, they are still talking about visions and the like. Except Slay. I think he's an outsider brought in at the last minute, probably to replace that Lindsay Blair woman. Do we know what happened to her?"

"She went back to London. Beck had her tailed to her home. Apparently she's locked herself away."

The woman nodded. "I'm ready with the other stuff. We can plant it at the hotel."

"That's the plan. We were lucky to get a room at the same hotel."

"No such thing as luck. It was strategy. Just like making reservations as a married couple."

"I thought that was just a bonus."

The woman glared viciously at the man. "One more comment like that and I'll break your ribs. We'll see how amorous you feel then." She reached up and put the headset back over his ears, then quickly turned her back on him.

In many ways, Dick felt as if he had been to the island of Karpathos before, even though he had never left the States, except for his military service. The sense of déjà vu was directly attributable to Martin's lectures, which he drilled into Dick's head. Martin even made Dick and the others memorize the hotel's number, made them practice placing international calls, and briefed them on the history of the Greek islands.

Now, standing in the bright open lobby of the Romantika hotel, Dick felt right at home. Romantika was one of the larger hotels on the island of Karpathos, but it was far from large with only 36 rooms. But a 500-room hotel would be overkill on an island of only 116 square miles. There were three other hotels of similar size in Pigadia, Karpathos, but the Romantika was right on the beach and came recommended by Pruit's travel agent.

Karpathos, an island approximately sixty miles northeast of Crete and midway between Crete and Rhodes, was a slice out of time. The ancient island boasted many ruins, including those of the classical town of Arkaseia and those of fifth-century Byzantine churches.

Even the island's name was intriguing. Karpathos was most likely derived from Árpaktos—Robbery Island. Pirates, who made their living plundering and terrorizing ancient ships, made use of the many inlets that surrounded the island. Dick couldn't help but wonder if what they were looking for had been brought to this island by seafarers who lived several millennia ago.

"Your room is ready," the hotel manager, a short, wiry, olive-skinned man, said with a smile that elevated his black mustache at least an inch. "You also have a message from a Martin St. James in California."

"Already?" Dick was surprised. "Martin must be putting in overtime."

"He said it was important and to call as soon as you arrived."

"He can't be serious," Katrin said, looking at the wall clock behind the check-in desk. "It's 4 P.M. here, that means that it must be 6 A.M. there."

"Thank you," Dick said to the manager. "I assume there is a phone in my room."

"Yes, of course," the manager smiled again. "I will find a woman to carry your things."

"Excuse me?" Dick said.

The manager laughed. "You are from America, no?"

"Yes," Katrin, who had been equally shocked, answered.

"On Karpathos," the manager explained, "both men and women do heavy work. Greece is the center of equality." He laughed again, and rang a bell. "The women here pride themselves on their stamina. It has been that way for many centuries."

A moment later a woman with dark skin and piercing black eyes appeared. She was wearing tall boots, into which had been tucked her white Turkish pants. She also wore a vest of the deepest blue. Black wisps of hair peeked out from the flower-print scarf she wore on her head. Wordlessly and effortlessly, she picked up the three large suitcases they had brought with them and headed for the stairs. The manager called out the room numbers to her as she walked past. Dick, Katrin, and Nick followed behind.

"Well, that was easy," the studious woman said as she stood in the lobby watching the trio they had been tailing walk up the stairs. "Now we have their room numbers."

"It pays to arrive on time," the man with glasses replied. "Luck is always prompt."

"Martin?" Dick said loudly into the phone. "Is that you?"

There was a hiss-filled delay, then Martin's voice, "Of course it's me; who else would answer my phone?"

"It's good to talk to you, too," Dick said sarcastically. "I didn't get you out of bed did I?"

Another delay as Dick's words were carried over the phone line, out of the building, across the island to a satellite dish that sent the signal to a geosynchronous-orbiting Syncom 4 satellite that relayed the message to a sister communication device hovering 22,300 miles over the equator. The signal was then downlinked to another dish and sent through a complex of computers and electronic devices to Martin St. James' mansion. It was a miracle of technology that people used every day without appreciating the science involved. Amazing as communicating across a dozen countries and several seas was, Dick was still annoyed by the short delay between the end of his words and the beginning of Martin's.

Standing next to Dick was Katrin, and seated on Dick's bed was Nick. Both had hastily followed the woman who had carried their bags to their rooms—the "bag woman" Nick whimsically called her—tipped her several hundred drachmae and then rushed to Dick's room. When they had arrived, Dick was already on the phone.

"We're all here," Dick said into the phone, "so what's up?"

(Pause)

"Things are changing here," Martin said with a barely perceptible snicker. "Literally. I have more information for you. You still have the equipment I sent?"

(Pause)

"Nick wanted to sell it so he could buy some baklava, but we persuaded him to hold out for a higher bidder."

(Pause)

"Stop kidding around," Martin snapped. "This is serious."

(Pause)

"All right, all right," Dick soothed. "Talk to me."

(Pause)

"I want you to set up the equipment and then call me back. I'm going to send you some things. Do you remember how to set the equipment up?"

(Pause)

"Martin, I've owned and operated my own trucking company for nearly twenty years, I think I can handle this."

(Pause)

"You better have Katrin do it. She seems to have a head for these things."

(Pause)

Dick scoffed. "Bye Martin, we'll call you back in a few minutes." Dick hung up the phone.

"Well?" Nick asked. "Anything new?"

"Sounds like he has a lead. He wants us to set up the computer and stuff." Dick turned to Katrin. "He said you should do it because you have a head for these things."

"It's not that hard," Katrin said. "I think he was just trying to get your goat."

Dick frowned deeply. "Well, he got it. Let's set up the stuff and call him back. I'm dying to know what he thinks is so important."

Opening one of the two suitcases in his room, Dick began extracting electronic equipment and handing it to Katrin, who set each device on the small table in the corner of the room.

"OK," she said. "First we open the laptop." Katrin pulled open the top to the Toshiba laptop computer. "Next we attach the printer." Moving effortlessly, she connected a gray cable from the back of the laptop computer to the small printer. "Then we attach one end of the phone line to the modem and the other end we place in the adapter. It's a good thing that Martin knew that telephone jacks in Greece are different from those in the United States, otherwise, we would be in a world of hurt."

"He is a smart cookie," Nick agreed.

Next, Katrin turned the computer on and waited for it to boot up. A few moments later they were ready to start.

"Now," Katrin began, "we activate our communication software so that we can receive messages over the phone." She paused as the screen flickered and changed to show that the software was up and running. "We go to our directory," Katrin moved the mouse she installed then clicked the left button. "Up comes the directory and there's Martin's name. Actually it's there twice."

Dick leaned over Katrin's shoulder and looked at the screen. Martin's name was listed as: St. James—voice, and St. James—data. Katrin clicked on the second listing. Seconds later a whine followed by several beeps emanated from the computer as the modem began dialing Martin St. James' phone number. His computer's phone number, actually.

The computer screen changed as the connection was made. Moments later the words Incoming Fax appeared on the monitor. A small hollow bar was slowly filled with a blue ribbon that indicated the percentage of the transmission received. When the indicator reached 100 percent, it was replaced by the words: Fax Received.

"Got it," Katrin explained. "Now let's print the fax and see what we have." Two keystrokes later the small printer was spewing out a four-page document.

"Is Martin still on-line?" Nick asked.

"No," Katrin answered, "he disconnected immediately."

"What? No good-bye?" Dick teased.

"I think he's just being cautious," Katrin offered.

"Cautious about what?" Dick said. "No one knows we're here except those who are supposed to know. I think he's just being paranoid."

"I don't know," Katrin responded. "My mother always said, 'Just because you're paranoid doesn't mean that they're not out to get you.'"

"Your mother said that?" Nick interjected.

"My mother is a very unique person," Katrin said evenly. "She's a good mother, but she is unique."

"Is it coming through clear enough?" the studious woman asked.

"Muffled, but it'll do," the man with the glasses answered. He was holding a flat black plastic square against the wall. "I wish we could have done this right. This microphone is pretty good, but we could have done better with an in-the-room bug, not to mention the video cameras."

"Well, Ross, there just wasn't enough time. We'll have to do it when they go out to dinner or something."

Ross Helms raised a hand to quiet his partner, Mickie Moore. "They've stopped talking," he said in a hushed voice. "But I can hear papers shuffling. They must be reading the fax."

Silence prevailed in the two rooms.

"Wait a second," Ross said as he closed his eyes to block out all distraction.

Frustrated at not being able to hear, Mickie stepped quickly into the bathroom and then returned with a glass tumbler, which she pressed against the wall. Placing her ear next to the glass she said, "It's not very sophisticated, but it works."

She placed the glass just in time to hear a male voice say, "Incredible. Just incredible."

Thirty-Seven

Addis Ababa, Ethiopia

"We were lucky," Ted said as he guided the ancient Toyota Landcruiser down a rough dirt road, oblivious to the washboard texture that rattled the vehicle so vigorously that it made speaking below a shout impossible. "Our phones work pretty good most of the time, but things sent by computer can get real garbled. There's a lot of noise on the line, you know. I have a computer and an Internet e-mail address, but the country's network system is so unreliable that it can take up to two weeks for me to get my messages."

With a quick turn of the wheel, Ted avoided a large pothole. He continued: "Of course, after what you three told me last night, I shouldn't call it luck. More like providence I would say."

"That's closer to the truth," Adam said loudly. "I can see why you decided to leave the Volvo home and take the four-wheel drive." Adam's back hurt from the rough ride.

"Yeah," Ted shouted back. "We're going to run into some rough road up ahead. Most of the roads in Ethiopia are unpaved. The farther you get away from town, the worse they get."

"There are roads rougher than this?" Pruit asked in dismay.

"This isn't rough," Ted replied evenly. "This is pretty good, actually. Not much worse than Park Avenue, wouldn't you say, Pruit?"

Pruit looked at Rachel, who shared the back seat with him and rolled his eyes.

"Good?" Rachel exclaimed. "Tell me you're kidding. You could use this road to dislodge kidney stones."

"I guess I've gotten used to it." Ted chortled. "It doesn't seem that bad to me."

Adam laughed. "How much longer before we get there?"

"In time or miles?"

"Time."

"The better part of the day, assuming we don't break down on the way."

"There's a comforting thought," Pruit offered as he once again adjusted his position on the seat.

"Are you sure your friend will help?" Adam asked as the vehicle lurched and bounced Adam up so that he hit his head on the ceiling of the cruiser. "Shouldn't we slow down?"

"Yes and no," Ted answered. "Yes, he will help. He knows everything there is to know about the area. He has to since he makes his living as a guide for hunters and adventurers. And no, we can't go slower. If we go too slow, the vibrations get worse. Pretty soon the whole car is rattling. It's like being inside a tin can rolling down a cobblestone road."

Adam looked out the window at the serrated, sharp-edged mountains. Distant ridges hued blue served as a majestic backdrop to the closer ranges that were dressed in variegated greens. Acacia trees punctuated the hillsides and softened their steeply angled slopes. The sky was a rich blue, deep as the ocean, and lightly augmented with a sparse collection of innocent-looking marshmallow clouds.

They were descending from Addis Ababa's 8,000 feet toward the Abbay River northwest of the capital city. They had lost no time in leaving after receiving Martin's fax. They each felt that they were on the brink of discovering what tens of thousands of others have hungered for, even died for.

Last night they sat with Ted and Lisa and poured out their story. While all had agreed that secrecy was paramount, none could see how they could progress without the aid of someone intimately familiar with Ethiopia. So they shared their remarkable tale, holding nothing back.

Ted and Lisa listened politely and intently, asking no questions and never interrupting. When Rachel and Pruit had finished describing their experiences, and after Adam filled in the details of his and Martin's research, Ted leaned back and closed his eyes.

For long moments he sat still, neither moving nor speaking. He revealed no emotion, offered no opinions. Five interminably long minutes later, Ted leaned forward and said: "Well, I can't speak for Lisa, but I can say this. If anyone, anyone at all, had come here and told me what you've just told me, I would have been quick to recommend professional help from a mental health expert. But since it's you, Adam, and since I've known you for so many years, I am left with no other option but to believe you."

Lisa agreed, but looked shell-shocked.

"I assume," Ted went on, "that you've considered the ramifications of such a find. You know the world will never be the same."

"I know," Adam replied thoughtfully. "I don't know what the world will do. I don't even know much beyond our next step, but I do know that we have no choice. We have been given a challenge, a mission from God, and we could not turn it down."

"Of course not," Lisa agreed. "Who could? You have displayed remarkable courage and faithfulness."

"I just wish we knew more," Rachel confessed. "It's like walking across a raging river by hopping from one stepping-stone to another, but never quite knowing when or where the next stone will appear."

"But that's the whole point," Ted offered. "Faith isn't faith until acted upon, is it?"

"I suppose not," Rachel said. "But it's hard."

"If it were easy," Lisa said, "then anyone could have done the job. Apparently you have something that God finds valuable and useful."

Pruit listened quietly, stoically. Ever sensitive to those around him, Adam could see that Pruit was struggling with his own spirituality. Without Pruit uttering a word, Adam knew the question the advertising man was asking himself: "What is it that God sees in me? Needs from me?"

"That bump on the head knock you senseless, buddy?" Ted asked, rousing Adam back to the present.

"Just thinking," Adam answered. He unconsciously rubbed the top of his head where he had smacked it on the ceiling of the Land-cruiser.

"Share those thoughts," Pruit encouraged. "We have an awful lot of hours to kill."

"I was thinking how amazing it is that three weeks ago my biggest concern was what I was going to preach the coming Sunday." Adam laughed. "Now I'm being bounced down a dirt road in Ethiopia, surrounded by some of the most beautiful scenery I have ever seen."

"You should see the landscape during the rainy season," said Ted. "Not even Ireland is as green."

"Don't you ever miss the States?" Rachel inquired.

"Sometimes," Ted answered. "I miss first-run movies and popcorn. I miss sitcoms on the television and easy access to bookstores. But it's a small price to pay."

"You really have come to love this place, haven't you?" Rachel asked.

Ted nodded. "I see things here that others only read about or experience through a "National Geographic" television special. I was far more comfortable in the United States, but I'm far more alive in Ethiopia."

"Well," Pruit offered loudly to be heard over the road noise. "Get us down this road in one piece and I'll buy you the best TV satellite system made."

"Really?" Ted said with glee. "You're on."

"I can see why you love it here," Adam interjected. "It's captivating."

"Careful, buddy," Ted responded quickly, smiling like a beacon. "Ethiopia is a seductive mistress. She'll lure you in as sure as the sun rises."

"Is that a bad thing?" Adam asked.

"No, but it's not for everyone. Life here is hard and filled with disappointments. True, there is great beauty here, but there are also many anguished souls. The people are scarred, wounded by the former socialist government, civil war, ethnic schisms, uncertainty, and famine. Outsiders who stay do so because they have to, compelled by some pressing reason. For me, it is my work."

Silence. Self-examiniation. Soul-searching.

Adam thought about Ted's words. In three weeks his life had abruptly changed. He did feel more alive, that he was involved in something greater than he was capable of imagining. The sense filled him with awe, wonder, and excitement. And, for some reason, it filled him with the sharpest fear.

Ahead of them was the greatest historical achievement ever. Intuitively, however, Adam knew the future also held the greatest danger. Still, he was almost overwhelmed with an exuberance of excitement and a sense of well-being.

Adam broke into song.

Less than one mile behind the foursome a dark brown Ford Explorer bounced roughly down the dirt road. The lone occupant swore loudly and frequently. Used to tailing "marks" on paved streets in major cities, he was finding this jaunt into the countryside to be no pleasure trip. The vehicle was new, strong, and capable of handling the road easily. The driver, however, was a different matter.

Still, it was his job to keep track of the people in front of him. The goal was to follow without being seen, an easy goal on crowded city streets, an impossible task on a deserted dirt road. The rooster tail of dirt kicked up by the Toyota made it easy to follow. Unfortunately, the dirt kicked up by his own four-by-four made it simple for him to be spotted.

"Come on!" Hector shouted through the windshield. "Slow down! This isn't some off-road race."

Ted's vehicle didn't slow. Consequently, neither did Hector's.

"OK, talk to me," Quince ordered within minutes of his arrival in the Addis Ababa hotel where Hector and Carl had set up operations.

Quince was wearing his trademark jeans, boots, and golf shirt. Dr. Julian Newton, who had begrudingly left his home in San Diego for a grueling set of flights to Addis Ababa, lay on the hotel bed, no longer caring if his tan slacks and silk shirt became any more rumpled. He wanted sleep, and everything else was secondary.

"Don't start napping yet, Newton," Quince said sharply. "You need to hear this."

"We've been traveling nonstop for days," Newton whined. "I'm not sure I'm capable of a sustained conscious thought."

"An archeologist like you should be used to travel," Quince barked.
"Travel, yes. A race around the world, no."

"Sit up and listen, Newton, or I'll leave you here in Africa."

Slowly Julian Newton rose to a sitting position, considered saying that being left in Ethiopia was preferable to the company he had been keeping, but decided against it.

To Carl, Quince snapped: "Fill me in."

Carl gave a short nod, made eye contact with his troubling gray eyes, and spoke: "We arrived the same day as our targets and immediately set up temporary operations here to await your arrival. While I was setting up communications and transportation, Hector—using the information provided us by the wiretaps on Adam Bridger's home—took up a position outside the Hawthornes' place. They live in a school for adults. He teaches them to read, and she's a nurse.

"That's intelligence you already have," Carl continued. "Hector had no trouble tapping the phone line. He also picked up a great deal of information from their conversations outside."

"How can he do that without being seen?" Newton asked groggily.

"With a simple listening device that comes with a parabolic dish," Carl offered. "That night, after they had all gone to bed, Hector was able to make secret entry into the house. He placed several bugs and a relay transmitter to boost the signal. He had a good copy on them from that time on. Using our satellite linkup, Hector has made contact every two hours."

"Where is he now?" Quince was pacing impatiently.

"On the road to Abbay River."

"Abbay?" Newton wondered aloud.

"Also called the Blue Nile," Carl added. "Martin St. James faxed something to Bridger. Unfortunately, we had not expected a fax, so we couldn't intercept it, but we could listen in on the subsequent conversation. It seems that the paintings that St. James is using as a guide . . . well, this is a little hard to say because it is so outrageous . . . but the paintings are changing. Now you and I know that's crazy, but they believe it."

"You had better believe it, too," Quince snapped. "I know Martin St. James and he is a bonafide genius. We even hired him once to help us with a development problem. Our people had

worked on it for two months—and I hire nothing but the best—
and they came up empty. St. James solved the problem in a week.
And I know for a fact that we weren't his only client. He doesn't
exaggerate."

"But sir," Carl objected quietly. "Paintings that change by themselves?"

"It may be a code phrase," Quince snapped. Weariness was
making him edgy. "Go on with your report."

Carl cleared his throat. "Anyway, the material St. James sent really lights a fire under them. They begin planning their next move.
First they told their stories to Ted Hawthorne . . ."

"Cut to the chase," Quince demanded.

"You got it. Based on what St. James sent them, they packed up
and took off for the Abbay River. There's a small town near the river
and a guide lives there. Hawthorne knows him and is going to ask
him to guide them to the river."

"Do we have this guide's name?"

"Yes. His name is Galefo."

"Is that his first or last name?" Quince asked.

"That's all we have on him so far. Just the one name. Galefo."

"Do we know the name of the town in which he lives?" Newton
asked, attempting to be part of the discussion.

Carl shook his head. "No idea but we could find out in short order.
Since we couldn't see the faxed material, we have no idea where
on the Abbay River they're going. That's why Hector is following
them."

"He has good transportation?" Quince inquired.

"Yes sir, just as you ordered," Carl shifted on his feet. "We were
able to purchase a new Ford Explorer. He's probably riding in the
lap of luxury right now."

"Good." Quince smiled for the first time. "It seems like our forward thinking may pay off. Did you make the rest of the arrangements?"

"Yes," Carl answered confidently. "I have a vehicle ready to go
right now. It's also a four-wheel drive. I thought we might be traveling off-road some . . ."

Newton groaned loudly and lay back on the bed.

Carl looked at Quince and smiled. Quince shook his head in disgust.

"I also have made arrangements for a helicopter for short hops and a plane for longer flights. We're ready to cover every inch of Ethiopia."

"Search equipment, too?" Quince inquired.

"Yes, sir," Carl answered proudly. "We're ready for every situation, and we're ready now."

Unconsciously, Quince rubbed his hands together in anticipation. "So all we have to do is wait for them to find the ark and then snatch it for our own."

"But will we be able to get it out of Ethiopia?" Newton asked from his supine position on the bed. "If anyone finds out what you're up to, then you're in big trouble. Real big trouble."

"If anyone finds out what we are doing," Quince said emphasizing the word "we," "you're as much a part of this as I am. And to answer your question: Yes, we can get it out of Ethiopia. Plans have already been made. Haven't they, Carl?"

"They have indeed, Mr. Quince," Carl replied with a sinister grin. "They have indeed."

"Get Hector on the radio," Quince ordered. "I need him to do something for us."

Thirty-Eight

Karpathos, Greece

The sun, a golden disk of waning light, was slowly sinking toward the azure waves of the Aegean. Above, the sky was transforming from brilliant blue to dark, somber grays. The sky was a reflection of the mood shared by the two despondent people who sat at the white metal table on the open patio outside the Romantika Hotel.

"Somehow I thought this would be easier." Katrin sighed heavily and rubbed her eyes. "I don't know why I thought that, but I did."

"I suppose when you're on a mission from God you just naturally expect things to go your way." Nick offered his words without turning his head, keeping his eyes fixed on the ocean that was now sparkling with the light of the setting sun.

"Is that wrong?" Katrin asked. "Is that a misguided expectation on my part?"

Nick shook his head. "You'll have to ask Dick when he gets back. He's more of an expert in spiritual matters than I am. I'm still new to all this."

"You don't seem too upset about our failings?"

Turning to face Katrin, Nick smiled. "I suppose not. Things will work out. I don't know how. I don't even know why I think that, but I feel that things are going to work out just fine."

"You've changed, haven't you, Nick?" Katrin asked. "I don't know you that well, but from all that you've said, you used to be pretty bitter."

"I was very bitter," Nick agreed, taking a sip of the strong coffee the waiter had brought. "After the accident I hated everyone and everything. I was impossible to live with. Just ask my ex-wife."

"What happened to your wife?"

"She remarried about six months later. I heard it was a nice wedding."

"Do you miss her?" Katrin asked, averting her eyes.

"Yes," Nick answered honestly. "But we didn't have a strong marriage to begin with. Even before the accident, I was self-absorbed. I don't think I was a good husband. I was a good provider, but that's not the same thing."

There was silence as Katrin took in Nick's confession, and as Nick wondered about his newfound ability to be honest about himself.

"How about you?" Nick inquired. "How come you haven't married?"

Katrin didn't answer immediately. She was uncomfortable about personal questions. Turning her head she stared out over the ocean. "Men aren't interested in me," she replied with a shrug, her voice barely above a whisper. "What I mean is, I'm not the type of woman men like."

"What type of women do men like?" Nick asked, puzzled.

"I don't know," she said, "but whatever it is, I'm not part of it."

"Nonsense," Nick blurted. "I know dozens of men who would be interested in you. Not all men are alike, you know. We aren't produced in cookie-cutter fashion. One man can be very different from the next. Just look at the difference between, say, Adam and Martin, or me and Pruit. We're not the same."

"Still . . ."

"Still, nothing. You are an attractive woman. You are bright, personable, and talented. Any man not interested in you would be an idiot. And that includes me."

A slight red tint crept up Katrin's face. She struggled not to make eye contact. "That's . . . that's a nice thing to say, but I'm not sure it's true."

"It's true," Nick said firmly. "To be honest, I'm attracted to you."

Katrin's head snapped around, her eyes wide at the revelation.

"I'm sorry," Nick said. "I shouldn't blurt out such things. I'm not a refined man like Pruit. I'm just a broken former fireman who let a bad situation get worse."

"I don't know what to say."

Nick shrugged. "I didn't mean to embarrass you, Katrin, but it's the truth. I find you very attractive, and it just rips me up to see you so down on yourself. As far as I'm concerned you stand head and shoulders above every other woman I've met."

"I wish I had your optimism," Katrin replied quietly. "It's clear that your vision has changed you, but mine has only confused me. One moment I'm excited to be here in Greece on this expedition, the next I'm afraid and feel lost and alone."

"You're not alone," Nick assured her. "We're in this together, all of us. It's going to work out, and all of us will be changed. I don't know how, when, or even why, but I know it's going to happen."

"After today, I'm not so sure. All we had to do was rent a boat, and we couldn't even do that."

"You couldn't?" A voice said behind them. Turning they saw Dick Slay.

Shaking his head, Nick said, "It was unbelievable, Dick. There's not a single boat to be chartered, leased, or rented. Every one of them has been rented by someone else. It's as if someone has purposely secured the rights to every boat on the island."

"What about a fishing boat or a sponge boat?" Dick asked.

"Same thing," Katrin answered. "Not only that, but they've been rented for days in advance. Not only can't we get a boat today, we can't get one anytime this next week."

Dick pulled up a chair and sat down. "This isn't good," he admitted.

"What about you?" Katrin asked. "Did you have any luck?"

"No," Dick replied, shaking his head. "This is weird. I tried to hire a pilot to fly us over some of the islands, but I was turned down every place I went. I couldn't find a private plane or helicopter pilot who would do the job. They said that they were booked up."

"I didn't think there were that many tourists around here," Nick said. "It sure seems suspicious."

236

"Not really," a man's voice interjected. Seated at a table next to them were three people, two men and a woman. "I'm sorry," the man said. "I'm afraid I've been eavesdropping for the last few minutes. I don't mean to be rude, but it's always so good to hear a voice from home when you're in a foreign country."

The man rose and approached their table. "I'm Jason Beck," he said, extending his hand to Dick who shook it, and then to Nick and Katrin. "I and my colleagues are here on a little vacation. Let me introduce Mickie Moore and Ross Helms." The two smiled and nodded. "Actually I should say Ross and Mickie Helms. They were married a couple of months back. I have trouble remembering that." Jason turned and faced the two. Ross reached out and took Mickie's hand. "We're from Seattle."

"Pleased to meet you," Dick said. "I'm Dick Slay from San Diego. This is Katrin Couer from Ojai, California, and Nick Stern of Fort Worth."

"I apologize for listening in," Beck said apologetically. "I also want to apologize for interrupting, but I think I can help."

"Help?" Katrin said. "Help us?"

"Exactly," Beck answered. "May we join you?"

"Sure," Dick replied. "Pull up a chair."

The three did just that. It was crowded around the small table that was meant to seat four people but was now pressed into service seating six.

"Let me explain," Beck began. "We work for Datadyne in Seattle. Ever heard of it?"

"It's a big computer company, isn't it?" Nick answered.

"Software actually," Beck said. "We don't make computers; we design and market the software that operates computers. Anyway, I'm one of the many corporate vice presidents and I'm here with two of our employees." He nodded in the direction of Mickie and Ross. "Datadyne is very successful and our founder, Gerald Quince, enjoys rewarding his employees. So, several times a year he selects two employees for an all-expense-paid vacation to the Greek islands. Quince's grandmother was Greek so he's always had a soft spot in his heart for this place. Anyway, Ross and Mickie were chosen to go as a wedding gift. I got to come along because they work in my department."

"He's trying to marry off some more people in the department so he can come back," Mickie said with a laugh.

"She's not kidding," Beck said with a broad smile. "I could learn to love it here."

"It is beautiful," Katrin agreed.

"When I overheard your dilemma," Beck continued, "I couldn't help but interrupt to offer my services. We have a boat available to us."

"You do?" Katrin said excitedly.

"A yacht actually," Beck answered. "It belongs to Datadyne, but we have use of it for our trip. Since no other boats are available, I thought you might allow us to take you where you need to go."

"That's a very generous offer, Mr. Beck," Dick said.

"Not really," Beck answered, "and please call me Jason. We were planning on sailing around a few of the islands tomorrow anyway and maybe doing some skin diving, so it's no bother to us. We had no special destination in mind."

"You operate the boat yourself?" Nick asked.

"Oh, no," Beck said quickly. "I'm into software, not sailing. The yacht has an experienced crew, so we will be safe. How about it? Let us help out. We would enjoy the company of fellow Americans."

"I would enjoy the company of another English-speaking woman," Mickie said with a smile. Katrin returned the smile.

Dick made eye contact with Nick and Katrin. Nick nodded and Katrin shrugged. "OK," Dick said. "If you're sure you don't mind."

"It will be a pleasure," Beck replied. "Just where is it you want to go?"

"We thought it might be interesting to look at some of the uninhabited islands around here."

"I understand there are a lot of those," Mickie offered.

"Quite a few," Dick agreed, "but they should be close enough."

"It doesn't matter," Beck offered. "We can always sleep on the yacht. That way we don't have to rush. We are equipped to stay out for days if necessary."

"That must be nice," Nick intoned.

"It is," Beck answered. "The yacht is a 103-foot Westport McQueen motor yacht, with enough room for everyone. We have every luxury, including an onboard hot tub. Have you ever been on a yacht before?"

"No," Nick answered.

"Then you're in for a treat." Turning to Dick, Beck asked, "What time did you want to get underway?"

"Tomorrow morning sound all right?"

"Absolutely," Beck answered quickly. "I'll let the captain know so he can prepare."

"We sure appreciate this," Katrin said. "You're a godsend."

"See," Nick said confidently to Katrin. "I told you it would all work out."

The *Quintessence* rocked lazily in the gentle swells as it slowly sliced through ocean water. The day was bright, the breeze warm and embracing, and the sea hypnotic.

"Not even the chamber of commerce could improve on this day," Katrin said as she lay sunning herself on the foredeck. She wore a modest dark-blue swimsuit that she had purchased the evening before at the insistent encouragement of Mickie.

"It's a shame we can't bottle this up and take it home," Mickie agreed as she rolled over onto her stomach to allow the sun's rays to caress her already bronzed skin. Unlike Katrin's conservative swimsuit, Mickie wore a close-fitting bikini that revealed enough skin to not only embarrass most of the men onboard, but even the gulls that followed overhead.

"You did put that sunscreen on as I suggested, didn't you?" Mickie asked. "With your light skin you could burn to a crisp before we get where we're going."

"I bathed in it," Katrin replied jovially, glad she was not the only woman on board.

"Good," Mickie said in a muffled voice. "Personally, I plan to roast myself through and through."

"Living in Seattle as you do, I'm surprised that you have enough sun to get a tan like that."

"That's a misnomer about Seattle," Mickie responded dreamily. "We get plenty of sun, just not much in winter, but then that's what tanning salons are for."

"Never been to one," Katrin said. "Too busy painting pictures, I guess."

"You need to treat yourself more," Mickie replied. "Life's too short to be locked away in a studio."

"You're probably right. How long have we been out here on the deck?"

"There are only two times in my world, Katrin—too long and not long enough."

"Let me guess. Your answer is, not long enough."

"Now you're catching on." Mickie laughed.

"I like you, Mickie," Katrin confessed. "It's good to have a woman to talk to. I certainly wouldn't be out here sunbathing if you weren't around."

"I'm just trying to save you from committing a horrible crime. You know it's illegal to come to the Greek isles and return home without a tan. They could lock you away."

"With my white skin, they'd have more than enough evidence to convict me."

"Stay with me, kid, we'll have you bronzed and beautiful in no time."

"That's a pretty big task," Katrin said.

"Not at all." Mickie propped herself up on one elbow and looked at Katrin, who lay on her back. "You're gorgeous; you just don't know it. All you have to do is let it out."

"Now you're exaggerating."

"Give yourself a break, girl. Being a woman in this world is hard enough without us turning on ourselves. You've got more going for you than you realize. Nick certainly thinks so."

"Oh, I don't know . . ."

"Don't argue with Mother Mickie. I've seen how he looks at you. I think he's slipping down the slope of love, kiddo."

"He's just being nice."

"My mother used to say, 'The lies we tell ourselves are the lies we believe the most.'"

"Meaning?"

"Meaning, the man has his eye on you. All you have to do is look at him to see it. You give the guy a chance and he'll come running."

Katrin said nothing.

"How do you feel about him?" Mickie asked.

"I don't know," Katrin answered honestly. "I've never thought of him or anyone in those terms."

Mickie lay on her stomach again then said, "Well, it's time you started thinking about it."

Katrin fell silent and let her eyes fix on one of the brown-and-white gulls that paced the yacht as it coursed slowly through the water. Could Mickie be right? she asked herself. And if so, how should I feel about it?

"This is great," exclaimed Nick. "I can't believe you had fishing poles stowed away on this tub."

"We have almost everything on this, as you call it, tub," Beck said. "We have diving gear, video games, a VCR with all the latest movies. We even have a small library. Mr. Quince doesn't skimp when it comes to his employees."

"I bet you don't have water skis," Dick interjected good naturedly.

"You've got me there," Beck answered. "As good a boat as the *Quintessence* is, I don't think she is fast enough to pull a skier behind her."

"She doesn't seem to be going all that fast now, either," Nick intoned.

"That's because we're trolling lures behind us," Beck responded. "If we go too fast we can't fish. And on a day like this, that would be a crime."

"You got that right," Dick said. "I haven't been fishing in years. What about you, Ross. Do you like fishing?"

"This is my first time, actually. I've always been too busy with school-work or employment to do much else. But I think I could come to enjoy this."

"Don't get too used to it," Beck said. "We do have to go back some-day."

"Perhaps," Nick said, "but not today. Definitely not today."

"How long before we drop anchor?" Dick inquired, enjoying the use of nautical terms.

"The captain said we should arrive in . . ." Beck looked at his watch, "another couple of hours. He was confused about why we would want to go to an island that has nothing but goats on it."

"At least he knew where it was," Dick said. "I was afraid that he would think I was nuts."

"His charts are very detailed. There isn't an island out there that he can't find. But there are more than fifty islands and most of them are uninhabited. I don't imagine that many people go to them."

Dick offered no explanation as to why he had chosen that island, and curiously, no one asked. For a reason Dick could not define, that observation made him uncomfortable. But best he could tell, his discomfort was not shared by Nick or Katrin.

Thirty-Nine

Ethiopia

Rachel patted her stomach. "Ugh! That was quite a dinner," she said. "I may be eating that for a week."

Ted smiled. "*Injera* and *wat* take a little getting used to. But it is filling."

"Which was the flat bread?" Rachel asked.

"Injera," Ted replied. "The stew is called wat."

"I don't think it will catch on in the States," Pruit said. "A little too greasy."

"A little?" Adam said with surprise. "That may be an understatement."

"You seemed to eat your share," Rachel replied with a grin. "You should learn to make it. I'm sure it would be a hit at the next church potluck."

They all laughed, more from the weariness of the drive than from the humor of the comment. They were sitting twenty yards away from Galefo's small wooden cabin. The day had been long and the drive grueling. Sitting on the warm ground under the stars, surrounded by acacia trees, Adam, Rachel, Pruit, and Ted unwound.

The air was still and heavy with the smell of the trees, the dry grass, and the hard soil. Rachel leaned back against Adam who held her in his arms. From time to time he would lower his head so that his nose barely touched her hair. She smelled sweet to him. Not the sweetness that comes from perfume, body lotion, or deodorant soap, but the fragrance that was uniquely hers.

"That Galefo is an odd one," Pruit said, breaking the silence. "And tall too."

"He's six-foot-eight if he's an inch," Ted agreed. "But that's not what makes him unique. He's a much sought after guide in these parts. No one knows this area or this part of the Abbay Gorge as he does. He has spent most of his life living in the gorge or the surrounding forest region. But you would expect that from a former *shufta* rebel."

"A rebel?" Rachel exclaimed. "He is a rebel?"

"Was, actually," Ted answered. "He's been out of that line of work for more than five years now. That's when I first met him. He wanted to improve his son's reading skills. He speaks our language well, doesn't he?"

"Surprisingly well," Adam agreed. "Did you teach him?"

"No, he was already fluent in most aspects of our language. What he didn't understand was Western monetary terms. You know, dollar, pound, that sort of thing. Since he was changing careers from guerrilla warfare to guide for rich adventurers, he needed to know some of those things. His son was a quick study, too."

"I didn't see his son," Rachel said.

"He died about a year ago," Ted replied somberly. "He became ill with a fever. No one knows what disease he was infected with. Galefo was leading a team of scientists into the gorge when it happened. When he returned he found his son dead."

"How awful," Rachel exclaimed. "He just found him dead?"

"Sometimes Galefo will be gone for weeks and the boy would be left to fend for himself. That in itself was OK, since the boy was fifteen years old. That's adulthood around here. Especially when you're reminded that the average life span isn't much over forty or forty-five."

"So Galefo lives alone now?"

"Yes," Ted answered. "His wife was killed in the ongoing civil war more than a decade ago. He's never remarried."

"I know this is none of my business," Rachel said, "but I couldn't help noticing that he has a scar on the right side of his head and that a portion of his ear is missing."

"Bullet to the head," Ted replied. "It just grazed him. The scar you see is what's left of the injury. You probably also noticed that his right leg is crooked."

Rachel nodded. "I also saw a large scar on the leg. It looks like an old, badly healed compound fracture."

"Right. He fell down the gorge while attempting to evade government troops during his rebel days. His comrades set the leg the best they could, but they were far from being doctors. Since there was no hospital nearby, Galefo had to heal on his own. That's when he quit the rebel work. He couldn't keep up any longer. Rather than slow them down, he left. For him it was the ultimate sacrifice for the cause. He would rather have died."

"Incredible," Pruit said.

"But make no mistake," Ted continued. "He may have been too slow to keep up with his comrades, but he's plenty fast for us."

"Does the fighting still go on?" Adam asked, pulling Rachel closer and holding her tight.

"Some, but not as much. There is still some ethnic fighting going on, but we'll be safe with Galefo. He's a hero to many of the *shufta*. As long as we're with him we'll be safe. Without him we could be in big trouble."

"Doesn't he want to join us?" Rachel inquired. "I feel like we are isolating him."

Ted shook his head. "He is a very private man. He has isolated himself and that makes him happy. Most likely he has already gone to sleep."

"Speaking of sleep," Pruit said. "Where do we sack out?"

Pointing to a small shed near the broken-down cabin that Galefo called home, Ted said, "There. It's not much, but it has cots, blankets, and an oil lamp. You can sleep there or in the car."

"What about. . . ?" Rachel asked delicately.

Ted looked puzzled for a moment, then caught on. "Sorry Rachel, there are no . . . facilities here. There is only . . ." Ted extended his hand to arm's length and drew an invisible arch in the air to indicate the surrounding wilderness. "I'm afraid there's no indoor plumbing. Actually, because Galefo has chosen to live away from any village, there's no outdoor plumbing either."

"So we are going to rough it," Adam said. "Just like the Boy Scouts."

Just then a high-pitched, eerie sound drifted in from the distant night. Instinctively Rachel bolted upright, her eyes wide.

"Hyena," Ted said. "They sound like the Ghost of Christmas Past, don't they? I bet you didn't hear anything like that on your Boy Scout camping trips, Adam."

Adam just shook his head. "How anyone can call that noise a laugh is beyond me. It sounded more like a banshee's screech."

"Not if you're a hyena," Ted joked as he stood to his feet. "It's time for us to call it a night, too. Galefo will want to leave shortly after sunrise. And don't worry about the hyenas. They eat only dead things— usually. They're scavengers, you know."

"I feel much better," Pruit said sarcastically. "I'm sure I'll sleep well tonight knowing that."

"Coming?" Ted asked the group.

"In a minute," Adam said. "I want to take in the night a little more and let my dinner settle. We won't be long."

The three watched as Ted walked to the small wooden shack.

"Well?" Adam asked. "Are we all ready for the big day tomorrow?"

"I guess so," Rachel answered. "Ready or not, we'll be going."

There were a few moments of silence as each person wondered what daylight would bring.

"What about you, Pruit?" Adam inquired. "Are you ready?"

"I guess so," Pruit said shortly. "I don't think it would matter much if I weren't."

"You're not having second thoughts are you?" Adam asked seriously.

Shaking his head Pruit replied, "I don't know what kind of thoughts I'm having. To be truthful, I'm getting really edgy."

"That's to be expected," Rachel answered.

"It is?"

"Sure. Actually, you've been doing far better than I thought was possible." Rachel leaned toward Pruit. "Most people are extremely irritable when they come off a sustained cocaine habit. I've been waiting for you to blow up."

"I have moments when I think I might, but then it all melts away." Pruit looked perplexed. "I don't understand it. I've tried to kick my habit several times and it just makes me impossible to live with. But this time I've been off the coke for over a week and . . . well, it's different. I should be biting your heads off. Instead, I've gotten more mellow. I have my moments, don't misunderstand, but nothing like before."

"That's because you have help this time," Rachel said.

"I know, and I appreciate your support."

"She's not talking about our help," Adam interjected. "She's talking about God's help." Adam saw Pruit stiffen. "That's still hard for you to believe? After all you've seen? After all you've experienced? God has His hand on you, Pruit. Like it or not."

"That's all a mystery to me," Pruit confessed. "Spiritual things have always been something to be ignored. I'm not sure I even believe in God."

"Yes you do," Adam said. "You can sense Him in every fiber of your being. You just haven't acknowledged it because of the price it would cost you."

"What price?"

"Everything you've done in your life, every achievement you've attained has been the direct result of your personal efforts," Adam explained, "but now you are faced with something your clever mind can't manipulate. If you acknowledge that, then you also have to acknowledge that some things are beyond your planning and control. That would require that you have faith, something you've never had before."

"You're not going to preach me a sermon are you, Adam?" Pruit snapped. "I'm not in the mood."

"No sermon, Pruit," Adam replied sincerely. "Just trying to open the package so that you can see inside."

"What package?"

"The package of your life. Inside is everything that makes you you. But it takes courage to take off the wrapper and look."

"But what if I don't want to look inside my life? What if I don't like what I see?"

"Every man has to look sooner or later, Pruit. Sooner is better." Adam stood to his feet. Rachel joined him. "You are a courageous man, Pruit, perhaps the most courageous man I've met. You've achieved many things. You've built a business that has brought you wealth, power, and prestige, but you found that it couldn't make you happy. So you tried something else—cocaine. Instead of bringing you happiness, it has brought misery. Cocaine is expensive, Pruit, and I don't mean in dollars. I don't know you well enough to know what pieces of your life you're paying out, but I know this is your chance to be free of that debt."

"You mean by helping you find the ark of the covenant." Pruit broke eye contact.

"No, that's not what I mean," Adam said quickly. "This has nothing to do with our quest. Your quest is a personal one that can only be reached with the help of Christ."

"I don't know, Preacher. I just don't know." Pruit stood. It seemed to Adam that he stood a little shorter, as if he had been mildly deflated, some of his life leaking away through the hole in his soul. "This is natural for you, Adam. It's a whole different universe to me."

"I know just how you feel," Rachel spoke up.

"How can you know?" Pruit asked more harshly than he meant. "You don't have a drug problem. You're a believer. You're even married to a preacher. And your vision was one of beauty. I got physical affliction."

Rachel bowed her head for a moment, then lifted it to face Pruit. "What kind of car do you drive, Pruit?"

"A Jaguar. Why?"

"Did you build it?"

"Of course not! Don't be ridiculous."

"I have a reason for asking," Rachel admitted. "When you look at me you see a woman, a doctor, and the wife of a minister. And yes, you see a believer. But what you're seeing is a new Rachel— one built by someone else.

"When I first met Adam," Rachel continued, "I was as far from being a believer in Christ as anyone could be. I was not only not a believer, but I was also fanatical in my disdain for things spiritual. I was a proud, arrogant atheist who thought that only fools and children could believe in a loving God and a Savior named Jesus. But when Adam came into the hospital with a burst appendix— which was a real crisis since he ignored all the early warning signs . . ." Rachel cut Adam a playfully wicked glance. Adam responded with a shrug of the shoulders and a look of chagrin, "I discovered that people can really be changed."

Rachel sat on the hard ground again and patted a spot next to her for Pruit to join her, which he reluctantly did.

"There was a series of mysterious events happening at my hospital," Rachel went on, "and I was assigned by my hospital administrator to look into the matter."

"What kind of mysteries?" Pruit inquired.

"People were being healed, and I don't mean by the physicians. I mean miraculous healings: burn victims, comatose patients, terminally ill people. All of them suddenly and inexplicably healed. Scars disappeared, cancer evaporated. It was incredible, but I refused to believe any of it. Almost daily I was exposed to the miraculous and I just kept denying its existence. It's a long story, but Adam and I ended up working together to discover the mysterious healer. I did so because it was my job; Adam did so because he was looking for some missing members of his church."

"Missing?"

Rachel nodded. "The people who were healed turned up missing, sometimes under violent circumstances. Anyway, I was forced to work with Adam and I hated him. Boy, I hated him."

Pruit looked at Adam, who smiled and nodded. "Actually, she's being kind."

"How could you hate Adam?" Pruit was nonplussed.

"Because he stood for everything I despised. I was a person of science and he a man of faith. I dealt with human bodies and he with human souls. And because he was right about the miracles. That forced me, literally forced me, to see that there was more to the universe than my limited sight could see."

She became silent for a moment, then continued quietly. "Things got worse. We faced danger and death. The story's too long to tell now, but the Healer . . . well, the Healer saved our lives. Through it all, I discovered God, faith, and the fact that I was in love with Adam. It took awhile, but I began to see things differently. But it didn't happen by accident. God put Adam in my life. Now He's put us in your life. And now you have a decision to make."

Rachel stood to her feet. "No one can make this decision for you, Pruit. If I could, then I would, but I can't."

There was a long period of silence, then Pruit spoke: "Would you mind if I have some time to myself? I need to be alone."

Rachel sighed heavily. "Sure. But Pruit, you can never truly be alone. You know that, don't you?"

Slowly, almost imperceptibly, Pruit nodded.

Adam and Rachel walked hand in hand to the rugged wooden shed that would be home for the night.

Pruit lay back on the ground and closed his eyes tightly. Images began to fill his mind. Pictures of his wife and son; images of his hands bleeding with the stigmata. Inside him a war was going on, a battle of titanic proportions.

He became a seething caldron of emotions bubbling uncontrollably. For a moment he wished things were the way they were before. Sure he had a little drug habit. Sure his family was stressed and troubled. But he could make it all work. He could apply his mind and all his intellectual strength to solve the problems. And soon everything would be fine—better than fine—they would be great.

But he was lying to himself. He could solve nothing. His problems weren't small, they were monstrously large and far out of his control. He could work day after day, hour after hour, and a century later he would still be the shell of a man that he was right now. His family would slip from him, his business dissolve, and his life slowly flake away until there was nothing left of Pruit Bain. The world would go on without him, and his existence would be no more meaningful than that of an autumn oak leaf that falls to the ground.

Pruit felt a burning sensation . . . but this time the burning was not in the palms of his hands, it was in his eyes, as hot tears brimmed to the edge of his eyelids and trickled down his face to the dry ground below him.

"Oh, God," he cried quietly, "oh, God; oh, God; oh, God . . ."

In the distance, a pack of hyenas laughed in unison.

The sun had crested the horizon a scant thirty minutes before, sweeping away the darkness and replacing it with its pervasive golden light. The new day was announced with hoots, calls, chirps, and cries of wildlife that Adam couldn't begin to identify. The air was sweet with the smell of dew-laden grass, trees, and soil. A gentle breeze rolled in from the south, carrying with it the cooler air of the highlands.

Adam's back hurt. The night's sleep, intermittent as it was, had left his muscles sore and stiff. He rubbed his stubble-covered chin and wished for a sink with hot water. All he had was a bowl of tepid water with which to wash his face and brush his teeth. As a boy, Adam had gone camping several times with the local Boy Scout troop and each time he had hated it. Even at the young age of ten years, he knew that he was better suited to learning about the world through the reading of magazines and books than through actual encounter.

"Good morning," Ted offered as he stood up from the small green Coleman camp stove he had been hovering over. "I'll have some breakfast for us in a few minutes. We had better enjoy it; I think it may be a few days before we taste fried eggs again."

"Is there coffee?" Adam asked, his voice gravelly. "I'd sell my car for a cup of coffee."

"No need to do that," Ted replied. "I'll give you a cup just because I like you."

"Thou art truly a humanitarian, Mr. Hawthorne. A virtual saint."

"Well, don't canonize me yet. You haven't tasted the coffee."

Pruit exited the small shack and stretched. His eyes were bloodshot and his complexion flushed. That, coupled with his unshaven face, mussed hair, and rumpled clothes, gave the wealthy advertising executive the look of an urban derelict who had lived too many years on the streets.

"Do I smell coffee?" he asked as he rubbed his eyes.

"Ted claims it's coffee," Adam answered, "but the jury is still out."

"I'll take his word for it."

"So you decided to get out of bed," Rachel said. "Ted and I've been up since daybreak."

"You are truly of noble and hearty stock," Adam joked. "Where have you been, anyway?"

"You know better than to ask a question like that," Rachel retorted. "Some things are best not spoken of in polite company."

"Oh," Adam responded with sudden understanding. He walked over to her and kissed her on the forehead.

"I love you more than life itself," she said while waving her hand in front of her nose. "I would follow you to the ends of the earth—which it appears that I have—but there will be no embracing around here until you change clothes."

"What?" Adam feigned shock. "You don't like my new, rugged, outdoors man loo?."

"It's not the look I object to," Rachel replied.

Adam laughed. "All right. I'll be back in a few minutes. Save me some coffee."

A few minutes later, Adam returned, dressed in wrinkled jeans and a long-sleeved flannel shirt. Ted held out a metal cup of coffee, which Adam eagerly seized.

Ted had prepared a simple breakfast of fried eggs, Spam, and leftover injera bread. Unremarkable as the meal was in its simple composition, it tasted heavenly to the famished team of explorers. There was something about eating out-of-doors with the sun just freshly over the horizon. Even the coffee, which had been perked in an old aluminum pot, tasted wildly delicious.

"Isn't Galefo going to eat?" Rachel asked.

"He ate before the sun came up," Ted replied. "He's getting our gear ready. He wants to leave as soon as possible."

"The sooner we start," Pruit offered, "the sooner we finish. I discovered that sleeping on a cot is not for me."

"I know what you mean," Ted said, "but anytime I started feeling sorry for myself last night, I reminded myself that there are many in Ethiopia who are far worse off. For example, the meal we just ate contains more calories than some people in this land get in a week. Especially in famine years."

"Well, that puts it in perspective," Adam said. Rising from his seat near the portable cook stove, Adam asked, "Shall we find Galefo?"

Galefo was easy to find. Standing near the Landcruiser, Galefo stood like a statue staring west. His tall frame cast a long, early morning shadow on the grassy ground before him. He wore military fatigues that were too short for his six-foot-eight frame. Next to him, leaning against the vehicle was a black gun. Adam knew next to nothing about weapons, but he had seen enough pictures in news magazines to recognize a Russian-made AK-47.

Hearing their approach, Galefo turned to face them. His face betrayed no emotion and very little interest.

"Are we ready, Galefo?" Ted asked in English. "I hope you weren't waiting on us."

"We are ready," Galefo answered. His voice was soft and his words measured. "The vehicle is packed with the things we will need."

"Great," Ted said. "Is there anything we can do to help?"

The tall black man shook his head slowly. "The work is done. Now the trip begins. The Abbay is five miles that way," he held out a long, thin, but muscular arm and pointed west. "We will drive to the edge of the gorge, then we will walk."

"Do you think you can find the area we're looking for?" Pruit asked. Adam noticed Ted stiffen at the question.

"I have seen your picture. If it exists, I will find it."

Over dinner the night before, Adam had shown Galefo the faxed images than Martin had sent. There were several pictures to study. One clearly showed a large bend in the flow of the river as it left its headwaters in Lake T'ana. The river flowed southeast before making a near 180-degree turn west, where it continued to course into the country of Sudan and then on into the Nile.

The next picture that had been taken from the mysterious changing painting was more detailed. The Abbay River could be easily seen, and joining the Abbay was another river or stream. Galefo immediately recognized it as the Jamma River. "It flows not far from here," he had said. "It shares its water with the Abbay."

The third image remained a mystery. It indicated rugged terrain and a small dark opening. Pruit had said the opening reminded him of the mouth of some sea animal. Galefo said he had never seen such an opening in the gorge and doubted that it existed. Still he agreed to guide them to the area—for a price.

The drive to the gorge took less than an half an hour which, after yesterday's teeth-rattling ride, was fine with Adam. The conditions in the Landcruiser were beyond crowded. Adam couldn't help feeling that sardines in a can had more elbow room. Rachel, Adam, and Pruit were wedged in the backseat and with each bump the car took, their heads were assaulted by the gear stowed in the small, overpacked compartment behind them. Ted drove and Galefo sat next to him in the passenger seat, his long legs bent so that his knees hovered almost chest high. Between his legs, Galefo held the AK-47 assault rifle. The only person remotely comfortable in the car was Ted, who was singing softly to himself as he drove.

"We are here," Galefo announced firmly. "Stop under that tree." Ted complied wordlessly.

Before the Landcruiser came to a full stop, Galefo's door was open. He unfolded himself from the front seat, stood, and stretched his long frame, then immediately began unloading the back of the car.

He pulled five backpacks from the storage area and set them on the ground. Each was full of unknown items and a sleeping bag was tied to the top.

"What is all this?" Pruit asked.

"Here," Galefo said brusquely, "this pack is yours." He held the pack in one hand and extended it to Pruit.

Pruit took the bag, grunted, and then exclaimed: "You've got to be kidding. This thing is heavy. What's in it?"

"Food for you and some camping gear," Galefo answered nonchalantly. "You didn't expect me to carry your food for you, did you? I'm not a pack animal. If you want to eat, if you wish water to drink, then you carry the pack."

Galefo passed out the backpacks without further discussion and then swung his own pack onto his back. "There are more supplies in the Landcruiser. We will leave them there in case they are needed later."

"How long do you think it will take to find our destination?" Adam asked as he lifted his pack onto his back.

"A few hours," Galefo shrugged, "a few days. Maybe a few weeks."

"Weeks?" Pruit exclaimed. "Do you think we may be down in the gorge for weeks?"

"We can leave anytime you wish," Galefo responded easily. "We can leave now if you wish."

"We'll go into the gorge," Adam said firmly. "We're just not used to this kind of hard travel."

Galefo looked at Adam for a few long moments. "The trip just now becomes hard. Everything else has been easy."

Ted spoke up: "I didn't know what adventure you had in mind when you first called me, Adam. I guess I'm going to have to screen my calls more closely in the future." Ted followed the statement with a laugh. "In truth, I wouldn't have missed this."

"Do you think you can handle this?" Adam quietly asked Rachel. "The pack may be a little heavy."

"I'll have to make do, I guess," Rachel replied. "I think I'll adjust. I made it through medical school and an internship; I can make it through this. Underneath this delicate Southern belle exterior is one tough cookie."

"You're pretty tough, all right," Adam said as he helped her situate the pack on her back. "Think of the stories you'll have to tell the grandkids."

"We don't even have kids," Rachel replied. "It's too early to think of grandchildren."

"I don't know," Adam disagreed. "I may be of grandfatherly age by the time we get through all this."

Galefo picked up his AK-47 and began walking toward the edge of the gorge. The others followed close behind. Galefo looked every inch the wilderness explorer: pack on his back, heavy hiking boots, rifle in hand, pistol strapped to his side, and a large knife tethered to his leg. He was an imposing figure.

When Adam peered over the edge of the gorge, he saw that he was standing on the brim of a cliff that dropped several hundred feet to the roaring river below. On the other side of the gorge was a similar cliff, its red rocks bathed in light from the rising sun.

"How are we going to get down there?" Pruit asked somberly. "Not on a rope, I trust."

The only answer Galefo gave was a slight wave of his hand as he beckoned the others to follow him.

"You really trust this guy?" Adam inquired warily of Ted, who was also looking in stunned amazement over the edge of the gorge.

"Yeah," he said breathlessly, "I trust him. In point of fact, we all have to trust him." With that, Ted followed Galefo.

They had walked less than 200 yards along the ridge of the gorge when Galefo veered left toward the precipice. Dutifully, the others followed behind him like rail cars behind a locomotive. Galefo was following a narrow trail, no more than five feet wide but—because of the steep drop to the roaring, bubbling water of the Blue Nile below them—felt closer to just a yard wide.

Adam's stomach was turning somersaults. Not one who was plagued by phobias, he still held a healthy respect for heights. Concentrating on the narrow trail before him, he made every effort to put the gaping chasm next to him out of his mind. Still, his backpack felt heavier and seemed to lean away from the rock wall on his right and toward the drop-off to his left. It was his mind playing tricks on him, but the sensation was still real.

"This looks like a well-worn path," Adam said in a vain effort to distract himself and the others. "I don't think we are the first ones down here."

"Monks," Galefo shouted back. "There are several monasteries carved into the rock. The monks walk these paths to gain supplies or to travel to other churches. This path is not used very much."

"People actually live in the gorge?" Pruit asked.

"Oh, yes," Ted replied. "Their churches are wondrous. They're carved right into the cliff face. Solid stone churches, similar to those in the north part of the country."

This a strange land, Adam thought to himself. Roaring rivers, churches carved out of stone, hyenas that laugh wickedly in the night, and rebel soldiers living in the wilderness.

For Adam the walk seemed like hours. Each step became more uncomfortable, and while he was in good physical shape, the altitude, thin air, and strange setting made the hike all the more difficult. He also worried about Rachel and Pruit.

Behind him, he could hear the labored, raspy breathing of Pruit Bain. Pruit was a man who traveled by car, limousine, and airplane, not by foot. He was a New Yorker and unaccustomed to the kind of physical exertion he was now experiencing.

"How are you doing, Pruit?" Adam asked, amazed at how winded his own voice sounded.

"I'm still here," came an even more winded reply.

"How about you, kid?" Adam asked Rachel.

"Having the time of my life," she said. "I wouldn't miss this for anything."

"That sounds like sarcasm."

"It is."

They walked on for another hour. Below them the river drew closer and with it the increasing sounds of running water. Above them the cliff rose foot by foot. They were descending the gorge, leaving behind the wide flat land above for the narrow path below their feet.

The Blue Nile, or as the Ethiopians called it, the Abbay, was a bubbling, swirling caldron of green water topped with frothy white foam.

"The river is sure active," Adam remarked.

"It is calm now," Galefo replied easily. "It runs much faster in the rainy season."

"Is it all whitewater like this?" Rachel asked between puffs of breath.

Had she been looking at Galefo instead of the path in front of her she would have seen him shake his head. "No. Some places are calm and smooth. Only when the river drops in elevation does the water turn white."

"The Abbay provides 70 percent of the electricity for Sudan," Ted said, wiping large beads of sweat from his brow. "There's a hydro-electric dam at Roseires."

"Even out of breath you play the tour guide," Pruit chided.

"Sorry," Ted replied with a small frown. "I'm just trying to keep our minds occupied."

"How much farther. . . ?" Pruit asked breathlessly.

"We rest up there." Galefo interrupted. "The path widens so we can sit. But not for too long."

True to Galefo's word, the path widened sufficiently for the group to sit or lie down. Packs dropped from the backs of the travelers like bombs from an airplane and did so to a chorus of groans and sighs. Only Galefo remained standing.

Adam plopped down by his backpack and leaned against the vertical rock wall that formed the cliff above them. Rachel joined him, stretching her weary legs before her.

"I never thought sitting on the ground could feel so good," Rachel said as she leaned back and closed her eyes. "Right now, this hard ground feels as good as any easy chair."

"I think I could fall asleep right here," Adam agreed. "If I do, don't wake me. Just pick me up on the way back."

"We've only been walking for . . ." she paused as she looked at her watch, " . . . three hours, yet I feel like it's been days. I shouldn't be this tired. I'm in good physical condition, and I've had to stand for as much as ten hours straight during a single surgery."

"How often have you had to stand in surgery with a heavy pack on your back?"

"Not too often, I guess. But still, I'm winded as if I've been running a marathon."

"It's the altitude," Ted chimed in as he lay down on the path and used his pack as a pillow. "We've been descending from the top of the gorge, but we are still close to 4,000 feet above sea level, maybe more. You haven't been at this altitude long enough to adjust."

"Well, whatever it is," Adam said, "it's giving us a workout. Just think how we're going to feel tomorrow."

"Too sore to roll over in bed, probably," Rachel answered. She reached for the canteen of water that hung on the side of her pack, unscrewed the black plastic cap, and began to drink.

"Slowly," Galefo said firmly. "Drink only in sips. The water must last us and if you drink too much too fast you will get sick. That will slow us down."

"Your concern overwhelms me," Pruit responded.

"I am a guide, not a nursemaid," Galefo said firmly. "I do my job. What you do is of no concern to me." With that Galefo walked several paces from the small huddle of people and sat on the dirt path, his long legs crossed in front of him.

"It wouldn't do to antagonize him," Ted said to Pruit. "He is one of the few guides who would take us down here on such short notice."

"It wouldn't do to antagonize me, either," Pruit snapped.

Adam looked at Rachel who was studying Pruit closely.

"Are you all right, Pruit?" Rachel asked softly, casting him a concerned, knowing glance.

At first Pruit said nothing, but then he nodded his head slightly. "Yeah, I'm OK. Just irritable, that's all. Irritable and exhausted." Then to Ted, he said, "Sorry. I've been a little out of sorts lately, and this sudden trip is starting to get to me. I'll try to find a more even keel and keep to it."

"No problem," Ted replied. "After all you folks have been through, anyone would be irritable."

"If we had known what awaited us, we would have gone into training." Rachel said, sipping her water. "With more planning and different circumstances this might have been fun. Who knows, maybe we'll come back again."

Adam and Pruit groaned in unison.

Galefo allowed the group to rest for thirty minutes before mustering them into line and resuming the march down the narrow ledge. Adam's legs had stiffened during the past half-hour and protested his demands that they support his weight and movement.

Step followed step in a silence broken only by the muted footfall of four pairs of boot-protected feet. The weary travelers, their heads bent forward, their gaze fixed on the path, focused only on the next step. Only Galefo walked with his head held high. For him, this was just a stroll. From what Ted had told him, Adam knew that such long hikes were more than daily routine for Galefo; at one time such journeys had been a means of survival for the former *shufta* rebel.

The sun passed its zenith and began its slow plunge toward the western horizon. A shadow, as wide as the gorge opposite them, began to climb up the rock face toward the path upon which they walked. Soon, from their perspective in the ravine, the sun would set and they would be bathed in a consuming ever-darkening blanket of twilight.

It was clear to Adam that they would be staying the night in Abbay Gorge. Weary as he was, the thought of sleeping on the ground was welcome. The thought of sleeping anywhere was welcome, just so long as he could remove the infernal pack from his back, shed his shoes, and cease from hiking.

"What's that sound?" Pruit asked, breaking the long silence that had traveled with the party. "That roar—what is it?"

"Jamma," Galefo shouted back from his position at the front of the line. "The river falls into the Abbay."

"Falls?" Rachel inquired with surprise. "Do you mean a waterfall?"

"Yes," was Galefo's only answer.

Not breaking stride, Galefo continued on, followed closely by four fatigued travelers. The roar of falling water echoed off the red stone chasm. In some ways the powerful song of water was frightening, in other ways it was attractive, compelling.

Galefo led the group around a wide bend and then stopped. He raised his long arm and pointed at a massive, undulating sheet of water that was crashing down from the cliff above to the troubled green waters of the river below.

"Jamma," he said.

"How will we ever get past that?" Adam asked, awestruck by the beauty and force of the cascading fluid.

"We go behind it," Galefo said matter-of-factly. "We sleep there. Then you tell me where we are to go next."

"Where we go?"

"Your picture shows only this place and no more." Galefo swatted at a fly that attempted to rest on his face. "I need a destination before I can guide you farther."

Adam looked at Rachel who returned the glance. With nothing to offer she could only shrug her shoulders.

Bolstered by the news that they would soon be able to rest for the day, the group pushed on toward the rushing torrent of the waterfall. The ever-advancing shadow cast by the cliffs opposite them finally engulfed the team. They had reached their campsite just in time—

258

a testimony to Galefo's knowledge and skill. Soon the twilight would give way to the swelling night. Adam had no interest in walking the narrow footpath in the dark.

A cool mist that became thicker as they approached the falls filled the air. Tiny droplets of water attached themselves to the hair, face, and clothing of everyone. By the time they had followed the path behind the curtain of water they were soaked. No one, however, complained. Instead, they relished the spray as it refreshed both body and mind.

The roaring of the water was constant and Adam would have had to shout to be heard. The crescendo of thunderous noise eased as Galefo led his charges behind the wall of water and into a small, wide-mouthed cavern. It was more a depression in the chasm's wall than an actual cave. Still, it was deep enough for the travelers to step back from the unceasing spray of water. At the back of the depression the ground was dry, unlike that which was close to the mouth.

Scattered around the grounds were the signs of campfires; pieces of charred wood littered the floor.

"It appears that we are not the first ones here," Adam said as he eagerly slipped the heavy backpack from his aching and raw shoulders.

"The monks stay here when they travel the path," Galefo said. "It is a good place to rest."

Galefo quickly made camp. He set up a small electric light that resembled an old Coleman gas lantern Adam had seen as a child. He encouraged the others to drink water and to eat the prepackaged, ready-to-eat meals that he had placed in each person's pack.

"Eat only one meal," Galefo had said sternly. "Save the rest for tomorrow. After you eat, rest. There is a small stream near here. I will refill the canteens in the morning, so you may drink as much as you wish. Just do so slowly." Galefo then sat down away from the others, tore open one of the plastic packages of dried meat and began to slowly consume it in silence.

"I'm hungry enough to eat everything in my pack and in yours," Ted said jovially. "I bet you've never done anything like this before."

"You would win," Adam agreed. "I'll bet you've never done anything like this either."

"Too busy with my work," Ted acknowledged. "But I am glad for the opportunity."

"What do we do about tomorrow?" Rachel asked. "Personally, I have no idea what to tell Galefo about our destination. The junction of the two rivers was all we could discern from the paintings."

Adam slowly shook his head as he bit into a piece of injera bread. "I don't know."

"Well, we have to decide on something," Pruit remarked. "I'd hate to think that we walked all the way down here for nothing."

"Something will happen," Adam said confidently.

"How can you be so sure?" Pruit asked harshly.

"How can you not be sure?" countered Adam. "After all we've been through and seen, how can you not believe that God will not lead us to the next step?"

"But how is He going to let us know?" Pruit asked.

"I don't know the answer to that," Adam replied, "but I do know that God didn't lead us here to abandon us. There's an old saying, 'God may lead His people through a desert, but He never leads them to a desert.'"

"Meaning?"

"Meaning that we will be told—somehow, someway—what our next move will be."

"I wish I had your faith," Pruit said, taking a long drink of water from his canteen. He wiped his mouth with the back of his hand.

"You can have my faith," Adam said. "Anyone can. And if anyone should have faith, it should be you."

Pruit raised his hand to stop Adam from continuing. "Please, no more sermons. I'm still thinking about the one you gave me last night."

"I don't mean to preach at you," Adam said sincerely. "I'm just trying to help you understand the truth that has made all the difference in my life."

"I know," Pruit answered. "This is just proving rather difficult for me."

"You're doing very well, Pruit," Rachel added. "Considering."

Adam noticed that Ted wore a quizzical expression, but he said nothing.

The next hour was spent in exhaustion-induced silence. Each had eaten one prepackaged meal and consumed a canteen full of water. Their stomachs full, their thirst quenched, and their muscles slowly relaxing after enduring unaccustomed strain, Adam, Rachel,

Pruit, and Ted huddled quietly together. They were enjoying the act of doing nothing.

"I need to stretch for a moment," Pruit said. "It's getting dark fast, and that little light Galefo brought won't last but a few hours before the batteries die. I better find my way around before I can't see to do so."

With a slight grunt, Pruit rose and walked toward the opening of the cave but stayed back from the intrusive spray from the waterfall. He stretched his back, then bent forward, attempting to touch his toes. He moved his head in small circles to loosen the muscles in his neck.

"Do you think he'll be all right?" Adam asked. "He seemed a lot more sensitive today."

"He'll be fine," Rachel assured. "The strain must be tremendous." Rachel cut her eyes toward Ted and then back to Adam. Adam knew that she was uncomfortable talking about Pruit's problem in front of Ted.

Turning to face his companions, Pruit said, "A condo like this could fetch a pretty high price in New York City."

The others laughed. Adam instinctively knew that Pruit was making an effort to lighten his own burdened spirit as he entertained the others.

"Not much here, though," Pruit went on. "Not even a back door." Pruit strolled to the back of the cave. The stone wall was rugged and covered in dust. "I'll bet all kinds of African insects live in the nooks and crannies of this place."

"Now there's a disturbing picture," Rachel said. "If you have any other observations like that, I'll thank you to keep them to yourself."

Pruit shrugged. "Of course, the really big bugs must live behind there."

"Behind where?" Adam asked, turning to see where Pruit was looking.

"There," Pruit responded, pointing at a crevice that ran from the floor to the cave's ceiling. "The crack in the wall."

Adam rose and walked toward the vertical opening. "It looks like some kind of fissure."

"Could be," Ted replied. "Ethiopia is still geologically active."

Pruit approached the place where Adam was standing. "Feels like

261

a there's a breeze flowing from it." Pruit held up his left palm and placed it near the opening. "The air is moving all right. Not a lot, but enough to notice."

"I read once," Rachel said, "that caves breathe. It has to do with the changing air pressure outside the cave. When the pressure is lower, air rushes from the cave to the outside. When the air pressure outside the cave is higher than that which is inside the cave, then the reverse is true."

"That would mean that there is another cave behind this opening," Adam said. Ted stood and joined the other two men.

Pruit brought his hand down and unconsciously wiped his palm on his jeans. A dark smear stained the pant leg.

"Did you get something on your hand?" Adam asked. "Dirt or mud?"

"No," Pruit replied, "why do you ask?"

"You just smeared something on your pants."

Pruit immediately looked at his trousers. "I don't know what that could . . ." He stopped abruptly and quickly made eye contact with Adam. Slowly, Pruit raised his left hand and looked at the palm. A small, neat hole was in the flesh and a tiny trickle of blood oozed from the opening.

"Good Lord," Ted exclaimed. "I know you told me about this, but to see it with my own eyes is . . . is . . . Wow!"

Rachel sprang to her feet and raced to the others.

Quickly, Pruit raised his other hand but saw nothing. "That's strange," he said. "Why just my left hand and not my right?"

"That's the hand you held up to feel the breeze coming out of the hidden cave," Adam said.

Rachel took Pruit's hand to examine it. "It looks like a puncture wound—like someone has driven a sharp object through the hand."

"Like a nail," Adam said firmly. "It's a stigmata—the mark of Christ."

Pruit stared in disbelief at his two hands. Only the left showed the stigmata. His right hand was normal. "I think . . . I think we've got our sign, Adam."

"A pretty clear sign, if you ask me," Adam replied.

"Just a second," Rachel said. "Hold your left hand behind your back and put your right hand in the opening."

"Why?"

"It's the scientist in me," Rachel replied. "Please humor me. OK?"

Pruit complied, slowly raising his unaffected hand and placing it near the narrow opening in the wall. When he brought his right hand back, it was marked with the same stigmata.

"Quick," Rachel demanded, "let me see your left hand now." Pruit raised it for her to see. The stigmata was gone. "Incredible," she said. "Absolutely amazing."

A palpable stillness filled the cave; then Adam laughed, reached out, and hugged Pruit. Then he hugged Rachel, then he hugged Ted. "There's no arguing the fact. We've arrived at our goal, or at least very near the goal."

The laughter was contagious. Only Galefo, who still sat on the opposite side of the small cavern, remained quiet, his eyes moving as he studied the excited troupe.

"Now what?" Pruit asked.

"Now what, indeed," Adam responded.

Forty

Dodecanese Islands, Greece

Nick was enjoying himself—a fact that was given away by a wide and toothy grin plastered to his face. Seated at the back of the inflatable boat known as a Zodiac, he held tightly to the handle of the powerful outboard motor that propelled the light surface craft across the water, creating a saltwater spray all around.

The boat, which had been lowered from the deck of the *Quintessence* by a small onboard crane, was fast and easy to handle in calm waters. The versatile craft had gained global popularity and was used for rescue operations by the various navies, lifeguards, and coast guards of the world. Nick was controlling the craft as if he had been born to do so.

When Dick, Katrin, and Nick decided that they had indeed located the correct island and therefore should explore it, Nick volunteered to operate the Zodiac. When asked if he had ever handled a small craft before, he had replied: "Sure. Every Texan is required to go bass fishin' by the time he's three. It's a law, you know. Besides, I've handled lots bigger equipment on the fire department. They may not have run in the water, but the principle is the same. There ain't nothin' I can't drive, includin' a little ol' boat like that."

Convinced by his enthusiasm, Dick and Katrin made Nick "captain" of the little craft that now sped the three toward the small, uninhabited island.

The boat was fast, which was fine with Nick, but not so fine with Katrin and Dick, who clung tightly to the grab rope that was conveniently attached to the top of the float that formed the hull of the Zodiac. Neither Dick nor Katrin were enjoying the ride as much as Nick.

The island, a small rocky projection from the Aegean, loomed ahead of them. Waves crashed against a vertical rock face on the south side of the island, casting billows of white foam into the air. The sheer cliff was typical on all sides of the island. When they first spotted the tiny landmass, the captain of the *Quintessence* cruised around it in a lazy circle so that every side of the island could be examined through binoculars.

"It's no wonder the island has remained uninhabited," Beck said as he stood peering over the starboard side of the yacht, binoculars held closely to his eyes. "The waves would smash a boat to pieces. And on the sides where there are no waves, there's nothing but rock straight up and down from water to sky."

"Not quite," Dick replied as he studied the rock formation through his binoculars. "There's a small opening on the west face. I can see a little sandy beach. It looks like a tiny harbor."

Beck redirected his binoculars. "I see it. Sure doesn't look like much. Are you sure that is where you want to go?"

"That's it, all right," Dick answered. "It's hard to miss its unusual shape." Dick's mind flashed to the image that Martin St. James had faxed just two days before. The picture that was taken from the painting portrayed an island that looked somewhat like a mushroom— a "squashed mushroom," Katrin had observed.

Within thirty minutes, the captain had pulled close enough to the island to drop anchor, but not so close as to be affected by the ocean surge. Fifteen minutes after that Dick, Katrin, and Nick were bouncing along the water in the Zodiac.

Katrin, doing her best to disguise the fear she felt, turned and looked at Nick. He was still smiling. Katrin reluctantly returned the smile and then turned to make eye contact with Dick. An unspoken communication was shared between the two, a communication that said, "I hope we live to see landfall."

Nick backed off the throttle when the boat came to within a hundred yards of the island. Grateful for the reduced speed, Dick released a slow sigh. He pointed just off the port side and said, "Put us in there, Nick."

Nodding his agreement, Nick cranked the throttle again and made for the sandy inlet. As they approached they could see a small cove of peaceful water. Nick steered directly for it. Moments later, he had beached the Zodiac, rather roughly, on a thin strip of sand that sloped gently into the water. Dick immediately jumped from the craft, bow line in hand, and pulled the boat out of the water.

"We had better tie her off in case the tide comes in," Dick announced, grasping the boat's small aluminum anchor by its shaft. "I'd hate to have to swim back."

"I'm still undecided," Katrin said under her breath. "It might be preferable."

"I heard that," Nick said with mock offense. "You should have ridden with me when I was drivin' firetrucks. You haven't lived until you've seen an American LaFrance pumper take a corner on two wheels."

Katrin shuddered. Nick smiled. Dick laughed.

Feeding out the bow line, Dick walked up the sloping beach and buried the aluminum anchor into the ground. "That should hold her," he announced. "It doesn't look like the tide rises this high. We should be safe."

The beach was no more than 300 yards across and only a tenth of that deep. It was pristine and devoid of any footprints that might indicate the presence of others. Looking back over his steps, Dick wondered how long it had been since anyone had stepped on the unsullied sands.

"This is beautiful," Katrin exclaimed. Her voice carried on the gentle breeze that swirled in the cove, lightly caressing her fawn hair and causing loose strands to dance in the air. "This place is untouched."

"At least untouched in recent times," Dick acknowledged as he looked at the cliffs that circled the island. "This is like standing in the crater of a volcano. We're surrounded on all sides by cliffs."

"What now?" Nick asked as he struggled out of the boat.

"We're on our own now," Dick responded. "We've run out of pictures to follow, so it's pure exploring now."

A forest of small trees lined the beach like sentries at the gates to an ancient city. Behind the trees were more trees, whose canopy spread over low bushes.

"I suggest we start with the forest," Katrin said. "Perhaps we'll find something hidden in the trees."

"Off we go then," Dick said.

"Before we do," Nick interjected. "I think we need to make somethin' clear. As you know, I can't walk very fast, so if I start slowin' you down any then go on without me. I'll catch up later."

"No can do, buddy," Dick replied. "You're more a part of this team than I am. I came into the game from off the bench—remember? You're the one with a vision. If you need to rest, you just say so; we'll wait with you."

"But . . ."

"No buts about it," Katrin added emphatically. "You were chosen like the rest of us. We started as a team and we'll continue as a team. Got that?"

"Yes, ma'am," Nick said, standing erect and offering a salute.

Dick laughed and began to move toward the trees. "Ready or not, here we go."

"How long do we give them?" Ross asked. He was watching the island closely.

"Doesn't really matter, does it?" Beck replied. "Where are they going to go? It's not like they can swim back to Karpathos."

"True enough," Ross replied. "Still, I'd hate to wait too long."

"We'll follow in an hour," Beck said. "You and Mickie be ready."

"Do you think they'll be hard to find?"

"No. As far as we know there hasn't been anyone on that island in a long time. No matter where they go, they're going to leave fresh tracks. All we have to do is follow them. And with that Nick fellow with them, they'll be moving pretty slow. We'll have no problem in hunting them down."

Slung over Dick's shoulders was a small backpack filled with a canteen of water, some sandwiches prepared by Mickie, a flare gun in case they got into trouble, and a first aid kit. It was a light load, but that was all that was needed.

The plan was for the three to spend the afternoon looking around the island, return to the *Quintessence* before dark, and return the next day if necessary.

That part of the plan rested easy on Dick's mind. What didn't rest easy was the part they couldn't plan. What if they found what they were looking for? Would they take the items with them back to the yacht? Or would they leave them, tell Beck and the others that nothing was there, and then make arrangements to come back another time?

Tempted as they might be to remove anything that they might find, Martin St. James had made a strong argument that any and all artifacts be left untouched. Taking the artifacts would constitute a criminal act, and getting out of a foreign jail could be difficult.

Other questions floated freely in Dick's consciousness. What if they found nothing at all? What then? How patient would Beck and his friends be? They couldn't wait around forever while the three searched every foot of the island.

The search shouldn't take that long, Dick reasoned. Shouldn't being the operative word. There were still many unknowns, such as terrain and Nick's ability to walk long distances. At least the island was small, not covering more than a couple of square miles. A good hike for most people, but not out of reach.

They walked into the grove of trees, pushing aside the small bushes that stood in their way. All plant life on the island was stunted. The lack of cultivation, the small number of animals, and the rocky soil had allowed for only limited growth.

"How you doing, Nick?" Dick asked over his shoulder.

"Still here and bearin' down on ya'."

"Need a rest?"

"Not yet. I wanna find what we're looking for."

"You and me both, friend, you and me both."

Katrin was nearly overcome by the beauty and primitive nature of the island. Having spent her entire life in suburbia, she was impressed with the stillness, the quiet, the solitude. There was something immensely attractive about being one of just three people on an island.

She saw the place as paradise. Here there were no expectations of social behavior, no demands to rise to the expectations of family and friends. Here there was just beauty. Here the senses were awash in color, smells, and sounds that would be drowned out in any civilized area. Here a person could be shy without criticism. All around her were peace and serenity, and Katrin wished deeply that such a peace could seep into her life.

Every step was painful. With each bending of the knee, with each extension of his legs, with each shift of weight, a stab of pain bolted through Nick. A month ago one tenth of the suffering he felt at this moment would have exiled him to his easy chair, where he would sit motionless, watching television. But there were no easy chairs on this island, and even if there were he would walk past.

Something had changed in Nick. It happened the day of his vision and he had never—nor would he ever—be the same. Before, his pain provided him with an excuse to avoid life. It hurt too much to leave his chair, to leave his apartment, to leave his self-imposed exile.

Now he was different. Sure, the pain was the same. His skin was still stiff. He still hobbled when he walked. But he was different. The pain no longer pushed him into idleness or bouts of self-pity. Instead, the pain was a constant reminder that he was alive. He could have died in that fire. Others did. He could have perished right there in front of that frightened child he had tried so hard to rescue. But he didn't. And now he had another rescue to make—himself. He had to snatch himself from a different kind of death—the kind of death that is protracted and lengthy. The kind of death that begins with rigor mortis of the soul. The kind of death that begins to decay a person from within and then slowly works its way out.

One of the most hideous things Nick had ever seen was in a documentary about insects. With graphic video footage the film showed a tarantula hawk—which was really a type of wasp—attack and paralyze a large tarantula with its sting. The wasp then laid its eggs inside the spider. When the eggs hatched, the larvae ate their way out. Nick felt a sense of disgust when he initially watched the program, and he relived that disgust as the vivid pictures came clearly to his mind again.

In many ways, Nick realized, life had done to him what that wasp had done to the tarantula. The accident had infected him with something that was destroying him from the inside out.

Nick was tired of being destroyed, eaten alive by his pity and the pity of others. After his vision, he knew that he had a purpose, and nothing, not even scorched, scarred skin, would keep him from fulfilling his destiny.

In his mind, there was only one certainty, only one absolute fact: he was going to find the golden jar of manna and Aaron's rod on this island or die trying.

"What's that?" Nick asked loudly.

Dick turned to face Nick, who had fallen about a hundred yards behind him and Katrin.

"What's what?" Katrin asked.

"That," he said, pointing through the trees. "It looks man-made."

Squinting, Dick struggled to find the object of Nick's attention when he saw it—a white, flat, vertical surface.

"You're right," Dick shouted. Dick and Katrin jogged back to Nick's position.

"I see it now," Katrin said excitedly.

"I don't know how I missed it," Dick exclaimed. "Now that you point it out it seems obvious."

Katrin was ecstatic. "That's it. That must be it."

Without another word, Nick began to make his way through the brush toward the large white object, crushing plants under his feet, breaking small branches off the undergrowth, and sounding like a loose moose walking on potato chips. He struggled against the brush as he pushed himself to move faster. Dick could have easily overtaken him, but he chose instead to bring up the rear. This was Nick's moment to shine, and as eager as Dick was to investigate, he held himself in check. He had no desire to eclipse Nick and Katrin's enthusiasm.

Nick ran as best as Nick could run. Katrin followed close behind. Dick walked. All had their eyes fixed on the still-mysterious object.

They quickly closed the fifty or so yards that separated them from their goal when they realized that the object was a building.

The three broke through the growth and found themselves standing in a clearing. The ground was covered in a coarse grass from which protruded large, rectangular stones—building stones. Before them stood the remains of a stone structure, now broken, weathered, and fragile. Four large pillars marked what was once a grand entrance. Each column was red, narrower at the base than it was at the head. On top of each column was a three-layer crown made of a dark slatelike stone that sandwiched a thicker, yet smaller stone. It reminded Dick of an ice cream treat he ate as a boy: an Eskimo Pie.

The pillars supported the remains of a pitched stone roof that had long ago broken into large chunks. As much of the roof lay on the ground as rested on the columns.

The main structure was a brick mason's nightmare. Blocks of hewed white stone had been stacked one upon the other like giant bricks. A single doorway lay in the wall behind the porch formed by the pillars and stone roof.

"This looks familiar," Katrin said slowly.

"This looks familiar?" Nick was shocked. "How could this look familiar? It's something out of the ancient-history books."

"That's it," Katrin replied. "History! When I was in college I saw a picture of a structure like this."

"I thought you were an artist," Dick said.

"I was an art major," Katrin explained. "Part of the course work included a class called 'Art in Ancient History.' I remember we had this professor who was a nut for detail. He made us memorize different types of ancient architecture. I remember seeing a picture of a building that looked like this. Not exactly like this, but very similar."

"Can you remember anything else?" Nick asked breathlessly. The struggle through the brush had winded him severely.

"Well, I know it's Greek, which makes sense, of course, since we are on a Greek island. But there was something else, something special."

Katrin lowered her head and raised a hand to her chin as she thought. "It was so long ago. I'm not sure I can . . . Wait! Minoan. Yeah, that's it. This building is like the ancient temple on Crete . . . Kron . . . no . . . Kos . . . Knossos. The temple at Knossos. Its ruins are near the city we took the ferry from."

"Iraklion?" Dick asked.

"Right," Katrin answered. "There's a temple like this one near Iraklion."

"What else?" Nick inquired, his breathing less labored.

"That's it," Katrin replied. "That's all I remember and I'm lucky I remember that much. I hated the class."

"Well, then," Nick said. "I suggest we see if anyone's at home."

Despite Nick's suggestion, no one moved. The three stood as still and as quiet as the stone pillars before them. Dick's heart was pounding so hard that he was sure that others would turn to him any minute and ask, "What's that sound?"

"Nick's right," Dick intoned softly. "This may or may not be what we came here for and I know only one way to find out." With that Dick took a step forward to cross the grass-carpeted clearing and enter the ancient temple that had been so carefully built by a culture that ceased to exist millennia ago.

"I wonder," Katrin thought aloud as they strolled toward the building.

"What do you wonder?" Dick asked, mesmerized by what may lie in the structure.

"Why build a temple here? I mean, this island is too small to support much of a community. Just sailing into the tiny little port would be a challenge for an ancient sailor in a day without gas engines. The stones don't look like they come from this island, which means that they would have to have been brought here. That's an awful lot of trouble to build a temple that most people would never see."

"Perhaps that's the point," Dick responded. "Perhaps they had something they wanted to hide, something to protect."

"Do you know what a temple like this would be used for, Katrin?" Nick asked.

"No. I know the Minoans worshiped a female god—a great mother goddess and that some young male god was associated with her. But that's all I know."

"Wasn't the Greek god Zeus supposed to have been born in one of the many caves on Crete?" Dick inquired as he reached the first step of the temple.

"Yes," Katrin answered. "Something like that anyway. Why have we stopped?"

Dick shrugged. "Anticipation. Fear. Savoring the moment. I don't know."

Nick paused for only a moment then began to climb the six steps that would place him under the covered portico. Dick and Katrin watched as he swung a leg up to the next step before dragging the other foot along. When he had climbed four of the six steps the others began their climb. Moments later the three stood at the threshold of the stone doorway. After a brief pause, Nick stepped in.

The four-foot-wide opening yielded to a sepulchral room which, fortunately for them, was dimly lit by sunshine that poured in through holes in the deteriorating walls and ceiling. The floor was covered in a thick, almost viscous layer of dust and rubble. Dick judged the chamber to be about 150 feet square with a ceiling that hovered 40 feet above them. Supporting the ceiling were several rows of stone columns evenly arranged throughout the large room. Building such a structure today would be relatively easy, Dick thought, but to do so twenty or thirty centuries ago was remarkable.

"Look," Dick said, gazing at the floor.

"What do you see?" Katrin asked, letting her eyes scan the ground.

"It's what I don't see," Dick responded. "No footprints. No footprints of any kind."

"That means we are the first ones to set foot in here in a very long time."

"Maybe as much as 3,000 years," Katrin added. "It kind of puts things in perspective, doesn't it?"

"So does that!" Nick exclaimed loudly, his voice ricocheting off the walls.

All eyes turned to see where Nick was pointing. Katrin gasped and Dick swallowed hard.

Across the room, and through the dusty, dimly lit air, was a large wooden structure. Its shape was easily recognizable, a fact that only heightened the confusion felt by Dick and the others.

"What . . . What would a ship be doing in the middle of a building like this?" Nick asked.

"I don't know," Dick and Katrin replied in unison.

"It looks old," Nick commented slowly. "It looks real old. Like it has been here since Creation."

Dick studied the boat. It was about a hundred feet in length with a curved prow and stern, and stood—propped up on large stone blocks—close to twenty feet tall. The ship was dilapidated. A large section of the stern had broken off and lay on the floor in heaps of rotting wood. No mast could be seen, but then the ceiling wasn't high enough to accommodate one.

"This is unbelievable," Dick said in awe. "A ship, a fully functioning sailing ship in the middle of a stone temple on a deserted Greek island. Who would believe this?"

"I'm not sure I believe it," Nick commented "and I'm standin' here seein' it with my own eyes."

"Look at the size of that boat," Dick continued. "How did they get the thing in here in the first place?"

"They didn't," Katrin replied. "My guess is that they built the temple around it. And I bet they did it because of what it contains."

Both men looked at her.

"I hope what we're lookin' for is in better shape than that old tub," Nick said. "Otherwise, we will have wasted an awful lot of time."

"It's there," Katrin said. "I can feel it."

"Well, let's have a look," Dick said as he started for the ship, taking careful, deliberate steps on the dust-blanketed floor.

"Wait a minute," Nick called out. "Not so fast. We need to do this right. That thing looks pretty rickety and if all three of us go charging in there without some plan, then the whole thing could come down on us. We could be stuck in there waitin' for help, or even killed."

"He makes sense, Dick," Katrin said. Then to Nick she asked, "So what's the plan?"

"Only one person goes in," Nick replied authoritatively. "That leaves two to conduct a rescue if one is needed. And I should be the one to go in."

"Why you?" Dick asked.

"Two reasons. First, I'm trained to conduct rescue operations. That was part of my job in the fire department. Second, if somethin' does go wrong, you two are in better physical shape to get me out, than I am to get you out."

Dick wanted to object. He didn't like the idea of Nick going in alone, especially into something so obviously fragile. But everything Nick was saying made sense.

"OK," Dick said. "But the boat isn't very big; we should be able to hear you at all times. When you go in, start talking. Tell us what you see. That will help us know where you are and that you're OK."

"Sounds reasonable," Nick agreed.

"I don't know," Katrin said. "I'm worried."

"Thank you," Nick offered with a grin. "I haven't had anyone to worry over me in a long time. But don't fret too much. I'll be careful."

The three walked to the broken stern of the ship and peered in. The ship's cavity was strewn with broken chunks of wood from support beams, pieces of overhead decks, and planking.

"There's a lot of clutter in there," Katrin said, her voice filled with anxiety. "You will be careful, won't you?"

"Yup," Nick said with bravado. "One life-alterin' injury is enough for me. I don't need another one."

"Well, take it slow," Katrin advised sincerely.

"Lady, that's the only way I can take it."

Abruptly, Katrin leaned forward and kissed Nick on the cheek. Nick was shocked—pleasantly.

"Promise me another one of those and I'll race right back here."

"It's a promise." Katrin blushed red and so did Nick.

Emboldened by Katrin's encouragement, Dick's vigilance, and his own compelling desire to complete the mission revealed to him in a vision, Nick took his first tentative steps.

"I wish I had a flashlight," Nick said, beginning his required nonstop dialogue. It's pretty dark in here."

Nick had made only five steps into the belly of the ship when a loud crack was heard.

"Nick!" Katrin called out.

"It's all right," Nick said reassuringly. "I stepped on a piece of wood. You'll probably hear more of that. This place looks worse than a teenager's bedroom."

Dick and Katrin stood at the broken stern watching the now shadowy figure of Nick move deeper into the boat. The sunlight that filtered into the room through cracks and breaks in the temple walls was insufficient to light more than ten or fifteen feet of the long seacraft's interior.

"It looks like the upper decks have caved in," Nick called out. "I can see right through the top deck. Looks none too stable either. The good news is that the cracks in the upper deck give me a little more light.

"There are metal objects lyin' all over the place," Nick continued. "Nails mostly. To be truthful, it's like walkin' through a bombed-out lumberyard."

"How are you feeling?" Dick asked.

"Fine, but it's hard to move because of the litter, not to mention my bum legs. But I'm doin' just great."

A crashing sound emanated from the bowels of the ship.

"What was that?" Dick called into the dark hull.

"Nothin' to worry about, just movin' some lumber." Nick coughed harshly. "Man, it's dusty in here. I think I'm about halfway through now, maybe as much as two-thirds. There's a large pile of debris in my way. I'm going to have to move it."

"Work slowly," Dick advised. "And work easy. I don't want this thing coming down around your ears."

"Odd," Nick replied. "I feel the same way."

Dick looked at Katrin and smiled. "At least he has his humor."

"I'm moving some of the wood," Nick called out. "You're goin' to hear some noise, but don't worry about it. I never was very good at housecleanin'."

True to his word, noises rumbled through the ancient and decayed ship.

"Most of this wood just crumbles in my hands. It's rotted through. I'm surprised the hull is still standin' at all. Let's just hope it continues to stand while I'm . . . wait a minute. What's this?"

"What? What do you see?" Katrin shouted.

"It's a box of some sort," Nick answered. "I can't see real well, but it feels like it's made out of stone. It's maybe four feet square. It has a lid. I can feel the joint where the lid and the box meet."

"Is the lid stone, too?" Dick asked.

"Yeah, it sure is. I think this is it. I'm going to try and move the lid . . . it's heavy . . . seems stuck." Dick could hear Nick grunting as he struggled with the stone box. He knew that this couldn't be easy for him. He had been sedentary for a long time and he lacked the leg strength to achieve any leverage.

"You want me to come in and help?" Dick shouted.

"No, let's stick to the plan. I feel better knowing you're out there ready to save my hide should I get buried in here."

There were more grunts. Nick's labored breathing could be heard outside the boat.

"Whoa!" Nick shouted. "The lid just gave way. I moved it a few inches, but not enough to reach inside. Maybe if I make a lever out of one of these boards . . . I can pry the lid back far enough to . . ."

Snap! A resounding crack echoed down the hold of the boat, followed by a crashing sound. The entire ship shuddered and creaked loudly.

"Nick!" Katrin cried out. "Nick? Are you all right?"

No answer.

"Nick?" Katrin shouted louder.

"I'm fine," Nick responded. "My lever broke and I fell down. I'm glad you didn't have to see that. I don't fall pretty."

"But you're OK?"

"Yeah, Katrin, I'm fine. Angry. Embarrassed. Dusty. But fine." There was a pause punctuated by the sound of rustling debris. "I don't think there's a piece of wood in here that can help me. It's all just too old and brittle. Let me see if I can push the lid back now."

Grunting. Gasping. Straining.

"There it goes. There it goes!" Nick shouted loudly. "Maybe my lever did some good after all."

"Do you see anything?" Dick asked anxiously. He began to pace. "This standing out here waiting is killing me," he said to Katrin. "I'm not a patient man to begin with, but this situation is sending me up the wall."

"I can't see much," Nick replied. "The lid's back about halfway. I'm reaching in to see . . . if . . . I . . . can . . . feel . . . anything."

Silence was punctuated with more sounds of physical strain.

"I feel somethin'!"

Katrin raised her hands to her mouth, and Dick instinctively took a step toward the boat. The ship was moving, rocking slightly back and forth in response to Nick's physical efforts inside.

"Easy Nick," Dick called out. "You're rocking the boat."

"That's a cliché, isn't it?" Nick inquired loudly.

"It's a warning," Dick answered. "Take it easy."

"OK, OK, I'm just tryin' to . . . I feel something. It feels like wood, like a wooden dowel or maybe a . . . branch. Got it! I don't believe this."

"Don't believe what?" Dick stopped his pacing.

"It's still hard to see, but it looks like a branch. A branch with leaves on it. I don't know how, but the leaves are . . . are alive. At least they feel alive. Can you believe that! Locked up for centuries in a stone box and this thing is still alive. You know what this means, don't you?"

"We found it!" Katrin screamed then flung her arms around Dick's neck. "We found it. We found Aaron's rod!"

Dick returned Katrin's hug, then quickly broke away. "What about the jar? Did you find the jar of manna?"

"Not yet."

By the rocking of the ship, Dick could tell that Nick was searching the box again. In his mind's eye, he could see Nick leaning over the edge of the stone box, feeling for some object he could not see.

The moments crept by like hours pass. The ship rocked some more, Nick grunted some more, and Dick paced some more.

"Yes!" Nick screamed. "Yes, it's here!" Groaning and labored breathing. "I have it. Man, this thing is . . . heavy."

"It's made of gold, you big sap," Katrin teased loudly.

"Sap? Dick, did she call me a sap?"

"I think she's too exited to call you anything worse," Dick answered. The ship began to rock again. "What are you doing now?"

"Seein' if anythin' else is in here. Nope, just the branch and the jar. What do I do now, Dick? Do I bring them out?"

"No. Remember what Martin said. We should leave everything where it is."

"But I want to see them," Katrin protested.

"Me too," came a loud and unexpected voice.

Dick snapped his head around to see who was speaking. Standing just inside the room were Beck, Ross, and Mickie.

"What are you guys doing here?" Dick asked innocently. "How did you find us?"

Simultaneously the three interlopers raised handguns and leveled them at Dick and Katrin.

"Hey . . ." Dick began.

"Shut up!" Beck shouted harshly. "Step away from the boat and into the middle of the room."

"I don't understand," Katrin exclaimed.

"I said shut up!" Beck motioned to the middle of the room with his gun. "I assure you that I have no problem in using this."

Dick and Katrin complied by moving away from the ship to the center of the ancient temple.

"Kneel down facing the ship." Beck ordered. "Do it now!" Dick and Katrin turned to face the ship and then knelt in the thick dust.

"Hands behind your head; interlace your fingers."

As soon as Dick and Katrin had done as they were told, Mickie and Ross stepped forward and, with quick and practiced motions, placed metal handcuffs around their wrists, securing their hands behind their backs.

"Thank you for your kind cooperation," Beck said bitterly as he approached them. Then he turned his attention to Nick, who was still sequestered in the ship. "Mr. Stern, would you kindly come out and bring with you whatever it is that you have found?"

There was no response.

Anger coursed through every nerve in Dick's body. He was infuriated by the shock of being held at gunpoint, by the betrayal of those who pretended to be their friends, by the danger Katrin and Nick were in, and by his own gullibility.

"Please, Mr. Stern," Beck shouted. "Let's try and do this the easy way."

Still no answer.

Beck sighed loudly, raised his pistol, and fired a shot through the decayed wood of the ship. Dust flew everywhere, and the wood the bullet hit shattered into tiny shards of material that rained down to the floor.

Still no answer.

"OK, Mr. Stern, if fear of my shooting you doesn't carry any weight, then let's try this."

In a swift and brutal motion, Beck reached down, grabbed Katrin by the hair, and jerked her to her feet. She screamed in pain and struggled to find her footing. Tears filled her eyes and raced in a near torrent down her cheeks. The scream carried throughout the stone room and into the belly of the ship.

"All right, all right," Nick called out from inside. "I'm coming out. Just give me a minute. It's hard to move in here."

"You have three minutes, and bring everything you've found with you."

The seconds dripped by slowly. Then, like Lazarus from the tomb, Nick emerged carrying a large container that looked to be made of pure gold. It sparkled in the limited light of the room, giving the impression that it was emitting an aura of its own. Nick held the jar by cupping his hands under its base with his arms wrapped tightly around its body as if he were hugging it. The vessel was so large that, in that position, it reached Nick's chin, which he rested on the container's lid. Pinned to the lid by the force of Nick's jaw was a branch about three feet in length. Stemming off the central branch were several smaller branches covered in bright green leaves.

"Thank you, Mr. Stern," Beck said as he raised his pistol to Katrin's temple. "Please be careful. If you drop anything, I'll put a bullet in . . . no, through, this lovely lady's head. Do you understand?"

"Yes," Nick mumbled, his jaw still tightly pressed to the lid of the jar. "But this is extremely heavy."

With a quick motion of his head, Beck silently ordered Mickie and Ross to help Nick. Ross took the jar, staggered for a moment under its weight, then stepped back. Simultaneously, Mickie grabbed the branch while training her gun at Nick's head.

As soon as his burden was snatched from his arms, Nick collapsed to the floor. The effort he expended to bring out the golden vessel had exhausted him to the point of unconsciousness. For a man who had to struggle to walk, his recent exertion was phenomenal.

"You're a wise man, Stern," Beck said as he released Katrin, who dropped to her knees, her face a living portrayal of pain. With a slow and deliberate motion, Beck pulled a pair of handcuffs from his back pocket and approached Nick.

Dick looked at the expression on Katrin's face and then at a man who had become his friend, lying in the dust, and the anger Dick had initially felt mushroomed to uncontrollable proportions. Seeing Ross' arms filled with the golden jar and Mickie's gun aimed at Nick, Dick sprang to his feet, his hands still cuffed behind him, and launched himself at the small of Beck's back.

When Dick hit him, he did so with the full benefit of his rage. Beck was knocked to the ground in a heap, Dick's bulky body landing on top of him. For a moment, Dick felt as if he had the advantage, but Beck quickly rolled to his left, dumping Dick face up on the ground. Before Dick could respond or even take a breath, Beck was on top of him, pummeling his face with his fists. He hit Dick countless times until blood ran freely from his now-broken nose, split lips, and loose teeth.

"You want to play the hero?" Beck shouted loudly. "You think you're some comic book hero?" Beck hit him two or three times more until Dick was sure he was going to lose consciousness. "You're no hero. You're an impotent, useless, piece of garbage. I've killed men twice as tough as you and not even broken a sweat."

Standing to his feet, Beck reached down, grabbed Dick by the shirt with two hands, and effortlessly hauled him to his feet. Dick could barely stand. Beck took one step back and then threw a wicked punch to Dick's abdomen, putting his full weight behind the motion. Dick doubled over as the air was forced from his lungs.

"Stop it!" Katrin screamed. "You're killing him!"

Gasping and struggling for air, Dick tried to hold onto what shred of consciousness he had left and hoped—prayed—that his paralyzed diaphragm would recover so that he could breathe.

Dick opened his eyes just in time to see Beck's knee come crashing into his face. Dick staggered back, his legs buckling. But Beck was not finished unleashing his fury.

"No one touches me," Beck shouted, his face red with rage. "No one! Certainly not the likes of you." Stepping up to the staggering man, Beck seized Dick by the shoulder and then ran him into one of the stone columns that filled the temple.

Dick hit hard.

"Please," Katrin pleaded. "Please don't hit him anymore."

Beck pinned Dick's head face first to the pillar with an elbow. "Shall I kill you here, Mr. Slay? Shall I drop your lifeless corpse right here? How would your wife feel? How would Cleo get along without you?"

Hearing the mention of his wife's name stunned Dick back to near normal consciousness. "How do you know about my wife?" Dick had meant the words to come out in a threatening shout, but there just wasn't enough air in his lungs. Instead, the words trickled out.

Beck laughed loudly. "I know everything about you, Mr. Slay. I know about you and your wife and your business and your friends and what you had for breakfast yesterday. Shall I recite your Social Security number? Driver's license number? Your bank balance? Information is my business and I love it. The only thing I like more is what I'm doing right now. Beating arrogant little worms like you to death."

"Beck!" came a strong voice. It was Mickie. "That's enough. We may need him, and I sure don't want to carry him out of here. Do you?"

Snapping his head around, he cast an evil, withering look at Mickie. He stared for a long moment, then took a deep and noisy breath.

"You're right, Mickie," he replied. "I may have overreacted a little."

"A little? You almost killed him."

Beck stepped back and looked at the pummeled man who leaned against the white stone pillar that now bore dark traces of his blood. Tilting his head slightly, Beck studied him as a naturalist might contemplate some previously unknown insect. Then he stepped forward and viciously slammed his fist into the small of Dick's back. The searing pain of the kidney punch dropped Dick to the floor, where he lay in a deathlike stillness.

The temple was spinning. The floor was undulating. Strange whistles and crackles and tones filled his ears. Darkness was slipping into Dick's mind. The last thing he heard was Beck's voice:

"Well, let's see what our friends have found for us."

Dick surrendered to the sweetness of unconsciousness.

Forty-One

Abbay Gorge, Ethiopia

Adam raised a clinched fist and rapped his knuckles against his forehead. "Think, Adam," he said aloud to himself. "Think. What are we missing?"

"Maybe nothing," Pruit said as he stared at the narrow slit in the cave wall. "We've already established that the opening is too narrow for any of us to fit through. I don't mind telling you that the thought of being wedged into a fissure gives me the creeps."

Adam began to pace around the cave, his head bowed in deep thought. "Let's back up and take a running start at this thing," he said. "Pruit is right; none of us is going to squeeze through that crack in the cave wall. Yet we know that what we're looking for is back there someplace. We have Pruit's stigmata as proof of that. All that remains is figuring out how to get to whatever it is that is behind the solid rock wall. We've looked through the entire cave and found no other openings. We've followed the gap from floor to ceiling, to no avail."

"Maybe this isn't the entrance at all," Ted offered. "Maybe this is just what it appears, a crack in the wall."

Adam shook his head. "I don't think so. I mean, your point is logical, Ted, but when we factor in the images from the painting, we have got to believe that this is where we're supposed to be."

Facing the wall, Adam closed his eyes tight. "I'm overlooking something here, but I just don't know what it is. Galefo, do you know of any other cracks like this, or other openings?"

Silence.

Adam turned to discover that Galefo was missing. "Where did Galefo go?" he inquired. "He was here just a few minutes ago."

"I don't know," Ted answered with a shrug. "Maybe he had to answer nature's call. He is human, you know."

Adam frowned, then returned his attention to the puzzle before him. "I can't help but feel the answer is right under our collective noses. But we've looked every direction possible."

"Wait a minute," Rachel said. "Not under our noses, but under our feet. We've looked every direction but down."

"Down?" Pruit was nonplussed. "There's nothing but dirt on the ground."

"How do we know that?"

Adam looked at Rachel for a moment, then at the floor of the cave where it adjoined the vertical crevice in the rock wall. "You mean like a trapdoor or something?"

"Something like that," Rachel replied. "Not necessarily a trapdoor, but an opening or gateway. Listen, have you ever noticed how old houses develop cracks in their walls? Those cracks occur where the building material is the weakest or where the ground has settled. Maybe this crack in the cave wall is here because there's been some settling over the years."

Stepping toward the back wall of the cave, Adam knelt down in front of the fissure and began scraping away the dirt at its base with his hands. The dirt was densely packed and gave way reluctantly. "Is there anything we can dig with?" Adam asked.

Rachel rummaged through her backpack. "There's a metal plate in here. Will that help?"

"Couldn't hurt." Adam took the plate from Rachel. It was a simple aluminum plate with high edges to keep food from falling off. Just the kind of thing a camper would carry along. "Bring the light over here so I can see what I'm doing."

Ted grabbed the electric lantern and set it near where Adam was digging. He then, like the others, watched in silence as Adam, on hands and knees, dug into the earth.

Six inches deep the metal plate released a scratching sound as it struck something hard. Adam continued digging until he had uncovered an area of the floor half a foot deep and three feet square.

He stopped to catch his breath. "This is too much like work," Adam said glibly, his breathing labored.

Pruit knelt down by the exposed area. "You've found solid rock, my friend. You won't dig through bedrock with an aluminum plate."

"Look," Rachel said excitedly, as she too knelt on the cave floor. Bending over to bring her face close to the ground, she took a deep breath and blew through pursed lips. Dust flew in the air, forcing Adam to wave his hand in front of his face to keep from inhaling the fine particles. "See," she said, pointing at a line in the stone.

"It's a flaw in the rock," Pruit said. "Big deal."

"Not a flaw," Rachel rebutted. "A joint. See how straight it is, even the edges. This is not a natural occurrence, it's man-made."

"She's right," Ted exclaimed excitedly. "That's no crack. Let's keep digging."

Together the four scraped with hands and metal plates taken from their respective packs until three sides of a rectangle could be seen. One side remained hidden under the cave wall.

"Now what?" Ted asked.

"That depends," Adam said. "That depends on whether this doorway—and that's clearly what it is—was ever meant to be opened again."

"What do you mean?" asked Pruit.

"If the builders of the door wanted to seal it forever, then the stone covering is probably too heavy for us, or even a dozen of us, to move. But if they wanted access to whatever is behind the cave wall, then there must be a way to open this."

"Do you mean like a secret lever that will cause the stone to slide out of the way?" asked Ted.

"That works well in the movies, Ted, but I don't think we'll be that lucky." Adam stood and stretched his back. "We need to be looking for something else."

"Like?" Pruit inquired.

"I haven't the foggiest idea," Adam confessed. "My guess would be that the stone is counterbalanced or set on a fulcrum and held in place by some key."

"What kind of key could open this?" Ted sat back against the wall.

"I'm not talking about a house key," Adam explained. "I mean something like a keystone, a wedge that keeps the stone door from moving."

"But we've uncovered the entire perimeter of the door," Rachel objected, "and there's nothing there."

"Which means, my dear Watson," Adam replied with a mock British accent, "that the keystone must be elsewhere."

"If there is one," Pruit remarked. "But I don't have any better ideas, so let's start looking."

"Wait," Rachel said. "Just how far could the key be from the opening? Not very far, right?"

"I guess so," Adam answered.

"So if it's here, then it must be nearby," Rachel glanced around. "Like maybe in there." She pointed to the split in the wall.

Picking up the light, Adam held it to the opening. "I don't see anything."

"Look lower," Rachel said. "If there is a key it would be close to the ground."

Adam held the electric lantern near the junction of the floor and the wall fissure. "I think I see something." He reached into the opening in the rock face. "I hope nothing is crawling around in here. It's a rock but it has an odd shape. It's wedged into the ground." Adam began to push and pull the stone, jiggling it. "It's coming loose." Grunting and groaning, Adam put his weight into it. The stone wedge gave way suddenly, causing him to plop ungracefully to the cave floor.

There was a grinding, rasping, abrasive sound as the large rectangular stone in the cave floor began to slip, the edge nearest the cave wall falling, the opposite edge rising into the air.

"It's hinged," Ted exclaimed. "It's balanced on hinges."

"Unbelievable," Pruit said softly. "This whole thing keeps getting crazier and crazier."

"So the crack in the wall isn't from settling after all," Rachel offered. "Whoever built the door must have made use of an already existing fault in the wall."

"Well," Adam said, standing to his feet again, "shall we all be good little Alices and go down the rabbit hole?"

"What about Galefo?" Ted asked.

"He's a big boy," Pruit replied. "He'll see the opening and follow. I say we go now. I'd just as soon have this whole thing over."

"I'd like to take more light with us." Adam walked to his backpack. "Check your packs. Galefo must have put a flashlight or something in our supplies."

Each pack was searched and each pack yielded a flashlight and extra batteries.

"Boy," Rachel intoned. "Galefo really knows how to pack. I even have another electric lantern. That means we can leave one for our trusty guide."

"Off we go then," Adam said. "I'll go first, if that's all right." No one objected. "OK then, how about Rachel following me, then Pruit, then Ted. Does that work for everybody?"

Each affirmed the idea. Adam then walked to the opening in the floor, stepped onto the slanted stone lid that now formed a ramp, inched his way down, and held out the electric lamp. "I feel like I'm being swallowed."

Adam disappeared into the dark, open maw.

Each in turn followed him down.

The downward edge of the stone lid rested on the landing of a set of stone stairs. The stairway tunnel was about four feet wide but the enclosed, dark passage made it seem much narrower. Slowly Adam made his way down the steps, one at a time, being careful not to trip and fall. A broken leg here could mean enduring hours, even days of pain before help could be found—if such help could be found.

"How far ahead can you see?" Pruit asked, his voice rebounding off the hard stone walls and ceiling and rumbling down the corridor.

"It's hard to tell," Adam replied. "But it looks like the stairs end soon. I wish I had thought to count them."

"Forty so far," Rachel called out. "At six inches a step that means we've descended twenty or so feet."

"You're a clever girl," Adam said. "I did a good thing when I married you."

Rachel laughed. "I agree."

With his attention intently focused on his feet, Adam pressed on. "Anyone ever read, *Journey to the Center of the Earth?* This is how

I imagined it—dark, confining, and a little scary."

Adam's words were light and playful, but his heart was pounding hard and his breathing was shallow. He forced himself to focus on each step he took. Step by careful step he led the party deeper into the ground underneath the Jamma River. He was excited, but he also knew he was afraid. It had never occurred to Adam that he might be claustrophobic.

"I've run out of stairs," Adam announced suddenly.

"And none too soon," Pruit replied. "I was afraid we were on the stairway to . . ."

"You're not going to believe this," Adam said, his voice dripping with astonishment.

"You'll have to move," Rachel replied. "You're blocking the way."

Adam stepped aside as the others joined him at the bottom of the stairs. No one spoke. No one moved. No one could believe their eyes.

Before them was a cavernous room that extended beyond the reach of the electric lantern's light. The ceiling hovered sixty feet above them. The walls looked smooth and milled. Standing next to the walls on the group's right and left were massive statues of stone: angels with long, ornate wings extended before them, creating a canopy that covered the chamber.

"How far down did you say we walked?" Adam asked in hushed tones.

"I . . . uh . . . I counted seventy-seven steps," Rachel replied weakly. "That would make it about thirty-eight to forty feet. Give or take a couple of feet."

"I would guess that these statues are close to sixty feet high." Adam raised the lantern. "Of course we dropped several thousand feet of elevation on the path."

"Rachel," Pruit began, "is this the stone church you saw in your vision?"

"No," Rachel responded quietly, "but these statues of angels are like the ones I saw in the church—only larger."

"They form a hall," Ted offered. "It appears that we move straight ahead."

Holding the lantern at arm's length, Adam walked purposefully down the corridor formed by the ranks of angelic statues.

"What kind of angels do you call these?" Pruit asked. "Other than 'large,' I mean."

"Cherubim," Adam responded. "Sure does away with the picture of chubby bare-bottomed babies, doesn't it?"

"Oh, yeah," Pruit said. "You can say that again."

"It looks like we've run out of room." Adam took a few more strides then stopped before a pair of large wooden doors. The doors were covered in colorful pictographs. Adam gently blew on the doors to blow away some of the dust. "Do these look familiar?" he asked Rachel.

"Yes. This is what I saw in my vision."

"It looks similar to the Kebra Nagast," Adam said. "Different in some ways, but very similar."

"Do we knock or just barge in?" Ted inquired.

"Let me," Rachel said as she raised her hands and pressed on the doors. To Adam's surprise, the doors swung open easily, accompanied by a grinding sound at the base. Dust scattered into the air and hung there as if suspended in water.

"No need to stand on formality, I suppose." Adam took a long stride across the threshold and then stepped aside to allow the others in.

"It's a pyramid," Ted exclaimed. "We're inside a pyramid!"

The walls of the inner chamber were indeed sloped and met in a point at the top. Turning, Adam studied the inclined wall behind him. It, like the floor, the double doors, and everything else, was covered in a thin layer of dust which Adam lightly brushed away with his fingers. The wall was covered with shallow engravings.

"More angels?" Rachel asked softly, as if she were standing in a cathedral.

"Yeah," Adam answered, mimicking her tone. "But that's not all. The wall is covered in gold."

"Gold?" Pruit stepped to the nearest wall, held his flashlight beam on it, and wiped away the accumulated dust. "It is! The walls are covered in gold."

"I bet if we cleaned up those huge statues out there," Adam commented dryly, "we would find that they have their fair share of gold covering them, too."

Adam turned to face the room, holding the lantern above his head. The chamber was empty except for a large, rectangular stone table centered directly under the pinnacle. On top of the rock pedestal appeared to be a mound of dark, dusty, frayed rags. Adam's heart began to race and thump like a piston in a large engine. Pruit stepped next to him.

289

"Do you suppose that's it?" Pruit asked softly. "I mean, it doesn't look like much."

"In my vision," Rachel interjected, "there was a purple linen draped over the ark. When I touched it, it fell to the ground. The angel in my vision told me to unwrap it. He said, 'Uncover the Holy, Blessed Woman. The world will see through your eyes and theirs. Uncover.'"

With her eyes fixed on the bundle of drapes, she approached. The others followed closely until each stood within arm's reach of the object.

Taking his eyes from the lone object in the room, Adam stared at his wife. She was transfixed, her eyes wide, her mouth agape. He watched as she swallowed hard and then slowly, tentatively, extended her arm. As if deriving courage from the act, she quoted the angel's words again: "Uncover the Holy, Blessed Woman. The world will see through your eyes and theirs. Uncover."

Rachel gently tugged at the cloth. The slight pull was all that was necessary for the ancient material to deteriorate into a pile of dust at their feet. A cloud of fine powder filled the air, causing everyone to cough.

It took a moment for the dust-impregnated air to clear, revealing a chest covered in gold, topped with a lid of solid gold from which had been crafted two kneeling angels, their wings spread up and forward until their tips touched.

Heavy silence. Fate realized. The impossible seen. Eternity confined.

Adam grabbed his stomach, turned, and staggered to the inclined wall behind him.

"Adam," Rachel asked, her voice filled with concern. "Adam, what is it?"

He shook his head and pointed. "The . . . the . . ." Adam sucked in a massive amount of air. He was perspiring profusely, his breathing was ragged, and he felt nausea fill his stomach. "The ark of the covenant! The ark of God! It really is the ark."

Adam began to weep.

"Are you sick?" Rachel asked as she knelt beside him.

He shook his head.

Pruit and Ted just stared at Adam.

"Moses. Joshua. David. Solomon." He began to sob, not from illness, not from fear, but because he and he alone fully understood what he was seeing. He knew that the eyes of Moses had gazed on the most holy artifact in history. That Joshua carried it across the Jordan and had it transported upon the shoulders of the levitical priests around the walls of Jericho. Adam comprehended in both his mind and his heart that this was the same instrument that caused David to dance and the very object placed in the holy of holies in Solomon's temple.

For Adam, the ark was not an archeological curiosity or the subject for an adventure movie. God spoke to Moses from above the ark. God's very words had reverberated in resounding tones from the ark. Lightning had flashed. Thunder had fractured the air.

The ark. The ark of the covenant. The ark of strength. The ark of power, capped with the mercy seat upon which the blood of countless bulls had been sprinkled for the sins of Israel. The ark that foreshadowed the coming of Christ and foretold His death.

Ever since Rachel's dream, Adam knew that he would gaze upon that which no man has seen for nearly 3,000 years. But now to actually see the relic of God's specific design right before his eyes was more than Adam could stand. His soul was filled with such awe, such reverence, that his body felt as if it would explode.

Adam was not ill. Adam had not been struck by a sudden deadly plague as the Philistines had when they captured the ark. Adam was struck down by unadulterated, undiluted joy.

"Well, well, well." A new voice. A strange voice. An evil voice. "You are certainly industrious, I'll give you that."

The four turned to the chamber's doorway but could see only bright lights that were being flashed in their eyes.

"Who are you?" Pruit demanded.

"Place the lights and take your positions," the voice said. The lights began to move as they were borne along by the people who held them. Moments later the chamber was filled with a bright effulgence that evaporated the darkness that had filled the room for so many centuries.

As Adam's eyes adjusted to the sudden influx of intense light he stood shakily to his feet. Spread evenly around the room were men, each with powerful, battery-operated lights. Adam recognized two of them: Galefo and Dr. Julian Newton, the president of the seminary where Adam taught. Only Newton was unarmed; the others steadily held military-type automatic rifles.

"Dr. Newton," Adam began. "I don't . . . I don't understand. What are you doing here? Who are these people? Why do they have guns?"

Newton didn't respond. His eyes were locked on the ark, his hand was raised to his mouth. He was having a response similar to Adam's.

"It appears that Dr. Newton is a little preoccupied at the moment, so allow me to do the introductions." The man spoke as one who was used to getting his way. "I am Gerald T. Quince. Just your knowing that is enough for me to order you killed, but I have need of you—for now."

"Quince?" Pruit intoned with disbelief. "The Gerald T. Quince of Datadyne Software?"

"It appears that my fame has preceded me." Quince gave a small bow. "And you, sir, are Pruit Bain. We almost did business together."

"I remember," Pruit said. "We lost that contract to BBD&O. Broke my heart. We could have done great things for you."

"Actually, you already have," Quince said, nodding at the ark. "You found that for me."

"For you?" Adam snapped.

"Ah, Reverend Bridger. Dr. Newton told me you were a lively one. Yes, indeed, I meant what I said. The ark is mine."

"If you think we're going to stand here and . . ."

Quince waved Adam off with a raised hand. "Look around you, Bridger. By my count there are four automatic weapons leveled at you. Since you have no weapons, the advantage would seem to be ours."

"I don't understand," Ted interjected. "How did you find us, and . . ." He turned to Galefo. "Are you with them, Galefo?"

Galefo stood straight and emotionless.

"We trusted you, Galefo," Ted continued, his words heavy with the pain of betrayal.

"Now Mr. Hawthorne," Quince interrupted. "Don't go impugning Galefo's loyalty. He is a very devoted man. He's just not all that devoted to you."

"But . . ." Ted began.

Quince cut him off with a raised hand. "We had your phone tapped and your house bugged. When we learned of your intentions to hire Galefo we simply made sure that he received an irresistible offer, an offer that Hector, who had been following you, made. He was easy to find, since he has such a fine reputation as a guide. We offered him more money, then sweetened the deal by providing arms and ammunition to his friends who aren't quite finished with the civil war yet. So you see, he is a man of loyalty. And in return for that little business transaction, he showed us another way into the gorge. He radioed us shortly before you left. Ninety minutes later we hopped into our trusty helicopter, flew to a path similar to the one you took, but about six miles farther north. We hiked in from the north, while you did so from the south. Then we waited to hear from Galefo. When he told us you had found something we decided to join you. Not very complicated, really."

Dr. Newton approached the ark and slowly walked around it, drinking in every detail of its construction, size, and craftsmanship. "Extraordinary! Magnificent! This is the greatest find in all of archeology. Nothing, not the pyramids of Egypt or Mexico, nothing in science is more important than this."

Adam was disgusted. Seeing his colleague in union with the people who were holding them at gunpoint nauseated him. He had trusted Dr. Newton; sought his advice. It didn't take much mental gymnastics to know that Newton had used the information shared in their meeting against Adam and the others.

"The workmanship is unlike anything I have ever seen," Newton went on. "Adam, did you notice the detail in the wings of the angels? Have you observed how the mercy seat fits perfectly in the gold crown so that it can't slide off when borne on the shoulders of the priests? And look here . . ."

"Don't speak to me like a colleague, Newton," Adam shouted. "You betrayed my trust and have endangered our lives."

"Oh, now, Adam," Newton replied with shock. "You exaggerate the point. All I did . . ."

"What do you plan to do with the ark?" Adam brusquely asked Quince. "Sell it, I suppose."

"Sell it?" Quince laughed loudly. "There's no price you can put on this object. You should know that. No, I have no plans of selling it. I plan to keep it. To admire it. To love it. You see, I collect antiquities—not always legally, but it is an obsession. This will be located in my vault, safe from others, and viewed only by me."

"Oh, but it must be studied," Newton objected. "The finest

scholars must be allowed to analyze it and describe it in the proper journals. This belongs to humanity."

"No it doesn't," Quince snapped. "It belongs to me. And when I get the golden jar of manna and Aaron's rod, I will be the sole possessor of the most important artifacts in human history, thanks in large part to you, Dr. Newton."

"No, wait." Newton was stupefied, and he swayed slightly as if his knees had gone weak. "I thought we agreed that . . ."

"For an educated man, Dr. Newton," Quince shouted roughly, "you are an idiot. A sniveling, whining idiot. Did you honestly think that I would allow the world to know of this treasure? You're a fool, Newton. A literal fool."

"What about the jar of manna and Aaron's rod?" Adam asked coarsely. "What have you done with my friends?"

Waving him off, Quince replied, "Friends are a dime a dozen. But not to worry. They're still alive—for now."

Quince stepped up to the ark. "It looks as if you have yet to open it, Bridger. I thought you would want to know if the Ten Commandments were still inside."

Adam said nothing. The onslaught of feebleness that had struck him at seeing the majesty and beauty of the ark had been supplanted with a barely controlled fury. His fists were tightly clenched, knuckles white, every muscle taut.

Cutting his eyes away from the ark for a moment, Quince studied Adam. "Watch him," Quince ordered. "He looks like a man who is thinking of heroics."

Galefo quickly crossed the chamber to Adam, placed the barrel of his AK-47 in the middle of Adam's chest and pushed him back against the sloped wall. Adam could feel the barrel dig into his flesh. Galefo wore no expression on his face. Clearly he was man whose emotions had dried out.

"Tell me, Dr. Newton," Quince began in a conversational tone, "do you think it is possible for a man to touch the ark without perishing?"

Newton shrugged his shoulders. "That's an unknown. We do have biblical accounts of the plague of mice and tumors the ark brought upon the Philistines when they captured it. And of course, there is Uzzah, who was instantly killed when he laid a hand on the ark to steady it when it appeared that it might fall from the cart upon which it rested. Now there has been much speculation over the centuries about the deadly nature of the ark of the covenant. Some for example . . ."

"The bottom line, Newton," Quince snapped. "Save the lecture for your students. Just tell me if I'm likely to be killed or injured if I touch this thing."

Shaking his head, Newton confessed: "I don't know. No one knows. The ark, except on rare and unusual occasions, was always covered. We are seeing what only a handful of men have ever seen. Whether it's still lethal is unknown."

"Hector, bring the woman here," Quince demand.

Stepping from his post by one of the walls, Hector did as his boss ordered, grabbing Rachel by the arm and jerking her to Quince's side. She stumbled.

Adam started forward, but Galefo shoved the barrel of his rifle deeper into Adam's flesh.

"Touch it!" Quince commanded loudly.

Rachel turned to look at Adam. His face was a mixture of pain from the intrusive gun barrel and fear for his wife.

"I said, touch it!" Quince's face reddened.

Rachel hesitated; fear draped her face.

"Galefo," Quince shouted. "I'm going to count to five. If she has not touched the ark by then, put a bullet in her husband's heart."

"No!" Rachel countered. "I'll touch it."

"One."

Rachel drew in a long breath.

"Rachel, don't," Adam pleaded. "We don't know . . ." Adam grimaced as Galefo leaned heavily on the AK-47, pushing it deeper between his ribs.

"Two."

Rachel looked at Pruit, then at Ted; their faces reflected her anxiety.

"Three." Quince said loudly.

Slowly, tentatively, Rachel raised her hand and let it hover near the ark. Adam wondered if she was remembering the part of the vision in which she had just lightly grazed the ark with her fingertips and the vision abruptly ended with her being catapulted back to her hospital bed. Was the sudden ending of the vision a symbol of instant death?

"Four. I'm losing my patience, Dr. Tremaine. If you don't think Galefo will . . ."

Suddenly there was a hand on the ark, laid squarely between the cherubim. It was Pruit's hand, and it was trembling. All eyes were fixed first on his hand, then on the man who dared touch the ark. Pruit Bain stood rigid as if someone had slid a steel rod down his back. His eyes were clamped shut; sweat oozed from his skin.

An eerie stillness flooded the room.

No one spoke.

No one moved.

All were transfixed by the unmoving man before them.

Then there was a slight whistle, as Pruit let out a long . . . easy . . . breath. A moment later he opened his eyes then smiled.

There was a consolidated sigh of relief.

"So its power is gone," Quince said. "I am both relieved and disappointed. At least it doesn't kill at the mere touch."

"Well, it didn't kill me at any rate," Pruit said glibly, emboldened by the fact that he was still very much alive.

"Enough of this," Quince announced. Reaching forward, he touched the ark without hesitation. Nothing.

"Hector, Carl, remove the lid. Let's see what's inside."

Obedient to the orders, Hector and Carl shouldered their weapons and, with each standing at an end of the ark, took hold of the mercy seat and lifted it. The lid moved easily and the two men sidestepped to make way for Quince.

Gerald T. Quince, billionaire businessman, stepped forward and peered into the golden chest of God. At first he gave no sign of what he saw, quietly letting his eyes dart over the contents. Then he lifted his head and laughed loud and long. With a flourish, he reached into the ark and pulled out a stone tablet.

Adam judged the tablet to be about two-and-half feet long and about eighteen inches wide. Unlike the image he had held of the stone tablets carried by Moses, these were thin, not more than an inch or two in thickness. The tablet had a greenish cast to it and clear markings that looked similar to ancient Hebrew.

"Behold," Quince said quietly, almost reverently, as if he possessed any reverence, "the Ten Commandments written by the very finger of God." Quince tenderly traced the engraved letters written in a language he could not read. "The words of God, and I own them."

"It's a shame that you hold no regard for the meaning of those words," Adam said forcefully. "There are several commandments there that you would find useful, such as no coveting, murdering, or stealing. No one owns the words of God, Quince, no one. The words of God own us."

Quince looked at Adam, his eyes narrow, suspicious. "Shut up, preacher. I need no sermon from you."

Newton raced forward, reached into the ark, and extracted the second stone tablet. He held it close to his chest, hugging it. He even kissed its edge.

Unable to believe what he was seeing, Adam ceased to feel the pressure of Galefo's gun in his chest. Before him was the ark of the covenant and the two tablets given to Moses by God—tablets of stone etched with the words that changed all of history—words inscribed by none other than God's own finger.

And both were in the possession of a madman.

Forty-Two

Aboard the *Quintessence*, northwest of Karpathos

Droning. Deep, resonant, droning. Dick couldn't tell if the sound he was hearing was coming from inside or outside his head.

He hurt, hurt everywhere. His throat was dry, his lips parched. Every breath brought a burning, searing pain to his chest. He coughed. Winced in pain. Coughed again.

"Dick?" a pleasant, soft, whisper said. "Are you awake?"

Dick licked his lips with a dry tongue and attempted to speak. A muted voice that was a mere shadow of his own oozed feebly from his mouth. "I'm . . . I'm awake. I think."

"We've been worried about you, Dick," the voice said. It was Katrin. "I was afraid that you had slipped into a coma."

The only response the beaten man could offer was a slight shaking of the head. "Still here, still alive—sorta."

"Do you remember anything?" Katrin asked softly as her gentle hand touched his forehead.

Thinking hurt. Breathing hurt. Remembering hurt. "I remember fighting Beck. I think I may have lost." Dick attempted to laugh,

298

but his aching body wouldn't permit it.

"You were very brave to stand up for us like that."

"Aw, shucks, ma'am," Dick replied lightly, "it weren't nothin'.'"

"Sorry I wasn't much help," a man's voice said.

Dick opened his eyes and tried to focus. His eyelids were heavy and puffy, allowing him only a small slit through which to peer at his friends. Nick and Katrin stood over him, each with an expression of deep concern.

"You took quite a beating," Nick said.

"I wasn't hit by a truck?" Dick asked.

"Not in the literal sense," Nick answered. "But that man is clearly a trained killer. I thought he was going to break you in two."

"It feels like he broke me into a hundred pieces." Dick attempted to sit up.

"No you don't," Katrin said. "You're not moving. Best I can tell, you have some broken ribs. I wish Rachel were here. She'd know what to do with you."

"Where . . . where are we?" Dick asked weakly.

"On the *Quintessence*," Nick answered. "We've been on board about three hours."

A frown crossed Dick's face. The *Quintessence*? How did he get back on the yacht? Slowly the memories returned. He recalled being hoisted onto his feet and made to walk from the ancient Minoan temple. He could barely stand, but they kept pushing him. When he fell, Beck would swear at him then lift him back to his feet, all the while threatening to leave him behind on the deserted Greek island. So Dick walked, or better staggered, through the small forest, stopping frequently to lean against a tree. Each stop angered Beck, who would then slap Dick to keep him conscious.

There was a vague memory of tumbling into the Zodiac and an even more misty memory of two jet skis that he had previously seen onboard the yacht. Everything else that came to mind was muddled and draped in dreamlike unreality.

"Where are we?" Dick watched through his swollen lids as Nick and Katrin exchanged knowing glances.

"Don't you remember our telling you that we are on the *Quintessence*?" Nick asked with concern.

Dick nodded. "I remember. I mean, where is the *Quintessence*?"

"You mean, where are we headed?" Katrin offered.

"Yes."

"We don't know, buddy," Nick said. "Katrin noticed that the sun is behind us, so it appears that we are headed east. I think he plans to dock in Rhodes."

"Rhodes," Dick repeated. "Not Karpathos?"

"No," Nick replied. "These people are smart. They're not going to take us someplace where we might be recognized by the staff of the hotel. I think they have another plan."

The hatch door to the lower deck of the yacht swung open with a bang and Beck stepped down the small ladder, followed by Mickie and Ross. Everyone carried a pistol.

"I couldn't help but overhear," he said. "You are smart people. Rhodes is exactly where we're headed. It's a beautiful place I'm told, with a nice yacht facility, pretty harbors, and a rich history. It's a pity we won't be taking any of that in. Our schedule is just too tight." Beck nodded to Ross, who holstered the pistol he had brought with him. Beck and Mickie kept their guns raised and pointed at their hostages.

Ross quickly made his way to the small windows that provided light below deck and began to pull closed the heavy curtains that covered them. Then, peeling off a long strip of duct tape from a roll he had brought with him, he began taping the loose ends of the drapes to the bulkhead.

"We can't have you waving at anyone on the docks when we arrive," Beck explained. "We want to keep a low profile. So here's the plan: We'll dock in Rhodes one hour after sunset. We will all stay on-board until midnight, at which time a van will brought as close to the *Quintessence* as possible. My crew will by then have our little prizes crated and ready for transport. After the items are loaded into the van you will disembark one at a time, under guard, and enter the vehicle. I will hold young Ms. Couer as a hostage. If you try to run, shout, or draw attention to yourself, I'll put a bullet in her spine. Assuming you behave, I will then escort her to the car and off we go."

"To where?" Nick asked, making no attempt to hide his anger or disdain.

"To the airfield," Beck answered nonchalantly. "Then we fly to Cairo."

"What's in Cairo?" Katrin inquired.

"That's all the information you need for now," Beck snapped. "I only tell you this much so that you know what's expected of you."

"Why not just kill us now and throw us overboard?" Nick spat.

"I like the idea," Beck said. "But I have my orders, and my orders require me to bring you along—for now."

"Orders?" Nick responded. "Who's behind all of this, anyway?"

"You ask too many questions," Beck answered, then, noticing that Ross was finished taping the curtains to the bulkheads, said, "I want to remind you that Ross and Mickie are right outside the door. They can hear everything you say. Any attempt to escape will make me angry. And you don't want to see me angry, do they, Mr. Slay?"

Dick didn't respond. He was using all his strength and will-power to remain conscious.

"I think you get my point," Beck said. He then turned and stepped back up the ladder.

The sound of a latch being thrown and a lock being snapped shut put the final exclamation point on the truth. They were trapped and powerless.

"There has to be something we can do," Katrin exclaimed. "We can't just sit here."

"I suggest prayer," Dick said with a cough. "I suggest prayer." Unconsciousness overtook Dick once again.

Forty-Three

Over Egypt

Small wisps of gossamer clouds flickered past the window of the Bombardier's Global Express jet as it cruised at more than 500 miles per hour high above southern Egypt.

Adam continued to gaze out the window as he had done since take off. Seated in the plush seats next to him, Rachel slept fitfully. She was exhausted as were Pruit, Ted, and himself. He wanted to sleep, to close eyes, weary from the stress and strain of the past days, but his overactive mind wouldn't let him.

They were in mortal danger, kidnapped and held captive by a greedy and very powerful man—a man who seemed to hold all the cards. A small voice in Adam's mind kept chanting the same theme: "There's nothing you can do."

It did seem that fate had turned against them. Hours ago, they bathed in the light of the greatest discovery in human history. Now they were handcuffed to the seats in which they sat. The center section of the jet had been modified to a conference roomlike setting, with high-back leather chairs situated in a near circle so that everyone could see the faces of the others.

But Adam wasn't a fatalist. He was a man of faith and a man of action. He believed and taught that God works His will through the actions of His people. Adam had never been content to simply sit back and wait for God to do something. Instead, he felt it was his duty to do as much as possible within God's will and let God bless the work.

But what could he do here? He felt weak physically from the arduous journey forced upon them by Quince and his cohorts. It was clear that Quince was a man of planning. It took less than half an hour for him to lead the others in the discovery of the gold-coated poles that were used to carry the ark. Adam, in his astonishment, hadn't even realized that the rods were missing. Newton found them tucked securely behind one of the large angels that watched over the entrance.

Under Quince's orders the rods were inserted through the gold rings mounted on the feet of the ark. Minutes later, under gunpoint, Adam, Pruit, Ted, and one of Quince's men, Carl, had shouldered the holy object and were marching it under the outstretched wings of the giant cherubim statues at the inner chamber's entry.

Getting the heavy object through the long stone corridor and up the stone steps had been laborious and extremely fatiguing. The ark was heavy, encased as it was with gold sheathing inside and out. Adam could only be thankful that the ark had not been constructed of solid gold instead of gold laid over wood. If it had, the weight would have been impossible.

It was while carrying the ark on his shoulder as the ancient levitical priests used to do that Adam was reminded of one of the traditions he had discovered in his research. There were some who held that the ark was not really borne upon the shoulders of the priests as a burden, but that the priests were levitated by the power of the ark so that their feet hovered a few feet off the ground. The tradition held no place in Scripture and therefore Adam doubted that the account was more than the fancy of some ancient storyteller. But by the time he and the others had carried the antiquity through the rock tunnel, he began to wish the tale were true.

Adam and the others were allowed a small measure of rest as Newton, Hector, and Galefo lowered the counterbalanced stone hatch back to its original position and replaced the keystone. The small mound of dirt dug up by Adam and his team was carefully replaced so that the secret doorway was concealed once again.

"Do a good job, gentlemen," Quince had said. "There is still much to be harvested from those two chambers. We don't want others to know it's there. Which brings me to another point. Hector, if you don't mind."

"Not at all," the swarthy thin man said. Hector smiled at Quince, then with incredible speed raised his automatic rifle, leveled it at Galefo, and squeezed the trigger. A dozen rounds erupted from the barrel in less than two seconds' time.

Rachel screamed. Pruit covered his head. Galefo fell to the ground dead.

Dr. Newton, a quiet, reserved, scholarly man, swayed, grabbed his stomach, and then vomited.

Hector and Carl wordlessly took hold of the now lifeless arms of the tall Ethiopian, dragged him to the edge of the small cave and dropped his body over the edge. It fell 300 feet to the churning river below, the force of the waterfall pressing the body below the surface.

Newton was on the verge of a nervous breakdown. "Why did you do that?" he screamed. "He was on our side."

Quince shook his head. "He was on his side. He betrayed these people here," he motioned to Adam and the others. "He would betray us, too. You saw how much gold is still down there. Do you really think that he would hesitate to come back with his rebel buddies after we were gone and strip the place clean?"

"But his body could become evidence against us," Newton exclaimed as he bordered apoplexy.

Again, Quince shook his head. "The crocodiles will eat him and be glad for the free meal. Now, let's go."

"But how do I know you won't have me shot in the back?" Newton asked.

"You don't," Quince said easily.

The journey back up the cliff face was shorter than the one they had taken down, and fortunately for those toting the ark, the path was considerably wider. Galefo had apparently chosen a longer route to allow Quince and his team time to travel to the site. Yet, despite its shorter length, the trek up was still taxing. Several times they had to stop, set the ark down, and rest. Quince would allow pauses of only five minutes and no more.

Things might have been easier had the sun not set. The only light Quince permitted was that which was broadcast by the moon. And Adam felt that Quince would have ordered that light extinguished if he had the means of doing so.

Quince took on the role of a taskmaster driving his slaves, as if he were overseeing the erection of an ancient pyramid. If Adam, Pruit, or Ted were slow in picking up the ark, Quince would place the muzzle of his weapon to Rachel's temple and order, "March!"

Every step had become an agony for Adam, and judging by Ted and Pruit's labored breathing it had become torture for them as well.

When they finally reached the top of the cliffs, Adam saw a large helicopter parked in a clearing away from the scattered acacia trees. It was an old Huey, the type that U.S. forces used in Vietnam. One man, armed with the same type of automatic weapon, was laying out items on the ground.

"Set it here," Quince ordered the bearers of the ark. "Hector, Carl, let's get this thing packed and get out of here."

Without hesitation and despite their own weariness, Hector and Carl wordlessly began to assemble a prefabricated wooden shipping container. The golden poles were removed from the ark's rings and slipped into long, sturdy, cardboard tubes. The tubes were then filled with tiny Styrofoam balls. The wooden crate was built around the ark and then filled with large, peanut-shaped Styrofoam packing material. The lid was nailed down.

On the sides of the crate, Adam could read the stenciled words: "Medical Supplies, Great Britain, Perishable." It appeared that Quince had thought of everything.

At gunpoint Adam, Rachel, and the rest were commanded to board the helicopter. Ten minutes later they were airborne, flying low over the Ethiopian countryside. The former gunship flew dark, without the beacons required by every airport and air travel department in the world.

"I suppose we're headed to Addis Ababa," Adam said to Quince.

"Don't be stupid," Quince snapped. "Too many people, too many police, too many government agents. We're flying to Derbe Markos. There's a small airstrip there. I have a plane waiting."

"Then where?" Adam asked.

"Not that it matters much to you," Quince offered harshly, "but then we fly to Cairo. I plan to meet some friends there. Come to think of it, you will have friends there, too. Assuming my people don't get spooked and kill them first."

The pit of Adam's stomach dropped and a wave of anger, sorrow, fear, rage, and sadness passed over him. Dick and the others were indeed in the control of Quince's men. That couldn't be good. And if Adam knew Dick—and Adam knew Dick—there was a struggle involved. Adam could only pray that his trusted friend hadn't bitten off more that he could chew.

The transfer at Derbe Markos went smoothly. Both people and cargo had been moved from the helicopter to the multimillion dollar private jet that sat on a narrow concrete runway.

Pruit, who had kept his own counsel over the last few hours, spoke: "Nice plane for a middle-class vehicle."

"Middle class?" Quince said. "This thing set my company back more than 34 million dollars."

"I paid 38 million for my Gulfstream V," Pruit said with a smile.

"Are you trying to antagonize me, Bain? If so, I'm not in the mood. Besides, I own three of these."

"Just chatting, that's all," Pruit said. "I figure I can say what I want, since you plan to kill us anyway."

"What makes you think that?"

"I didn't build the largest advertising agency in the world by being stupid, Quince. I've been around the block as many times as you. True, your net worth may be greater than mine, but your intellect is substantially lower."

"You're smarter than me?" Quince said with a chortle. "How do you figure that? I'm the one with a multibillion dollar international business. I'm the fifth richest man in the world. Last time I looked you didn't even make *Fortune* magazine's top 100 list."

"Well, you got me there, Quince old man," Pruit's smile broadened, making him look like the cat that ate the canary. "You do have more money, and we all know that money is the measure of success. Don't we?"

"What else is there?" Quince responded. "Money, possessions, and power."

"Two out of three ain't bad, I guess."

"What do you mean, two out of three?"

"I'll grant you that you have money and that you have possessions. You even possess the very ark of God—for the moment at least.

But one thing you don't have is power."

"You're being ridiculous," Quince retorted loudly. "Of course I do. You see how people jump at my every word."

"That's not power," Pruit said shaking his head mournfully, like a parent who can't make a child understand a simple but necessary truth. "Giving orders is not power, it's control, but a very tenuous control. It could all fall in around your ears in a minute."

"Not bloody likely," Quince responded.

"Face it, Quince, you're on thin ice." Pruit nodded across the aisle at Hector and Carl. "What do you suppose they're thinking right now?" Hector and Carl looked at Pruit. "They saw you order Galefo's death, and now their wondering if you're going to order theirs. How does Hector know that you won't order Carl to blow his brains out sometime soon? After all, he does know where the chambers are, and he knows that you have the ark."

"Shut up, Bain." Quince snapped. "You're making a fool of yourself."

"On the contrary, I'm making a fool of you."

Quince leaned forward and struck Pruit with a wicked backhand. Pruit's nose gave a snap as it broke. Blood ran down his face. Looking at Quince, Pruit smiled and said, "No power. You can hurt me. You can kill me. But you will die powerless, always looking over your shoulder. Always wondering who is finally going to turn you in—and there's nothing you can do about it."

Quince brought his hand up again to strike Pruit, but then stopped. Slowly he lowered his hand. "Pruit Bain, I'm going to enjoy killing you."

Turning, Quince began to slowly walk to the front of the plane.

"Quince! Behind you! Look out!"

Spinning on his feet, Quince raised his rifle, ready to fire. There was no danger. Everyone was still seated.

Pruit began to laugh. "See? Do you see? You have no power. All you possess is fear, and fear is a leech that will suck you dry of life. Trust me, I know. Everyone is your enemy. Everyone a potential assassin. You can't even trust your own crew." Pruit began to laugh hysterically. "You have money. You have position. But like me, you never have had peace of mind. You're poverty stricken, Quince, just like I was. We're two peas in a pod, old man. Two peas in a pod. We sit in our lifeboat of image and position, but find that we are sinking in a sea of money. And money doesn't buy peace of mind, Quince. It won't buy a good night's sleep or the hug of a woman who loves you. As a businessman you're wealthy, but as a human being you're the poorest pauper. Face it, you are pathetic."

Adam couldn't believe what he was seeing or hearing. Pruit, handcuffed to the seat of the plane, was challenging a man who could order him killed with a word.

Quince's face grew crimson as the rage grew inside of him. Slowly he raised his rifle to his shoulder and aimed the barrel between Pruit's eyes.

A large, confident smile spread across Pruit's face. "Go ahead. For the first time in my life, I'm really ready to die."

"Uh, boss," Hector interrupted. "I hate to get in the way of a man and his work, but if you fire that in here, the slug is likely to blow a hole in the side of the plane and we'd lose pressure or sever a cable or something, maybe even crash."

There was a long, silent, heavy moment. Then Quince closed his eyes, turned, and walked briskly toward the pilot's cabin.

Adam saw Hector and Carl exchange glances; he saw Rachel, who had been awakened from her light sleep when Quince slapped Pruit, stare at Pruit in disbelief; he saw Ted look across the aisle, his eyes wide with fear. Only Pruit seemed calm and assured. Ignoring the blood that ran from his nose, Pruit closed his eyes and slipped off to sleep.

"Something has gotten into Pruit," Adam said to Rachel. "I don't know what it is, but it's in there good."

Forty-Four

Cairo, Egypt

The Global Express jet was towed into a large hangar at the extreme southern end of the Almaza Airport, a smaller airport than the Cairo International Airport a few miles northeast.

Inside the hangar harsh overhead lights cast long shadows from the plane. With hands cuffed together in front of them and under the watchful eyes of Carl and Hector, Adam, Rachel, Pruit, and Ted were allowed to deplane. A dark-skinned man in a uniform was speaking with Quince. At first Adam's pulse raced. Perhaps the uniformed man would rescue them, but that hope quickly evaporated when he saw Quince pass a large brown envelope to the stranger. A payoff.

There would be no customs inspection, no evaluation of the cargo. Most likely the man in the uniform just received two or three times his annual salary.

Adam let his eyes trace the hangar. He was looking for an escape route, a phone from which to call for help, a weapon to use, anything that might offer hope. He saw nothing. But he did see something that made his heart stop. A small group of people were huddled together next to some wooden crates. One person, a man, lay on the cold concrete. It was Dick.

Immediately, Adam started toward the group, but Hector stepped in his path. Adam said nothing as he ignored the raised gun and walked around the armed man. If Hector wanted to stop Adam from reaching Dick, then he would have to shoot him in the back.

"Dick," Adam called, breaking into a trot. "Dick!"

The others looked up. A man and a woman, each holding a pistol in one hand, stiffened at Adam's noisy approach.

"Adam," Katrin called as she stood up. "We were worried about you."

"With good reason," Adam replied. "What happened to Dick?" He looked down at his longtime friend who lay motionless on the floor. His face was bruised, and his eyes swollen. Streams of dried blood were caked to his face.

"He's been beat up pretty bad," Nick said sadly. "He keeps slipping in and out of consciousness."

"He . . . he was trying to protect us," Katrin said, her eyes flooding with tears. "He attacked that man over there, but the man was too fast, too strong."

"Not to mention Dick's hands were cuffed behind his back," Nick added. "He never had a chance."

Turning, Adam looked at the man Katrin had singled out. He didn't recognize him.

"His name is Jason Beck," Nick explained. "We found the island just as Martin said we would, and on the island we found an old temple. Inside was a large, very old wooden boat. Inside the boat was a stone box with a golden jar of manna and that rod thing. We used Beck's boat to get there. They followed us in and ambushed us after we found the artifacts."

Kneeling down, Adam shook Dick's shoulder lightly. There was no response. His friend was breathing, but it was clear that he was in deep trouble. Standing again, Adam turned to face the plane. "Rachel, come here. Dick needs you."

Without hesitation, Rachel made her way to the others, followed by Pruit and Ted. Fortunately, Rachel's hands were cuffed in front of her so that she had some use of them. She placed two fingers on the inside of Dick's wrist and felt for a pulse.

"His pulse is weak and thready," Rachel said in clinical tones. Adam could almost hear the wheels turning in her brain. "Color is ashen. Respiration below normal and shallow. I don't like this. Did he complain of any pain or make any comments at all?"

"He said it hurt to breathe," Katrin answered. "I think his ribs may be broken."

Deftly as her cuffed hands would allow, Rachel unbuttoned Dick's shirt and pulled it back. The left side of his chest was dark blue. She palpated his abdomen and Dick groaned.

"He's coming around," Adam said excitedly.

Rachel shook her head. "No, he's just responding to the pain. He's bleeding internally. I don't know how much or how fast, but he needs medical help and he needs it now."

Adam looked around. The man and the woman who stood guard over Dick and the others looked unconcerned. Adam turned to Hector and Carl, who had joined them. "This man needs medical help right away," he said loudly. "Without it he will die."

Hector looked at Carl then shrugged.

"You," Adam cried out. "Hey, you in the uniform. This man is dying. Can you help us?"

The dark man smiled, offered a slight bow, then saluted with the brown envelope and made his way to the side door and exited.

"Are you all heartless?" Adam cried out. "Have you no feelings? No souls?"

"As a matter of fact, they don't," Quince said as he approached the gathering. "That's why I employ them. I don't think you've met everyone, Reverend Bridger. The young lady there with the nine millimeter is Mickie Moore, who was with the FBI until she was caught taking a bribe. Now she works for me. The stately gentleman is Ross Helms, one of the DEA's top agents until he started selling confiscated heroin. I gave him a new line of work. And this man," Quince said, putting his arm around Jason Beck, "is the finest spy in the business. He learned his craft first as a navy SEAL and then as a CIA operative. I offered him more money and a much more comfortable lifestyle. Now, instead of skulking around in dark little European and South American countries, he steals industry secrets for me. Your friend here made the mistake of attacking Mr. Beck. As you can see, he's sensitive about such things. And of course there are Hector and Carl, both of the Seattle Police Department until that unfortunate incident with a witness."

"Please," Adam pleaded. "My friend needs immediate care."

"You're married to a doctor, are you not?" Quince asked with mock concern.

"Yes!" Adam shouted. "A doctor who is handcuffed and without medical equipment or drugs."

"Now that is a shame."

"Are you just going to let him die?" Adam took a quick step toward Quince but was stopped by Beck's outstretched arm.

Raising a hand to his chin, Quince struck a thoughtful pose, then said, "Yes. I think I will." Then he laughed.

Adam started forward again, but Beck stepped in his path. Beck was so close that Adam could smell his sweet breath and see the pores of his skin. Nose to nose their eyes met. Adam saw nothing but greed and anger in Beck's eyes. He was a man with a soul so callused that he was immune to the pain and suffering of others.

"What do you want me to do?" Adam's voice betrayed his desperation. "Do you want me to beg? Is that what you want?"

"You miss the point, Bridger." Quince grinned. "You are all going to die anyway. So what if your friend goes first?"

There was nothing Adam could do. No action he could take. He was as helpless as a baby left in the woods. He could not overpower the small army of soulless mercenaries Quince had assembled. For the first time in his life he lost all hope. He wanted to be strong, to be filled with faith, but now he was too exhausted, too strained, too confused, and too emotional.

Adam bowed his head in resignation. So this was the end? Maybe God had led them to a desert. Adam felt his heart, his courage, his hope fade away. The consuming blackness of despair was about to devour the last of Adam's strength and determination.

With head bowed, Adam felt hollow, impotent, useless.

It was his position that suddenly changed Adam. It was the bowed head, the position of prayer and supplication, that changed him. A light—small and distant, but warm and unavoidable—began to glow in the abject darkness that swallowed Adam's heart.

Submission?

Adam couldn't give up. The others depended on him. The others were looking for him to provide leadership and direction. That's why he was part of the team. God had chosen him as He had chosen the others. Adam had a role to play, a job to fulfill.

A voice wormed its way into Adam's clouded consciousness. A familiar voice carrying familiar words. He heard Pruit say, "Not to a desert, but through a desert."

The words made the small light, the tiny flame in Adam's heart, grow. And as it grew it pushed back the tenacious darkness that would absorb Adam's faith. Adam reached a decision. If he was going to die, then he was going to die a man of faith. If Dick was going to die, then he was going to die for something worthwhile and far more important than anything he had done to date.

The fire grew.

No, there would be no surrender here. Adam would not abdicate the throne of his life to anyone other than his God. Not to fear. Not to terrorism. Not hopelessness. If death awaited him, then bring it on. If pain and suffering were standing in line for a crack at the preacher, then let them come.

Adam made a decision: No matter what happened, he would die with God's name in his mouth.

The fire spread.

Raising his head, Adam looked deep into Jason Beck's cold eyes and said, "I don't fear those who can kill the body, but if I were you, I'd fear the One who can destroy both soul and body."

"What's that mean?" Beck asked coolly.

"I think you know," Adam replied. "It's from the Gospel of Matthew."

"I don't believe that stuff." Beck declared arrogantly.

"I think you do," Adam replied easily.

Something flickered in Beck's eyes. A split second of doubt, a chink in the armor that shielded his emotions. It was then that Adam knew the fight was far from over.

A loud, protracted squeak tumbled through the air. All eyes shifted to a side door of the hangar where light from a mercury vapor lamp was pouring in the opening. A lone man crossed the hangar, his shoes squeaking on the slick concrete floor. The door shut behind him.

"Mr. Quince?" The voice called out in a thick and proper British accent. "It's me, Peter Straub."

"Come in Mr. Straub," Quince said as he crossed to meet the man. "I've been expecting you. I trust all is in order."

"Yes, sir." Straub was a thin, wiry man with an oily complexion.

His hair was undecided between brown and black and his thick eyebrows each charted their own course. "And let me say thank you for your generous advance."

"You're welcome," Quince said. "You have always proved discreet as well as effective."

Straub looked over at the odd mix of people standing around the prone Dick Slay. "Oh my," Straub intoned. "Looks like he's had a rough day."

"That he has. Have you made arrangements?"

"Yes, but this is a tough one. I've had to go to extra lengths to be sure things will work out."

"You're not asking for more money are you?" Quince asked suspiciously.

"Of course not. The original price is fine. I'm an honorable man." Despite himself, Adam guffawed.

"Shut up, preacher!" Beck shouted. Adam raised his hands, acquiescing.

"All I'm saying," Straub continued, ignoring Adam's outburst, "is that I retained some help. Quality help. Getting stolen items from Cairo to America can be touchy, you know."

"I don't like working with unknowns, Mr. Straub," Quince intoned darkly. "You know that."

"Indeed I do; that's why I chose this person. She's worked for you in the past—indirectly, of course. She's only let me down once and that couldn't be avoided."

"Let you down? She?"

"Yes, she was to steal a Peruvian artifact for one of my clients, but the deal went bad. She was lucky to get away, actually. Too close for comfort, don't you know."

Adam saw Beck stiffen.

"What's this woman's name?" Quince asked.

"Blair. Lindsay Blair. When I briefed her on the mission, she jumped at the chance to be of help. I think she's trying to make it up to me. You'll like her. She's lovely and . . ."

"Blair!" Beck said loudly. "Quince, she was with them, before she bailed out."

"With whom?" Straub asked, taken aback by Beck's unexpected anger.

"With them, you idiot," Quince shouted. "Where is she?

Where is she right now?"

"Getting some needed things out of the car," Straub replied. "I'm afraid I don't . . ."

"Ross, Mickie, go get her," Quince ordered. "I want her standing right in front of me in the next five minutes. Do you hear? Within the next five minutes."

Ross and Mickie ran for the door.

Adam turned to the others; their eyes were wide with confusion. Glancing down at Dick, he saw something that made his heart skip a beat: Dick was conscious and smiling. He had heard, and somehow he knew that having Lindsay Blair back in the picture was a good thing.

Weakly, Dick winked a puffy blue eyelid at Adam.

Forty-Five

Cairo, Egypt

Lindsay felt that she had lost her mind. What was she doing here huddled in the dark Egyptian night waiting for angry and armed people to come storming out an airplane hangar? A sane person would have stayed home, built a fire in the fireplace to ward off the cool English night, and sipped tea from china cups while reading a good novel.

But not Lindsay Blair. No, she chose instead to travel to Cairo with that slimy dealer in stolen art, Peter Straub. It was the last thing she wanted to do, but it was the first thing she had to do.

There was no time to second guess decisions now. In for a penny in for a pound, and judging by what she saw through the open door when Straub went in, her very life was invested heavily in the next few minutes.

She had wanted to be rid of all of this. She had left the others with absolutely no inclination to ever see their faces again. Self-righteous they were, at least a few of them. But the passing of the days did not, could not, erase them from her mind. She dreamed of them at night, and when her mind wandered during the day it always wandered in the same direction—straight to those dysfunctional zealots.

No matter how hard she tried to discipline her mind, she thought of them. Worse, she worried about them. Lindsay Blair had never worried about anyone before. So unique was the emotion that she didn't even recognize it at first.

Her greatest fear was that she would have another vision of hell and once again see her father in torment. But no vision came to plague her. Instead, she was beset by a simple warming of the heart. It was a passive force, but nonetheless irresistible. Stress, she had told herself. That's all it was, just simple stress, but it was much more than that. She had come to care—even if on a primitive level—for those odd people.

The faces of the backward artist, the self-obsessed advertising man, the piteous firefighter, the holier-than-thou preacher, and his self-righteous wife swirled constantly in her brain, demanding to be seen, to be noticed.

Except she didn't see them that way at all now. She didn't know why, but the image she held in her mind had given way to a far different view. Now she saw them as that gifted artist, Katrin; that heroic firefighter, Nick; that creative genius, Pruit; that noble doctor, Rachel; and that caring pastor, Adam.

Strange how she now thought of them by name as well as by their attributes. None of this made sense. This was not the way Lindsay Blair thought. "I am a thief," she reminded herself repeatedly, but the occupation had lost its appeal. That fact alone shook her to the core.

Regardless of what had happened to her, she was in Cairo and she was in danger. She had committed herself to helping the others the moment Straub called and told her that Quince had the ark of the covenant and needed it smuggled into the United States. Such was not her normal line of work, but she was an expert on concealment and she had the worldwide connections to get the job done.

But the value of the ark was not what occupied Lindsay's thoughts. If Quince had the ark, then something had gone terribly wrong with the quest. That meant that the others were in trouble. Why should she care? No reason. But she cared nonetheless and that irritated her enormously.

"Time to rock and roll," she said softly to herself. "Better start concentrating now or someone will need to rescue you—assuming you're still alive."

Quickly she stripped off her clothes. Underneath she wore a tight-fitting, all black outfit. It was the uniform she wore when working at night. She pulled a black ski mask over her face, not to conceal her identity, but to cut down the amount of light her skin might reflect and thereby give away her location. There was also the added advantage of the momentary shock and fear the mask brought. It was a small thing, but then it was always the details that made the difference between success and failure, between life and death.

The trick here was to disable Quince and his men without getting herself or the others shot. For that reason, she chose not to carry a gun. One shot could set off a frenzy of gunfire and the wrong people could die.

Stealth and cunning were the tickets here.

Darkness was her friend. She had spent years training to work on moonless nights or in dark rooms. She doubted the others had that type of training. Still, she had to assume that Quince would not bring along Boy Scouts on the trip. Most likely, his friends were as deadly as they came.

A mercury vapor light that hung high and out of reach on the side wall of the hangar was casting an eerie blue glow on the black pavement. The light had to go. There were a dozen different and high-tech ways of dealing the with light, but Lindsay had time for none of them. Instead, she chose a speedier, albeit low-tech approach. Picking up a rock from the litter-strewn grounds she threw it at the large bulb. It shattered into a thousand glittering pieces which fell in front of the door.

All the better, she thought. The thin shards of glass would come in handy.

Had she been able to come alone, Lindsay would have carried the tools of her trade which would have been enormously helpful. But explaining the need for such tools to Straub would have been difficult. She was left to make do with what she could find around her.

Fortunately, the rented Ford van, which Straub had parked just five feet from the entrance door to the hangar, was well equipped with emergency equipment, including flares, jumper cables, plastic tape, nylon cable, and a few hand tools. There was also a jack and spare tire.

She wished for more.

Knowing that she had only a few precious seconds to act, Lindsay sprang into action. First she popped the car's bonnet—what the Americans called the hood—and removed the wire that ran from the ignition coil to the distributor. Disabling the auto was essential to prevent Quince or his people from making good an escape with hostages. It was while she was looking under the hood that she got her first idea. Along with disconnecting the ignition wire, she also pulled the longest spark plug wire free. She now had her first weapon.

Ever so quietly, she lowered the hood, but didn't latch it. She threw the ignition wire under the car in case she needed it later. Then, walking to the far side of the van she opened the passenger door. The dome light inside came on and cast a weak umbrella of light throughout the vehicle.

Jogging quietly, Lindsay rounded the corner of the hangar closest to the door, placed her back next to the wall, and listened carefully.

A small click emanated from the door handle, betraying its use. Lindsay forced her breathing to slow and her mind to sharpen. She was in the "zone" now. She was as ready as she could be. It seemed that all her training, practice, and study had been preparation for this time.

Suddenly the door sprang open and light from the hangar flooded the immediate area. Lindsay had been right to separate herself from the door. Had she been standing at the side of the hangar instead of the front, the light would have both blinded her and made her an easy target.

Lindsay couldn't see around the corner, but she knew everything that was going on. No more than two people had been sent after her. She could hear the footfalls on the broken glass from the lightbulb over the door. In her mind she pictured the two assailants with guns drawn and held at arm's length in typical police fashion. That is, if they weren't carrying automatic rifles.

"Roof clear," a whispered male voice said.

"Side clear," a hushed woman's voice uttered.

Footsteps on pavement instead of glass. They had moved away from the door.

"Car clear," the man said.

The open door of the van had indeed attracted their attention. Now it was Lindsay's turn to act. Since they knew she wasn't on the roof, next to the building, or in the car, they would begin to search the structure's perimeter. The question was, would they travel as a pair, or split up?

Lindsay hoped for the latter. She was not disappointed. As she strained to listen to their movement, she could detect that one set of steps was receding from her, the other drawing closer. They were hoping to surround her.

In Lindsay's right hand was the spark plug wire she had taken from the engine. Taking each end of the thick, black rubber-coated wire, she formed a loop about eighteen inches in diameter. She held the loop tightly in her right hand. This had to be done right the first time. One mistake and she would be dead.

The slow and cautious footsteps grew closer. Lindsay silently took a deep breath and held it. She bent her knees slightly, crossed her arms in front of her, right over left, and prepared to spring into action.

Ross Helms had been a highly trained agent for the Drug Enforcement Agency. He knew police procedures backward and forward. He had made hundreds of arrests and participated in dozens of raids before his indiscretion was discovered and he was released from active duty. He had been lucky to avoid jail. Yet all his training and experience could not prepare him for the surprise that awaited him.

Holding his nine-millimeter pistol with both hands and extending his arms before him, he fully expected to pin Lindsay Blair in his gunsights. Instead, as he rounded the corner, he felt a hand grab his wrist and pull him forward a step. So shocked was he by the brazen act, he didn't see the woman's elbow flying toward his face. The impact rocked him. He stood stunned for a second, but that was long enough.

The next thing Ross knew was that a loop of rope or wire had passed over his head and clamped down on his neck. He felt his windpipe crimp shut. Then he felt someone's back against his, a swift and painful tug on the binding around his neck, and Ross watched as his feet sailed into the air. He was being flipped over the woman's back, like a duffel bag being tossed to the deck by a sailor.

Ross didn't see the ground racing toward his head and he only felt it for a moment as the force of the throw and his own weight combined to form a skull-crushing result.

Lindsay rubbed her elbow. The man had a hard head, but not hard enough to stop a fast-moving elbow in the nose. It was then an easy matter to loop the spark plug wire over his head and flip him over her back to the ground. The hardest part of the whole move was assuring that the opponent landed on his head and not flip all the way over and land on his hands and knees, which, although painful, would not incapacitate him.

The basic rule that Lindsay had lived by was: Never give anyone a second chance to attack.

With an ease that came from practice, Lindsay picked up the man's gun that still lay in his unmoving hand, ejected the clip, and cleared the chamber. She took the clip with her as she approached the other corner of the hangar, from which she expected the man's partner to emerge.

Lindsay was forced to wait in silence again. As she did, a strange thought popped into her mind. What she had just done to the man could have been much worse. Normally she would thrust him down with such force that he would run the risk of a broken neck. But this time Lindsay had held back. To be sure, the man was unconscious and would be so for hours. Even upon waking he would be in no condition to fight. But why had she held back?

Footfalls. Heavy breathing.

Closer.

Lindsay crouched next to the wall again. When it sounded like the woman was just two or three feet around the corner, Lindsay threw the clip of bullets she had taken from the man's gun over the corner of the roof. She heard it rattle loudly on the ground behind the would-be assailant.

The distinct sound of shoes turning quickly in place let Lindsay know that the woman had gone for the bait and spun around to see what had caused the noise. Lindsay stepped around the corner. When the woman rotated back around she was met with the heel of Lindsay's hand crashing into her chin.

The woman staggered, her arms limp at her side. Lindsay took one step forward and delivered the same hand to the same face. The woman dropped in a heap.

Quickly Lindsay disarmed the gun and threw the clip and bullet from the chamber as far as she could.

"Well," she whispered softly to herself. "Isn't this sweet? Matching pistols!" Lindsay allowed herself the luxury of a small, quick grin. "Now the easy part is over."

"What is taking them so long?" Quince demanded. "They should have been back with that Blair woman."

"Lindsay is quite proficient," Straub said casually. "She can be determined."

"Well, she can't be anymore determined than me," Quince shouted. "I want that woman in here now! Hector, Carl, go get her."

"No, wait," Beck challenged. "That's what she wants. Don't you see, she has the advantage. If she has taken out Ross and Mickie, then she has at very least two nine-millimeter pistols. She also has the advantage of position and surprise. She can take us out one by one if we give her the chance."

"Well what do you suggest?" Quince snapped. "We have limited time. The air traffic controllers we bribed will change shifts in a couple of hours. If we're not in the air soon, we'll be stuck here in Cairo."

"I don't know," Beck confessed. "Give me time to think. I'll come up with something. We're OK as long as we have her friends."

"Friends?" Quince was surprised. "She's after the ark. She's a professional thief and doesn't have friends."

"It's not the ark she wants," Beck said. "If she wanted the ark she would have laid low until it was released to Straub. Then it would be her possession. She'd do in Straub and keep the ark for herself. No, if she just wanted the ark there would be better ways to get it. She wants her friends."

Quince thought for a moment. "You may be right. You may be right after all. As long as we have them, we have the advantage. Listen up everyone. I want a gun at the head of every hostage. If she looks in here, I want her to see the muzzle of a gun pressed into the ears of her comrades."

Carl, Hector, Beck, and Quince slowly approached the handcuffed hostages.

Lindsay leaned back against the wall of the hangar. She had been peering in one of the windows and saw the weapons trained on Adam and the others. It was clear that no one else would be coming out to find her. That had been her only hope. Alone, she could handle one or two at a time. She had trained for such things all her life. But she couldn't take them all on at once. There were too many, and they were too well armed.

What to do now? If they wouldn't cooperate by coming out, and she couldn't go in, then they were stalemated. She needed a new plan, but she was coming up dry.

"Think, Lindsay," she whispered to herself. "Use your brain. It's the most powerful weapon you have. But think quickly."

Nothing. No ideas. No plans.

She had failed. She had failed in her life. She had failed those who were depending on her. This wasn't the way it was supposed to work out. Soon they would do what terrorists typically did: shoot a hostage to make a point, to force her hand. Lindsay knew it would work.

"Help me here, God," Lindsay murmured quietly. "Those are Your people in there." Lindsay had never prayed in her life. Never sought God or His presence. She preferred the real, cold world of facts. But now there was a new fact in play: she was helpless, and in minutes people might start dying.

"I know I haven't been Your sort," Lindsay continued, "but I need You now. More importantly, they need You. What do You want me to do?"

There were no voices from heaven. No peals of thunder or flashes of lighting. No words were whispered in her ears. No visions. No dreams. No angels.

But there was God nonetheless.

Lindsay smiled for a moment, stepped away from the wall. She had to act quickly. Seconds mattered. The value of a single minute could be weighed by the price of a life. It was a crazy idea, but then crazy ideas seemed to work.

Sprinting around the hangar, Lindsay slipped into the van through the open door. There she reached under the dashboard, seized a handful of wires that ran to the radio, the clock, the cigarette lighter, and the like, then yanked with all her might. She had to jerk fiercely several times until a bundle of wires came loose in her hand.

Pulling the mask from her face, she walked quickly to the back of the van and opened the emergency road kit from which she removed four flares, a roll of plastic tape, and a small screwdriver.

"Quince," Lindsay called through the slightly opened door. "Can you hear me, Quince?"

"I hear you, Ms. Blair, but be careful what you say, or one of your friends may die."

"I'm coming in, but don't shoot me. I have a surprise for you, but if you shoot me it will ruin your whole day."

"What are you talking about?" Quince shouted back bitterly.

Slowly the door opened. Beck raised his AK-47 assault rifle to his shoulder and took careful aim, but Lindsay wasn't what he sighted.

"Does this look familiar to anyone?" Lindsay asked as she slowly entered the hangar, her right arm extended in front of her. She was holding a package wrapped in black plastic tape. The bundle was threaded with wire, two strands of which extended above the rest. The package, which Lindsay held by the two wires, gently swung back and forth like a large pendulum.

Pulling the door closed behind her, Lindsay quickly assessed the situation in the room. As she crossed the hangar, she could tell that her point had been made. The blood had drained from every face in the room.

"What is that?" Quince asked.

"What does it look like?" Lindsay countered.

"It looks like a bloody packet of dynamite to me," Straub cried out as he took several steps back.

"Very good, Peter," Lindsay said with a smile. "Any idea why I'm holding it this way?"

"Dead man switch," Hector said, his eyes wide. "We shoot you and the two wires you're holding separate, triggering the explosion."

"You must be very proud to be associated with such bright people, Quince." Lindsay placed her left hand under the bundle so that it wouldn't swing and then slowly moved it back and forth like a salesperson demonstrating a product.

"Where did you get dynamite?" Beck asked suspiciously.

"I'm a resourceful woman. You'd be surprised what they leave laying around airports."

"I don't have time for this," Quince shouted. "I don't believe you're ready to blow us all to bits, especially since you'd die in the process."

"Don't underestimate me, Quince," Lindsay snapped, her eyes narrow. "I'm not in a good mood and I'm more than willing to let my little device shred you to pieces. Are you ready for your eternity in hell, Quince? I can't say that I liked it much myself."

Quince didn't answer.

"Adam," Lindsay said, acknowledging him for the first time. "I need you to do me a favor. Do you see that old wooden office chair over there in the corner?"

"Yes," Adam said.

"Go over to it, please."

Quince leveled his gun at Adam. "I give the orders here."

"Not anymore," Lindsay retorted. "Adam, do it."

Slowly, Adam walked to the chair, waiting to hear the muzzle explosion and feel the impact of a bullet in his back. None came. Once at the chair, Adam turned to face Lindsay. "Now what?"

"Be a dear and break the window with the chair."

"What!" Quince said.

"Adam, do as I've told you."

Adam exhaled heavily, picked up the wooden chair, and threw it with all his might at the side window. The glass shattered loudly. A moment later a bell began to ring.

"She's triggered the alarm," Beck shouted over the earsplitting clanging.

"I rewired the alarm. I'm really quite good at such things." Lindsay was shouting, her voice was barely understandable over the noisy signal. "All right, listen up, everyone." "Here's how this works. I figure the police will be here in approximately five minutes. That means you, Mr. Quince, and your chums had better get back on your plane and get airborne. The ark is still on the aircraft?"

Quince nodded.

"In that case, you get what you want—the ark; and I get what I want—my friends."

"What if I don't agree?" Quince demanded. "What if I call your bluff?"

"We have nothing to lose and everything to gain, Quince." Lindsay shouted loudly. "You never would have let anyone in this room, other than yourself, live. They all know you and your business. You're too rich and famous to be a private man anymore. If you let them live, there would be witnesses around to identify you. No,

Mr. Quince, you planned to kill them as soon as you were done with them—including your employees.

"So if you think I'm bluffing . . ." Lindsay continued as she held up the package. "Then call me on it." She took two steps closer to Quince all the while rubbing the two exposed copper wires together.

A small bead of sweat appeared on Quince's forehead.

"I think you're down to four minutes, Quince, and you still have to back the jet out of the hangar." Lindsay smiled, then the smile faded as she looked at the injured Dick who lay on the floor, and the others, each with a gun pointed to his head. "If I were you, Quince, I'd leave while I still could."

Dr. Julian Newton who had kept to himself in the corner of the hangar, stepped forward. He was visibly shaken. "Please, Mr. Quince. We must go. I don't want to spend time in an Egyptian prison. We're foreigners, remember?"

Quince's face darkened and every pore seemed to ooze rage. His eyes flitted around the room looking for answers, a way out or someone to blame. He found the latter.

"Straub! This is your fault," Quince proclaimed angrily. "If you hadn't brought her with you none of this would have happened." Instantly, Quince raised his weapon and squeezed the trigger until a short burst of bullets erupted.

Katrin screamed, everyone ducked, Straub fell backward dead.

"You idiot," Beck screamed. "Now we have a dead body to deal with and the police on their way."

"In the plane," Quince ordered. Beck sprinted to the switch that would automatically open the hangar's large door, activated it, then led Hector, Carl, and Newton up the boarding ramp. "All right, Blair, you can have your friends, but I keep the ark." Then he ran up the ramp and closed the hatch.

As soon as the jet's door was closed, Lindsay began shouting. "Out. Everyone out of the hangar now." Rachel, Katrin, Pruit, and Ted headed for the side door. Nick took several painful strides toward his fallen comrade, arriving only a step or two behind Adam.

"I'm not leaving Dick," Adam cried. "No way am I leaving Dick."

Nick said something, but his words were swallowed by the high-pitched whine of the Global Express' two powerful turbine engines powering up. Inside the hangar, the roar was deafening.

Adam turned to see Lindsay standing in front of the jet, holding high the bundle in her hand and staring at Beck, who sat in the pilot's seat.

"Get out," Adam ordered Nick, motioning to the door with his hand. Hot choking jet exhaust began to fill the cavernous room.

Nick couldn't hear, but he got the message, then delivered a message of his own. "No."

In a feat of personal strength that defied anything Adam had ever seen, Nick straddled Dick, grabbed the front of his shirt and hoisted the semiconscious man to a sitting position. Then in a fluid movement that belied the piercing pain that it caused him, Nick reached around Dick's back, grabbed his belt, and with a herculean effort, heaved Dick's stocky body onto his shoulder. It was the typical fireman's carry, but the fireman that executed the move was far from typical.

Adam watched in amazement as Nick lumbered under the weight of Dick's limp body. Nick's legs, weakened by trauma, atrophied by forced inactivity, bore up under the load. Adam knew that it was not the strength of Nick's legs that made it possible, but the strength of his heart.

The jet backed out of the hangar slowly. Lindsay followed; her long black hair flowed like streamers in the potent exhaust. As soon as Beck had cleared the hangar, he reversed thrust and slowly started for the runway.

Before the jet could break inertia, Beck looked out the pilot's window at Lindsay, the woman who had defeated not only Quince but him as well. Through the darkness, he saw her—illuminated by the jet's running lights—hold up the bundle and then, with great flourish, released the two wires that made up the dead man switch.

Nothing happened.

Beck's eyes widened in rage.

To make her point, Lindsay quickly stripped off the black plastic tape, removed one of the sticks of "dynamite" and ignited it. The flare blossomed into bright flame that nearly obscured Lindsay's laughing face.

The slow-moving plane lurched to a stop. Beck's face disappeared from the cockpit window. A moment later the passenger hatch opened and Beck appeared. He raised his AK-47 and unleashed a hail of bullets. Lindsay dove for cover, but she was too late. While most of the rounds ricocheted off the pavement, three bullets found their mark. Lindsay Blair lay unmoving in an ever-increasing crimson circle of blood.

When Officer Ahmed was dispatched to the Almaza Airport to support the local airport police, he didn't expect to be the first on the scene, nor did he expect to see a woman with a flare in her hand being mowed down by a man with an automatic rifle shooting from the doorway of an expensive Western private jet.

Nor did he expect to draw his revolver and fire all six rounds until the assailant fell from the doorway of the plane to the tarmac. He didn't expect the need to call for backup and ambulances.

But he did. And his day was just beginning.

"Lindsay!" Katrin screamed. "Lindsay's been shot! They shot her. They shot her!"

Rachel was helping lower Dick from Nick's shoulder when she heard Katrin's frantic cry. Sprinting around the corner of the hangar, Rachel saw the jet slowly coasting along the tarmac, apparently without direction, a police officer cautiously approaching a man who lay facedown on the ground, and Katrin running to Lindsay's side.

Rachel ran to Lindsay and knelt at her side. She was lying facedown, arms and limbs akimbo. Gently, Rachel turned her over. Lindsay was staring through lifeless eyes.

"Oh, no," Rachel said. "No, no, no. It can't be."

Katrin was weeping uncontrollably.

Sirens echoed down the runway and tarmac. More police cars arrived, their emergency lights flashing like tiny lighthouses warning of immanent danger.

"Ambulance," Rachel called out as she struggled to contain her emotions. "I need an ambulance over here."

Rachel assessed the situation aloud. "Three entry wounds, pupils fixed and dilated. No pulse. Oh, God, help me—help me, please." Adam, Nick and Pruit joined her. Ted stayed with Dick.

"She's bleeding out," Rachel exclaimed. "We have to get her into surgery." Although Rachel knew it was a useless act, she began CPR. "One, two, three," she counted out loud. Nick, bending his knees farther than they had been bent since the accident, knelt near Lindsay's head and began mouth-to-mouth resuscitation, blowing air into her lungs each time Rachel's count reached five.

The ambulance crew arrived and pulled out a stretcher and medical kit.

"Start an IV with Ringer's . . ." Rachel looked up to see that the medics didn't understand her. They couldn't speak English, and she couldn't speak Arabic. Forcefully, she grabbed one of the men by the front of his uniform and pulled him down to her spot. "CPR," she ordered. He complied.

Snapping open the plastic medical kit, Rachel quickly searched the contents. The other paramedic took her hand to stop her, unaware that she was a doctor, and she had no way to tell him. She slapped his hand away.

She examined the medications and IV solutions. All the labels were in Arabic. Rachel began to cry with frustration.

Lindsay was dead. Dick lay dying.

A tube—white and warm. A path—clear and straight. An attraction—irresistible and captivating.

Calling.

Embracing.

Caressing.

Lindsay Blair felt alive . . . full . . . and at long last peaceful.

If love were light, it would be this light; if love were warmth, it would be this warmth; and if love were a calling, it would be this call.

The tube carried her along as gently as an oak leaf on the last warm day of fall. With each moment that passed something was stripped from Lindsay's mind, heart, soul. Bitterness left first, followed by doubt. Self-hate evaporated, mistrust dissolved, and disbelief died. In their place blossomed sweetness, assurance, love, trust, belief, and faith.

And they fit. They fit so well,that Lindsay understood that until this moment she had never been complete. Her construction had been faulty. Now she knew, she understood what life was supposed to feel like.

A silhouette distant. A silhouette drawing closer. A man. A smile that could warm any soul. A hand. A pair of arms. An embrace.

A word spoken.

A response given: "Yes, Lord. Oh, yes, Lord."

Epilogue

Steaming plates of spaghetti with deep red tomato sauce were set on the table. Leonardo himself served the food. It wasn't often that world celebrities dined at his little Italian restaurant. Now he had not one celebrity but six. Their pictures had appeared in *Time*, *Newsweek*, and *U.S. News & World Report*. They had been the subject of talk shows and news shows, and their story had appeared in every major newspaper in the world.

By comparison, however, they were merely a faint star when weighed against the objects they brought to the world's attention. The ark of the covenant, the Ten Commandments, the golden jar of manna, and Aaron's rod were now displayed to the public for the first time in more than 3,000 years.

And the public came by the thousands. Currently housed in the Cairo Museum of Antiquities, seekers traveled the globe to stand in line for six hours to peek at the holy objects for six minutes. But no one complained. People were remarkably patient, and remarkably grateful.

The Egyptians, knowing that in archeological terms possession is 100 percent of the law, were unusually magnanimous. The Egyptian president had stated in a United Nations General Assembly that the objects of God belonged to the world. Even a

Muslim president could see the importance of the Jewish antiquities. This was, of course, after six months' effort to authenticate the
artifacts. Not a single scholar who was asked to examine the
objects could provide any evidence that the artifacts were anything
other than what they appeared to be—the holy objects of the
Old Testament.

The world would share the treasures under the guidance of the
United Nations. Every three months, the ark and its companion pieces
would be moved to a new museum in some part of the world.
Sites were chosen by lottery. It was a logistical nightmare eclipsed
only by the diplomatic nightmare that preceded it.

Israel, of course, claimed the right of ownership, and there was
no doubt that the world court would ultimately declare the land of
the Hebrews the final resting place for the ark. But Israel's claim did
not go unchallenged. The Egyptians made claim to partial ownership since it could now be reasonably argued that the ark had
been removed from the Jewish temple to protect it from the evil King
Manasseh's blasphemy of placing idols in the temple proper.
Militant priests abducted the relic and sailed up the Nile to the island
of Elephantine, near Aswan. There they built a temple which
endured through portions of the sixth and fifth centuries B.C. It was
removed once again when the ancient Egyptian priests of the ram
god Khnum, in a plot with the local Persian governor, destroyed the
Elephantine temple.

The Ethiopians clung tenaciously to their belief that they should
be possessors of the ark since, according to Kebra Nagast, it was brought
to their land by Menelik I, son of Solomon and the Queen of Sheba.
Few scholars backed their contention.

Moving and displaying the objects required the highest security and the latest in protection devices. The ark's defense needed to
be invulnerable. New security systems were installed in each building in which the artifacts appeared. Supervising that security was
Lindsay Blair.

"The food smells great," Lindsay said beaming. "No offense,
Rachel, but hospital food just doesn't cut it for me."

"You needn't apologize to me," Rachel replied. "I work in a
hospital, remember? Hospital food is bad worldwide, even in
Egypt." Rachel paused as she twirled spaghetti on her fork. "You look
great, Lindsay."

"Thank you. I'm on the mend."

"I really thought we lost you there at the airport."

"You did," Lindsay said evenly. "It was the greatest thing that ever happened to me. Seeing heaven was a lot more pleasant than seeing hell."

"It's a miracle you're alive," Rachel offered sincerely. "And I mean that literally."

"I know." Lindsay took a bite of garlic bread. "But more amazing than that is how I'm living. Life is so much sweeter now."

"I'll say amen to that," Pruit chimed in, placing his arm around his wife. "Did I tell you? We leave tomorrow for a cruise in the Bahamas. Our son Michael is going to join us."

"That's great, Pruit," Adam said. "We didn't get to ride around on a yacht like some people I know." Adam cut a glance at Dick who was devouring the food on his plate as if he hadn't eaten since leaving the Cairo hospital six months previous.

"You wouldn't have liked it, Pastor," Dick replied. "Too much blue water and warm breezes. It would have only distracted you."

Dick's wife, Cleo, elbowed him in the side. "I'm ready for that kind of distraction."

"That sounds like a pretty good honeymoon spot," Nick offered taking Katrin's hand.

"So do I get to do the service, or what?" Adam inquired.

"We wouldn't have it any other way," Katrin answered quickly. "I want this knot tied tight."

"So where are you two lovebirds going to live?" Pruit asked.

"Fort Worth," Nick answered.

"Ojai," Katrin replied simultaneously.

Nick looked at Katrin. "Maybe we'll just move in with Martin."

Laughter filled the private dining room, and no one laughed harder than Anna St. James who sat next to her quiet brother. "It's a joke, Martin."

"I know it's a joke, Anna," Martin replied evenly. "I'm laughing on the inside."

More laughter.

"I wasn't sure you were coming, Martin," Adam said. "It's good to see you out of the house."

"Well, I'm still more comfortable at home, but this was important. We've had a hand in changing the world."

"It wouldn't have happened without your genius," Pruit interjected.

"If I hadn't involved myself, then God would have found someone else." Martin's words were soft, almost imperceptible.

Adam almost dropped his fork. Did he just hear Martin St. James speak of God as a real Person and not as an abstract concept? Conversation around the table continued, but Adam heard none of it. Instead he made eye contact with his old friend. Martin read the question in Adam's eyes, a question with eternal ramifications.

Martin nodded slightly. Adam swallowed hard and blinked back tears. Anna was beaming.

"I'm glad everyone could make our six-month anniversary." Rachel said. "Who would have guessed the effect the ark would have on the world?"

"It's affected everything," Adam said. "Church attendance has skyrocketed. Seminary enrollment is up. There's a new interest in the Bible. I think that's what God had in mind don't you."

"That and more," Lindsay said as she remembered the words uttered to her. "That and much more."

"How's Ted?" Pruit asked.

"Still working in Ethiopia," Adam replied. "He's still talking about the huge monetary gift you gave his school."

"That was my pleasure." Pruit said. "I've always worked for my benefit. He works for the benefit of others. This way I could participate."

"What's the latest word on Quince and his gang of thieves?" Nick inquired between mouthfuls of spaghetti.

Adam shrugged. "Still in an Egyptian prison. His money and name didn't impress them much. They take murder, theft, and kidnapping very seriously there. And if he and the others ever get out of there, they stand to face trial here in the States. The police found a huge collection of stolen artifacts in the basement of his office."

"Is his partner still running the show at Datadyne?" Lindsay asked.

"Yes," Adam answered. "It turns out that his partner was the real technical genius of the two, but Quince kept him sequestered away, and since Quince owned the bulk of the stock, his partner was helpless. Most people didn't even know he had a partner."

"At least no one at Datadyne lost his job because of Quince's greed," Rachel interjected. "They have a lot to be thankful for."

Adam thought for a moment, then said, "If you ask me, we all have a lot to be thankful for."

Afterword

No object in the Bible has captured the interest of so many people as the ark of the covenant. The number of theories regarding the final disposition of the ark is almost overwhelming. It has been reportedly found below the Dome of the Rock in Jerusalem, on mountains in the regions surrounding the Holy Land, and in various places in Ethiopia.

The truth of the matter is that no one knows the truth of the matter. While some scholars believe that the ark was destroyed in one of the several sieges against Jerusalem, there is sufficient evidence to believe otherwise.

The scenario presented in this work of fiction is only a possibility, and should be viewed as a contrivance of storytelling and little more. The underlying concept, while possible, is a creation of the writer's mind.

Most likely the ark will never be found unless God chooses to reveal it before the last days. Still . . . it is interesting to speculate.